To Suzane,
I hope you will find
Something in my book that
holds your interest

Frieda Infeber

Frieda's Journey   6/22/15

Frieda's Journey

Frieda Lefeber

To order additional copies of this book, contact:
Xlibris Corporation
1-888-795-4274
www.Xlibris.com
Orders@Xlibris.com
18778

Contents

I DEDICATE THIS BOOK WITH LOVING AFFECTION
TO MY DEAR FAMILY: HOPE, HOWARD, RACHEL, AND DANA.

Prologue

My life has been a journey of high peaks and deep gorges, a life of hope and joy, but also of disappointment and desperation. In this book I shall portray the hurdles I had to jump and the many obstacles that blocked my safe passage through life.

Most of life's lessons I had to learn on my own without much parental guidance. I had to pay dearly for my mistakes, but I learned from them in the end. My deep faith in God—in a force that guides me with intelligence—saved me from despair. Even in my darkest hours, I had hope for a better tomorrow.

In this book I shall reveal where I come from, my humble beginnings as a Jew in Germany, my escape from there, and the many incredible opportunities that presented themselves along the way. My life has been rewarding in many ways, and I am grateful.

My Family

Family Tree

My parents' families hailed from the eastern part of Germany, the province of Posen. But after World War I, according to the treaty of Versailles, that land was annexed to Poland and all my relatives migrated into Germany proper. There didn't exist any strong bonds between members of my father's family. After he married my mother, he didn't communicate with any of his siblings until my brother's Bar Mitzvah, when I was eleven years old. My father's two younger sisters never saw him again after he married my mother, and therefore I never knew them.

I know little about my paternal grandparents, Rosa Arndt and Mendel Graumann. They were born in the 1850s in the village of Wissek, and had five children:

Jacob, Else, Samuel (my father), and two younger daughters (names unknown). I only knew Uncle Jacob briefly. He lived with his wife, Frieda, and two daughters, Hertha and Trude, in Liegnitz, Germany. They later immigrated to Israel.

I met my Aunt Else once, at my brother's Bar Mitzvah. She was widowed and had two children, Manfred and Recha. She and Manfred died in Auschwitz, and Recha immigrated to Sao Paulo, Brazil.

Maternal Grandparents

I know more about my mother's family because she came from a close-knit family. My grandfather, Louis Salomon, was born July 24, 1848 in Posen, Germany. He married his distant cousin, Fradel Salomonsohn. They had eleven children, three of whom died in infancy. The names of the eight children are: Leo, Adolf, Max, Hugo Ella, Kate, Clara (my mother), and Olga.

Uncle Leo was married three times. He lived with his wife, Kate in Berlin, and had one daughter, Friedel, from his first marriage. Friedel married Arnold Jacobson and had one son, Alfred, who now lives in New York. Uncle Leo and his wife Kate died in Auschwitz.

Uncle Adolf and his wife Bertha lived in Kuestrin, Germany. They had two children, Hermann and Hertha. Hertha married Sam Oppenheim, and immigrated to Sydney, Australia. They had a son Jehuda Israel, and a daughter, Hannah Chalmers.

Uncle Max and his wife, Cilla, lived in Schneidemuhl, Germany. They had two children, Hilde and Alfred. Max, Hilde and Alfred immigrated to the United States of America.

Uncle Hugo, a widower, lived with his daughter, Rita, in Potsdam, Germany. Both took cyanide poison when the Nazis came to send them to a concentration camp and died instantly.

Aunt Kate and her husband Max Wiersch, lived in Kuestrin, Germany. They had two children, Brunhilde and Berthold. All eventually found refuge in the United States.

Aunt Ella married Samuel Reich, and they lived in Schneidemuhl, Germany. They had two children, Rosel and Achim. Samuel died in a concentration camp on Kristallnacht, but Ella and her children eventually found refuge in the United States.

My mother, Clara, and father, Samuel Graumann, lived in Kuestrin. They and my brother, Gerhard, immigrated to Israel.

Aunt Olga and her husband, Ernst Mainzer, lived with their three children, Ruth, Herbert, and Alfred, in Baden-Baden. Aunt Olga and her husband died in Auschwitz, but the children immigrated to Australia and the United States.

*   *   *

Most of my relatives have died by now; besides me, only

Rosel and her brother Achim survive. Those that survived the Holocaust reached their eighties or high nineties. Apparently I am blessed with good genes.

My grandfather Louis's grandfather reached the incredible age of 114 years. (In Germany birth registration was mandatory, and therefore his age is verifiable.) The story goes that he was always in good health and was independent until later in life when he had to move in with his granddaughter, my Aunt Cilla's mother. The old man used to go to the village saloon every night and to indulge in a glass or two of schnapps. But the last two years of his life he couldn't walk alone, and Aunt Cilla, who was a young girl at the time, had to bring him to the tavern because he was no longer steady on his feet. He died peacefully in his sleep.

All I know about my paternal grandparents is that they lived in a small house in the village of Wissek, in the eastern part of Germany. They were poor. My grandfather made his living as a glazier by cutting window glass.

My father was born on July 28, 1884. When he was ten years old his father became ill, with early signs of senility, and was therefore unable to make a living. His older brother Jacob and sister Else were already married, and were unable to help. For four years my grandmother had to carry the burden of supporting her family by selling housewares in flea markets. It was a hard life, traveling by horse-drawn wagon daily from village to village. When my father left school at the age of fourteen, he was able to help lift the heavy burden for his mother. When she died in 1910, at the age of sixty, my father became the sole breadwinner for his sick father and his two younger sisters.

My maternal grandfather was prosperous in his wholesale housewares business in Posen, Germany He was a handsome man, six-foot three-inches tall. He had a majestic appearance and sported a mustache, like the Emperor Friedrich Wilhelm I. As a young man, he served in the Potsdam Guard Fusilier (an officer of the Emperor's Elite Guard). He was always proud of his ancestry, which he could trace as far back as 1605. All his eight children received only elementary education. At the age of fourteen they were sent away to apprentice in other businesses for four years. He was very controlling and his children feared him. He expected his children to continue working for him after they returned from their apprenticeships, until they married.

My mother, Clara Salomon, was born November 15, 1884, in Posen. After her elementary education, she went to learn the piece-goods business. Upon her return, she too worked for my grandfather. She was a beautiful girl, tall and slim with striking gray eyes and auburn hair. When she was twenty-two years old, her parents arranged for her to meet a distant cousin, with possible marriage in mind. She thought her cousin was handsome and agreed to meet his parents in Berlin where he worked in their shoe business. The first thing he did was to take her to his parents' store and made her put on high-heeled shoes. She wasn't accustomed to walk in them and felt most uncomfortable. She was a girl from a small town, and she found city life overwhelming, and the cousin was too urbane and overbearing. Disappointed and depressed, she returned to her parents and broke off the engagement. She continued to work for her father and was not interested in meeting another man for the next five years.

When she was twenty-seven, her mother became gravely ill with cancer and expressed the wish to see her daughter Clara get married before she died. The young man my grandmother had in mind was Samuel Graumann, who was of the same age as my mother. He had been a customer of my grandfather's for years. My grandmother knew he was poor, but she thought he would be a good match for her daughter. Clara agreed to meet him. Grandmother invited him to a festive meal and introduced them. Samuel brought flowers and formally asked Clara to marry him. When she accepted, he tried to kiss her, but she rebuffed him by slapping his face, making it clear to him that she would not kiss him until they were married. In spite of this embarrassment, they set their wedding date for January 31, 1912, three months after they met.

On the day of the wedding, my father received from my grandfather Louis, a handsome dowry of twenty thousand German marks; a huge sum in those days. After the celebration, the newlyweds drove off to Wissek, to the house my father was born in, where they were to live with his sick father and two younger sisters. My mother, however, disliked the arrangement and insisted that the two sisters move out right away. They left and never spoke to my parents again.

Wissek was a village with just a few hundred inhabitants. My grandfather's house was built around the middle of the nineteenth century. It was a plain, box-shaped, two-story building with a huge, heavy wooden entrance-door, big enough to let horse-drawn carriages pass through, leading to the courtyard. The house faced the paved market square, where a red stone church stood in the center.

With the money my father received from Grandfather Louis, he enlarged the building by adding wings to either side in the rear of the house, creating a U-shaped structure. Grain was stored in the larger wing. The living quarters were in the smaller wing, from which steps led onto a paved courtyard. At the rear of the property was a beautiful garden with a lot of fruit trees.

With such substantial financial improvement, my father no longer had to struggle to eke out a meager living by going on the road and peddling housewares. He started to deal in the grain trade.

The marriage was harmonious. My father adored my mother. She had good business sense and took over all financial matters.

One year after their marriage, on February 6, 1913, my brother Gerhard was born. A boy, especially the first-born, is always a great joy and blessing to Jewish couples.

World War I

With the beginning of World War I on August 8, 1914, two and a half years after my parents were married, their lives changed forever. My father was immediately conscripted into the German army and fought as an infantry soldier against the enemy during the harsh winter months in Russia. My mother couldn't continue the grain business by herself. In order to make a living, she converted her living room into a store and sold housewares, which she obtained from her father. Life was hard; she was taking care of her little son and the business. She also had to deal with her sick father-in-law, who would often disappear, and later be found by the police, wandering on some lonely road totally lost, incoherent, and incontinent.

My father had been gone barely a month when my mother discovered she was pregnant. She didn't want another child and wanted to get an abortion. But her sister, Olga, talked her out of it. Olga lived across the market square with her six-month-old baby girl, Ruth. Baby Ruth never saw her father because Olga's husband was killed in France in the early days of the war. Both sisters shared their worries about the future and carried on as best they could.

World War I was raging in Europe when I came into this world, under the most foreboding circumstances.

My Birth

On March 21, 1915, my mother received a much feared telegram from army headquarters, informing her that my father had been wounded on the battlefield and had been sent to an army hospital in Stettin, in the northern part of Germany. In those days it was impossible to get any information by telephone about his condition. My mother must have been in agony not to be able to get in touch with him.

Since she was in her seventh month of pregnancy, she was in no condition to travel to Stettin, which was about a five-hour train ride away from Wissek. The shock about my father's injury caused her to start premature labor pains. She contacted the local midwife and later that night, at ten o'clock, she gave birth to me at home, with the help of Mrs. Goltz. I weighed in at a meager three-and-a-half pounds. In those days an infant with that low birth weight hardly had a chance of survival. There was no doctor in the village, the nearest hospital was more than an hour away, and incubators didn't exist. My mother took one look at me and was horrified. She prayed that God should take me. She asked Mrs. Goltz not to bring her baby to her again because she was sure I could not survive.

Mrs. Goltz cared for me for a long time. In order to keep me warm, she wrapped me in cotton dipped in olive oil. Luckily, she was able to secure a wet nurse who supplied me with milk, since my mother had none of her own due to her emotional state. Registration of a newborn had to be done within forty-eight hours of birth in Germany, so Mrs. Goltz took care of it. She gave me the name Frieda, which I hated all my life.

My mother thought it was a miracle that I survived under the care of Mrs. Goltz. When I was weaned away from breast to bottled milk, my mother bought a goat, and I thrived on its milk. By the time I was a year old, I looked like any healthy baby.

Childhood Memories

My father was recuperating from shrapnel wounds in both legs in the army hospital for seventeen months and walked with braces on both legs. I remember the day he came home. My cousin Ruth and I were playing in front of my mother's store. I saw a soldier in uniform watching us. He was smiling, and when he picked me up I was not scared. I was staring at this strange, stubbly beard. He walked into my mother's store, holding me in his arms. That moment of his return stayed clearly in my mind.

After his return from the army, my father resumed his grain business, and my mother continued to work in her store. A few Russian prisoners of war, who had not yet returned to their homeland, worked for him. Sometimes, Constantin, one of our Russian prisoners, played with us. I loved it when he perched us on his broad shoulders and then hopscotched up and down the long courtyard and into our garden behind.

The Iron Cross for Valor was bestowed upon my father. However, his wounds made him an invalid for life. They were a constant reminder of the senseless war he had fought in. Even years later, I would hear him waking up and screaming from nightmares. He would tell us about his experiences of the war. One story stands out in my mind: He and his buddies were starving in the bitter-cold steppes of Russia, when one day they found a raw pig's head lying in the field. Immediately, the soldiers started a fire, singed off the hair, then roasted the meat and devoured the head, like hungry lions. My Jewish father had never eaten pork before, but was so famished that he indulged in eating that meat.

My brother and I loved to play in the grain silos. We would

cover our bodies with grain and lie there pretending we were asleep. When we heard our feeble grandfather approaching the silo we called out, "Opshick." It was his nickname, which he disliked. Aggravated, he tried to find us, wielding his cane. Once he caught me and he hit me on my nose, and a small blood vessel broke, leaving a permanent mark. I ran screaming to my mother, who was furious at him. After that I stayed far away from him and never teased him.

I was four years old when Grandfather Mendel died. I watched the casket being placed onto the hearse. We were told my grandfather was resting in the casket and was being sent to heaven. It was a long walk from our house to the cemetery. My brother and I were first in line, walking in the funeral procession behind the horse-drawn hearse, followed by my parents, other relatives and villagers. Looking at the plain wooden box, I felt relieved that I did not have to be afraid of my grandfather anymore.

Adjacent to the grain silo was the big washroom with a big stove and a large, coal-fired oven. This was where the workers on the farm and the household help ate their mid-day meal. One day I was keeping everyone company in the washroom, sitting on a chair and rocking it back and forth, totally disregarding the maids' warnings that I might fall. The more they told me to stop, the more wildly I rocked the chair. Suddenly it toppled backward with me in it, the chair falling on poor Fifi, our dog, who was just passing by. Fifi was killed. I cried bitterly and I felt awful. It was entirely my fault. My father must have felt sorry for me. He came home the next day with a new puppy, one just like Fifi, a spotted terrier. I was thrilled and hugged him. We named him Fifi too. But I never rocked another chair again.

Every few weeks there was washday. First the laundress had to scrub the wash on a metal washboard with soap and then the linen was boiled in big metal vats on the coal fired stove. Two maids helped the laundress hang everything outdoors in the fresh air. I loved the smell of the freshly dried sheets. The maids would stretch them on all four corners while I was hiding underneath.

One corner of the spacious washroom had a large wooden closet. It was the smoke room, where all kinds of sausages and goose breasts were prepared and stored. Every Friday, huge loaves of multi-grain bread, challah, and strudel cake were baked. My mother added all the ingredients into a big earthware bowl, while a maid had to turn the heavy dough. I always watched and waited until I was allowed to lick the bowl, when we made our own butter by churning milk. I loved drinking the buttermilk with chunks of butter in it.

For us children, it was healthy country living and we thrived. But soon, all this came to an abrupt end.

Childhood Memories, Flight to Flatow

The war had ended on November 11, 1918, with the bitter defeat of the German Army, and, according to the treaty of Versailles, Germany lost the part of the country in which we lived, to Poland. Germans who lived in that territory were given a choice to adopt Polish citizenship and keep their property, or leave without compensation. In protest, German civilians formed a militia, and fighting ensued between Polish soldiers and German citizens, who resisted the takeover. Sporadic skirmishes went on for almost two years. The Poles advanced to our village of Wissek in the late fall of 1919. Nightly battles were fought on our land and even in our courtyard. Every night my mother and the maid dressed us in nightshirts and carried us, half asleep, into the cellar. I clearly remember the basement where we hid. All the family and household help, including the Russian prisoners of war, sought refuge in the cold basement. My brother and I were placed on the floor, tucked in warm feather beddings next to the harvested potatoes, where I would soon fall asleep. Once we woke up from the noise of shattering glass, as a bullet pierced through the cellar window with a wheezing noise and then lodged into the opposite wall. We were scared and cried, but were too tired to be kept awake.

On another night a loud knock at the iron cellar door woke me up and frightened everyone there. "Open up," a voice said in Polish. Constantin was chosen to answer the door because he knew some Polish. He walked up the steps that led outside and opened the heavy iron cellar door. A Polish soldier stood there, asking to see the master of the house. Constantin told him that my father was an invalid on crutches. He begged him not to do my father any harm because he treated all prisoners well. The Polish soldier left and everyone breathed a sigh of relief.

The shooting usually stopped at daybreak, and then everybody came out of hiding. Each morning, the men who had died during the night were laid on the ground alongside the church. As soon as my brother and I were dressed and had our breakfast, we rushed with our cousin Ruth to the church to count the dead. To me the men looked as if they were sleeping. Some of them just stared with their eyes open. I didn't understand yet the meaning of death and was not afraid looking at them, but I noticed that the villagers who had gathered there were crying.

One morning, my Aunt Olga's store window was broken by an artillery bombardment. After the broken glass had been swept away, Ruth and I were playing on the newly swept floor. Suddenly I felt a sharp sting in my calf, which started bleeding profusely. Horrified, I ran home across the market, screaming for my mother, who removed the piece of glass and bandaged the wound.

In January 1920, Wissek finally fell into the hands of the Polish Army. The village magistrate was my father's school friend, who had taken on Polish citizenship and, therefore, was permitted to remain in Poland. My father, however, had not yet decided whether to stay or to move to Germany, when an unforeseen event suddenly solved this problem. My father received a phone call from his friend, the magistrate, forewarning him that my mother was on the blacklist and would be arrested by nightfall. The reason for the impending arrest was that my mother's Polish washwoman, with whom she had had an argument, claimed to have seen my mother strangle a Polish soldier in our doorway during a night battle. The magistrate advised my father to leave town as soon as possible, certainly before dusk. Immediately after the shocking news, my father prepared the sled carriage and harnessed the horses, while my mother hastily gathered our most valuable belongings. Before dark, my parents put us in the carriage and covered us with our warm feather bedding. I remember how I cried about wanting to take Fifi along. To stop me from being noisy my father hastily pushed the dog into a trunk beneath the carriage seat.

On that stormy, late afternoon my parents, my brother, and I, with Fifi underneath our seat, gave up all our possessions and fled Wissek, never to return again. My father drove on the snow-covered road until total darkness. I had fallen asleep but woke when my mother carried me into a sparsely lit barn. I asked for Fifi. When I heard that he had suffocated in the trunk, I cried uncontrollably. But my mother laid us on the hay, covering us with our feather bedding, and soon we fell asleep.

At dawn we left, using the back roads, to avoid the border control. After a short ride, we arrived safely on German soil in the small town of Flatow. My father owned an apartment house there and we moved into an empty ground floor apartment.

Flu was raging in Europe, and my mother caught it, becoming gravely ill. For two weeks we children were not allowed to go into her darkened bedroom. I remember how I missed her and prayed to God to make her well. She recovered slowly, but developed asthma, and she subsequently often suffered severe attacks. She was very fearful of living in Flatow, which was only a half-hour ride from Poland. She had sleepless nights, always frightened that the Poles might come and take her back, so we only stayed in Flatow for one year. During that time, I was enrolled in a kindergarten, where nuns taught me to stitch the outlines of pictures of houses on cardboard.

I loved being in the playgroup, but the long, daily walk to the school always filled me with great apprehension. To get to school I had to pass a square, where gypsies lived in a red brick house. I was frightened of them because whenever I was naughty, my mother would pick up the phone and pretend she was calling the gypsies to come and get me. Although that resulted in prompt obedience on my part, it made me afraid the gypsies might spot me on the tree-lined square on my walk to school and steal me. To avoid them, I pretended to become a dog by walking like one, with both my hands and feet on the ground. One day, my father passed by in his car and spotted me in this peculiar position. He stopped and asked what I was doing. When I told him, he laughed out loud. I was very relieved when he ushered me into his car and took me to school. From then on, I was driven to school daily.

I loved my father much more than my mother. She was the strict disciplinarian, very often to the point of cruelty. Perhaps because of her suffering from asthma she had little patience with us. She had a "loose" hand. There was not a day that I did not get a slap in the face, and sometimes she would resort to a leather whip, which landed on my rear end and left red streaks. My father, however, only spanked me once in my life, and he did that under duress because my mother had ordered him to do so while she watched this ordeal.

That particular incident happened in Flatow when I was five years old. Fire had broken out at the local chocolate factory, which was not very far from where we lived. Without telling anybody, I followed the many townspeople who rushed to the scene to watch the flames. I don't know how long I stood there, mesmerized by the spectacle. It was already dark when suddenly, I heard my mother's voice saying, "There she is," pointing at me and rushing towards me with my father. She grabbed me angrily by the arm as she said, "Wait until you get home. You are going to get it." I could hardly keep up with her running home, while my father limped behind us.

When we arrived, my mother handed my father the whip and ordered him to give me a good spanking. For this procedure my father had to sit down on a chair, put me over his lap, and pull up my skirt. All the while I was screaming loudly and kicking my legs. But he was ever so gentle; the spanking did not hurt at all. I screamed until my mother told him to stop, and then she ordered me to bed without food. I learned my lesson, never to leave the house again without permission.

I am sure that this difficult period in their lives contributed to the lack of attention our parents paid us. Neither of them played games with us nor read us stories, so I did not learn to read or write until I went to first grade.

In the summer of 1920, we were vacationing with Aunt Ella and her family by the seashore. We children had a lot of fun building castles in the sand. We spent evenings alone, playing games in our adjoining rooms at the hotel while the grown-ups went out dancing. One day I got lost on the promenade. I was crying bitterly and was afraid I wouldn't ever find my parents again. I couldn't remember the name of the hotel where we stayed. Just then, two nuns came along and comforted me. They eventually found my parents.

The ocean air was very beneficial to my mother, but as soon as we returned to Flatow her fear that the Poles would come and arrest her came back, and her anxiety attacks returned.

Life in Kuestrin

In the fall of 1920, my father decided to move to Kuestrin, a town of 15,000 inhabitants, about four hours away from the Polish border.

My mother's sister Kate, her brother Adolf, and their families lived in this town. They had left Posen two years earlier and had settled there. Uncle Adolf and Aunt Bertha owned a dry-goods store there, and Aunt Kate and Uncle Max dealt in scrap metal. Both families had bought large, luxury apartment houses in the park section of town.

By the time we arrived in Kuestrin, a great housing shortage existed, and my father could not find a place to live. Aunt Kate took us in for several months. My father co-owned the apartment house where Uncle Adolf lived, but there was no apartment available. So my father constructed temporary living quarters in the courtyard of a building he and Uncle Adolf owned. Finally, in January 1921, we moved into the stone house that he had built there, although the walls were still damp, and my mother's health continued to deteriorate. Her asthma and emphysema worsened and she was eventually sent to Bad Reichenhall, a sanatorium in the German Alps, where she found relief in the pristine air and by using an atomizer and smoking a medicinal cigarette daily, the latter of which she continued to do all her life. Years later, in the corridors of my daughter's dorm at Penn, I recognized the familiar smell and realized my mother's medicinal cigarettes must have been marijuana.

I was happy in Kuestrin. I received a lot of love and understanding from Aunt Kate as well as from my beloved grandfather, Louis, who lived by himself on the ground floor of an apartment house near my school. He knew when I passed by his house each day and waited to give me a hug. When I was very young I loved to sit on his lap and he would show me magic tricks or allow me to open and close the lid of his gold watch. On Saturday afternoons, he took all his grandchildren to an ice cream parlor for sundaes. My favorite was vanilla ice cream with raspberry sherbet and raspberry sauce, topped with whipped cream. But mostly, Grandpa was very lonely. He, like everyone who had to leave the part of Germany that was annexed to Poland, had lost his fortune and was dependent on the mercy of his eight children. It was agreed amongst his children that he should receive twenty German marks spending money per month, as well as food. I once overheard when he complained to my father, "One father can support eight children, but eight children cannot support one father."

I don't know how many times I ran over to Aunt Kate's because my mother had punished me. Aunt Kate always comforted me and tried to alleviate my suffering by offering any food I desired out of her pantry. My favorite was her preserved sour cherries, and I usually emptied an entire jar. I was lucky to have had her. She meant more to me than my mother, who never allowed me to hug her. Perhaps it was because of her illness; most often she pushed me away, saying, "*Geh mir vom Leibe,*" ("Get off of me"). Ever so many times, my mother would say, "I'd rather have ten boys than this girl."

She never spent much time with Gerhard or me, leaving us instead in the care of the household help. Even at dinnertime we were allowed to speak only when spoken to. She was always much kinder to Gerhard and when I asked why, she would answer with a sarcastic smile, "Don't you know? Gerhard is the good boy and you are the stepchild." I knew it was not true, because she had told everybody what a difficult time she had when she was pregnant and how awful I looked at birth. Whenever I was bad she warned me by saying, "If you don't obey instantly, I shall hit you so hard, that blood will spurt out of your mouth."

Every Friday night, a chicken dinner was served. Without fail, I was served last and I always got the wings. Sometimes it annoyed me and I would ask my mother why. She would answer, "First comes Father, then I, then Gerhard, and then a long time nothing, and then you."

We had no electric refrigerator, and one day my mother told me to go to the ice-cold cellar and carry down a dish of hot chocolate pudding. I was scared to go and refused to go alone. The cellar had mousetraps all over, and, of course, I was afraid of mice and rats. Without raising her voice, she grabbed me by the arm with one hand, holding the bowl of hot pudding with the other. She hurried down the staircase with me, mumbling the same thing over and over again, "I am going to drive that fear out of you, if it is the last thing I do." She hastily opened the cellar door and walked down the steps with me, handed me the bowl, and ordered me to put it on a table at the far end of the cellar. Without any objection I obeyed, but while I did so, she quickly turned, walked up the steps and locked the door behind her. There I stood, petrified, in almost total darkness, screaming with fear. After a while, I stopped, in the hope she might think something had happened to me. Shortly thereafter, she appeared and asked me, "Are you now cured?" And in a low voice I timidly answered her, "Yes." She repeatedly tested me after that but I never again refused to go to the basement.

I feared my stern mother, but I still loved her and wanted to be loved, but she had an unapproachable, cold attitude towards me. As a child I yearned for affection, but was unable to receive it from her. She must have suffered from depression ever since the day when she heard that my father was wounded and she gave birth to me prematurely, with little chance of my survival. Perhaps the heavy burden that she had to carry while my father was recuperating away from home, and then the terrible, false accusation of her having committed murder, and the escape out of Wissek, whereby they lost all their possessions, affected her mentally. Maybe she loved me but couldn't show her feelings. She was too wrapped up in her own world.

When I was in my teens she was relentless in her punishments. One Saturday when I was about fourteen years old, I was late to come home for the "havdalah" prayer to close the Sabbath at sundown. In Jewish tradition, one couldn't eat supper or even light a cigarette without first saying that prayer. Everybody was angry with me for being late, especially my mother. She pulled my handbag from me, took out my compact powder case and my lipstick and threw them into the burning fireplace. My "precious" possessions were gone! I had only owned them a short time and had been so proud of them. They were presents from my cousin Rosel, who had come to visit me from Schneidemuhl. Oh, did that hurt me!

For a while I felt I was too heavy and was careful what I ate because I wanted to be slim. One evening, for supper, we had hot milk soup with egg dumplings and home-fried potatoes swimming in butter. I refused to eat it. As usual, she gave me a stern look, but I did not obey. Without raising her voice, she ordered me to go to bed without food. Angry with my cruel mother, I cried myself to sleep. The next morning at the breakfast table, my swollen eyes still burning, she placed before me the same food on the same plate as the night before, but cold. Without a word of objection, I ate the food, but with disgust.

When I was about fifteen, I tried to lose weight. Before going home for dinner I would pick carrots, cauliflower, or peas from our garden and eat them there raw. That way, I could only eat a smaller portion at the dinner table. I really lost a lot of weight. In the winter I would buy carrots, apples, and pears, which were slightly damaged, for a few pennies from the local fruit and vegetable store. The owner's wife would let me eat what I had purchased, in their room behind the store. Sometimes, my mother would come in, while I was eating, but she never caught me. At mealtime I ate so little that after some time even my mother became worried. She was afraid I would catch TB. One evening I was doing my homework and I had a craving for chocolate. I was surprised when she actually went to the candy store to get me what I wanted. She must have been concerned about my health and I liked that.

In contrast to my mother, my father was always warm and kind to me. As a young child I was allowed to sit on his lap and hug and kiss him. He would say, "My snuggly little pussycat." I always had great love and affection for him.

In Kuestrin my father started a horse and cattle trade. He bred and raised his own livestock. Later, he was elected president of the German cattle association and remained so until Hitler came to power. When the Depression came in 1922 and money devalued from day to day, he had the foresight to buy land to let the animals graze. These animals were then sold at auction in the fall. He also invested in real estate, buying three apartment houses. He intended to purchase many more, but my mother was very much afraid that it might be too risky.

I remember a heated argument on the subject of acquiring more real estate. It was the only time I ever heard them quarrel. It happened while we were still living in the stone house my father had built. All four of us slept in one bedroom and I still had a junior bed with railings. I was awakened by a loud argument my mother had with my father, threatening him with a divorce if he bought one more apartment house. In anger my father said he would leave right then. He walked out of the room, slammed the door behind him and got dressed in the other room. I was upset when I heard my father was going to leave us, and started to cry. Swiftly my mother, who was lying in her bed, ordered me in a low voice, "Go and beg Dad, tell him you want him to stay." In an instant I jumped over the bed railing and ran to my father and held his leg tightly so he couldn't move. "Please, Father, don't leave us, please," I cried. He gave me a hug and reassured me, "No, no I will not leave." Then he went back into our bedroom, lay down next to my mother, and I went back to sleep.

My father was a deeply religious man. The Morning Prayer took three quarters of an hour before breakfast, which included the laying of *Tiffillim* (a ritual which required putting leather strips around one arm and a small leather box on the forehead). A *Tallis* (a "prayer shawl") was draped around my father's shoulders while praying. For lunch he would return from work to say *Minchah*, the noontime prayer. After that he took his daily nap. In the evening, after supper, he prayed again the *Maariv* prayer, thanking God for food and health.

Unfortunately, he did not have much time for us, except every Shabbat morning, when he brought us to the synagogue. In good weather, all our relatives met either in a nearby forest garden restaurant for tea, or they would come to our house for coffee and home-baked cake, which, in good weather, was served in our garden. The garden was my father's pride and joy. It easily stretched over two acres. We had a big grape arbor and fruit trees (cherry, peach, apple, pear, and plum). We had gooseberry bushes, loganberries, raspberries, and big strawberries, and all kind of vegetables. He planted plenty of flowers. Wild roses on arches decorated the pathways. He worked hard on it with his crew. He cultivated long-stemmed roses of all colors. When they were in bloom, he brought bouquets of flowers to my mother.

In 1922, after living in the crowded stone house for more than a year, we moved into an apartment on Schueztenplatz 3 in Kuestrin. The house belonged to Uncle Leo, who lived in Berlin and owned a furniture store there. It was a beautiful house and had a balcony decorated with flowers. Our apartment was on the second floor. It had large rooms, but no modern improvements. At first it had kerosene light then gaslight, which later was converted into electric light. There was no bathtub, and the toilet was one half-staircase below our living quarters. Every nightstand had a porcelain potty, which was emptied each morning by the chambermaid. Every room had a decorative tiled oven, heated by coal, and every morning the maid had to remove the ashes before starting the fire. On a marble-top washstand in my parents' bedroom stood a large china bowl and pitcher. In the morning the maid had to bring in warm water for each of us to wash, and once a week, on

Fridays, we took a tub-bath in Aunt Kate's luxury apartment. Later we took the bath in the newly built hotel across the plaza from where we lived.

The apartment had five rooms: a library, a living room, a dining room, and two bedrooms—one was the master bedroom and the other my brother's room. I was bedded every night in the library on a most uncomfortable divan, which was covered in the daytime with an oriental throw rug. The household help occupied the top floor. Our apartment was a short walk from the stables and the garden.

My mother was content to live in Kuestrin in the company of her sister and brother. She hired Miss Gerson to be our governess and to oversee the household. Miss Gerson stayed with us even after we did not need a governess anymore. Every morning she prepared breakfast for us, got us ready for school, and made sure we had done our homework. We grew up under the supervision of Miss Gerson, who was very good to us and taught us good manners. Gerhard and I didn't get along too well and often quarreled. He especially hated to have me around when his best friend visited him daily and they played the piano. He chased me out of the room and threatened to hit me hard if I returned.

With time my mother's health improved. She knew how to take care of herself. She slept late in the mornings. At ten o' clock every morning, the hairdresser would come to the house to set her hair with a curling iron. My mother was a beautiful woman and she wore fashionable clothes. Sometimes she would buy her clothes in Berlin in couture houses, and much of her clothing was custom-made. For school, she bought me sailor dresses (a pleated, striped skirt and a top with a navy-blue sailor collar and cuffs), which were very fashionable at the time. When she went shopping in Berlin, she always came back with a few party dresses for me.

Her daily chores consisted of buying and preparing the food for the day, and then visiting her brother or sister for a chat, or meeting other distant relatives in town. Once a week she went bowling. She decorated the new apartment with beautiful hand-carved furniture she had bought from her brothers, Leo and Hugo, who had furniture stores. Uncle Max supplied her with fine china and silver. She bought Persian rugs and fine curtains and a piano for us children. My brother was very gifted, and after one year of lessons he could play any song he heard by ear. I, however, had to take lessons for years from a teacher I feared, because whenever I touched the wrong key, she quickly tapped my fingers with a bamboo stick, which frightened me. It took me forever to learn to play a decent piece of music. My mother would ask me, "Please, play the piece that cost me one hundred marks," and I knew exactly which one she meant.

My mother had her good side. She kept a beautiful home and was an excellent cook. On Fridays a lot of preparation was necessary to prepare for Shabbat. Friday mornings, Cantor Levy came to kill a live chicken by cutting its throat with a sharp razor to let the blood out. We children used to watch this religious ritual. The dead chicken used to flutter for quite a while after it was dead. The maid had to tear off the feathers and singe the skin of the chicken. My mother made noodles every week for the chicken soup. My mother loved to buy beautiful objects of art and bought decorative silver and china. She taught me to appreciate these things. I grew up in a very cultured environment.

The Shabbat table was always very festive, with a fine tablecloth, silver candles, wine, and beautiful dinnerware and silver. Mother loved to give parties and enjoyed having her sisters and my cousins visit us.

Every so often we had unexpected guests to Friday dinner, who stayed for the night in our guestrooms, which were in a separate wing in the courtyard. These were Russian or Polish Jews who had fled their country from persecution and were on their way to America. Because they had to stop their journey before sundown on Shabbat eve, they contacted Cantor Levy in Kuestrin, who sent them to us, as we did not live far from the railroad station. My father, being a pious Jew, considered it a good deed (a Mitzvah) to feed and house these poor people, much to the dismay of my mother. The people looked unkempt with their long beards and dark coats and hats. She was always afraid they might bring lice (*kinnim*) into the house. Also they only spoke Yiddish, and my parents understood only a few words. They did not know how to use their knives and forks properly either. She was prejudiced and had no sympathy for them. I wonder if she ever remembered how she had treated these sojourners when years later she arrived in Palestine and had to adjust to a strange, primitive life.

Most of the time she got along well with her brother and sister, but sometimes she would have quarrels with them that would last for extended periods of time. When she was not on speaking terms with them, she would not allow us to visit them. I was about thirteen years old when my cousin Brunhilde married Arthur Wolff. The wedding was celebrated at Aunt Kate's home. Shortly before the wedding the sisters had an argument and we were not allowed to join the wedding party. Gerhard and I stood in front of Aunt Kate' s house, listening to the dance music coming from Aunt Kate's apartment, longing to go up to the party. Aunt Kate spotted us from her balcony and urged us to come up. Gerhard had no fear of my mother, so he went. But I, who wanted so much to see the bride, did not dare go up, for fear of my mother's wrath should she find out. Instead, I just sat sadly on a bench in front of the house, listening to the dance music and laughter from above.

My mother had me under control at all times. When she scolded me, I bottled my anger up inside and my throat churned. All I could do was just cry and be upset with myself for not having the guts to defend myself. I was afraid of her. She gave me an inferiority complex and I developed a low self-esteem. I only had C grades in school and never had the ambition to do better. I don't think my parents paid any attention to how I did in school.

In school I had a few friends. My best friend was Dorothea

Mueller. We were friends from the first grade on and were inseparable. I spent more time in her house than in mine. Her mother adored her daughter and was always kind to me. I always wished my mother would treat me like that. Dorothea was an only child and was happy to have me as her playmate. When we were older we would go to the silent movies together to see Charlie Chaplin. Between five and six in the evening, it was customary for students to stroll in twos along the main street and flirt with the opposite sex. Dorothea was very popular. I had my eye on Ludwig Hirschfeld, my brother's friend, but he always ignored me.

Sometimes, after school, a group of classmates would meet at the spooky, local seventeenth-century fortress with the ouija board at hand. Everyone sat on the sandy ground around a round, low, three-legged table, touching each other's fingers, calling upon our dead relatives and asking them questions. If the table started to tremble, the answer meant "yes" to the question asked. We were scared to no end, but it was a ritual we enjoyed and when we were done we smoked hand-rolled cigarettes.

In 1932 I graduated from Lycee (high school) in Kuestrin and went on to Obereal Gymnasium (the Heinrich von Kleist Schule), which still exists in Frankfurt on the Oder. The school prepared us for graduate study at a university. Dorothea Mueller and a few of my classmates from Lycee attended the same school. Most students commuted by train, but I roomed with a Jewish family whose daughter was also in my class. I was no longer the only Jewish girl, as I had been in the Lycee in Kuestrin, and I did not feel so isolated. Since the family in Frankfurt did not eat kosher meals, my father did not allow me to eat with them. Little did he know that I had been eating ham (which is strictly forbidden under Jewish law) at Dorothea's house for years. I joined the local Jewish community center where there was a kosher restaurant, and where I also attended interesting lectures and occasional dances. I enjoyed student life, especially the independence that came with living away from the scrutiny of my strict mother. I even earned pocket money by tutoring a younger student in math.

January 1933 brought the rise to power of the fascist national-socialist party under the leadership of Adolf Hitler, and our freedom as citizens of Germany was immediately greatly curtailed, and our existence ultimately threatened.

The national-socialist party in Germany began forming as early as 1923. It was a small, anti-Semitic group under the leadership of Adolf Hitler, an Austrian housepainter, who, within a year, had enticed jobless workers in Germany to rebel against the ruling democratic party in Germany. In 1924, when I was only nine years old, Hitler staged an uprising and curfew was declared all over Germany for several days. After dark we heard shots being fired in the streets and we children were scared. I remember awakening at night and being so frightened that my mother had to take me into her bed. I heard her talk to Aunt Kate about Hitler, saying that he was a menace to us because he hated Jews.

Hitler received a year-long imprisonment in Landsberg, near Munich, Germany. While in prison Hitler wrote the book *Mein Kampf*, in which he stated his intention of annihilating all Jews in Germany; a policy known as *Judenrein* ("free of Jews"). At that time nobody thought this could ever be possible in a civilized society in the twentieth century. Every decent-minded person thought these words could only come from a maniac. Little did we realize how soon Hitler would be able to draw the German people to his banner.

By 1932, some of my classmates had already joined the Hitler Youth Movement. They did not show any animosity towards me, although I often heard them sing a song, which contained dreadful threats against Jews. I don't recall the exact words, but it said something about how Jewish blood would drip from Nazis' knives. The song was called, "The Horst Wessel Song." The melody still rings in my ears.

My school chum Dorothea Mueller, however, always stayed loyal. Even after Hitler came to power we kept in touch secretly.

Years later, when I was studying at the Jewish hospital in Berlin, she studied nursing at the Countess Rittberg Hospital in Berlin. Shortly before I emigrated, she took the risk of paying me a farewell visit in my nurses' residence.

How Life Changed After Hitler

I was a student at the Heinrich von Kleist Schule (a school of higher learning) in Frankfurt on the Oder when Hitler became chancellor of the German Reich. That day there were parades held all over Germany. Some of my classmates were happy that Hitler had been chosen to be the chancellor of Germany. They already wore to school the khaki uniform of the Hitler youth group, with the swastika emblem on the sleeves. Just as we were discharged from school the parade passed by, and many girls joined in the march, proudly singing the new Nazi lieder. They even wanted me to come along, but I felt it was wrong for me to be celebrating the victory of a party whose leader was a preacher of anti-Semitism, so I declined.

While the Nazis were jubilant about Hitler's rise to power, Jews in Germany began to worry about their future. Within weeks, life changed drastically in the Jewish community. Jews in government positions (judges, doctors, teachers, etc.) were forced to retire without pay. Hitler announced strict rules prohibiting Germans to socialize with Jews. Nazis stood in front of Jewish enterprises, daring anyone to enter the stores. Students of Jewish faith had to leave schools and universities.

I, however, was permitted to continue my studies, even though I was Jewish, because I was the child of a German Army veteran. I only had to finish that school year to get my baccalaureate degree, and then I intended to study dentistry.

But for my family and me, the good life soon came to an abrupt end. My mother had to discharge Miss Gerson, our beloved governess and housekeeper, and a maid. Both of them had worked for us ever since we lived in Kuestrin. According to new restrictions on Jews, Mother was only permitted to engage one maid, who was over sixty years old. Poor Miss Gerson, who was middle-aged, became very despondent after she left us, and committed suicide, leaving us a note about how much she missed us and how life was no longer worthwhile.

I was still attending school in Frankfurt in May 1933 when my mother called me, crying and in total despair, begging me to come home instantly, because my father had been taken away to the local prison in Kuestrin. I took the next train home and found my mother suffering an asthma attack from the excitement of my father's arrest. A doctor was attending her when I arrived. As soon as she could speak she told me what had happened.

The evening before, one of my father's foremen, Kurt, and two of his friends, came to my parents' home. Kurt recently had become the local group leader for the Nazi party, but was still working for my father. He came to tell my father that he would always allow him to continue his trade in livestock. Very happy about the good news, my father invited him and his comrades to join him for supper, which they gladly accepted.

My mother's seamstress had just finished her day's work in our home, and as she left she saw the men eating supper and drinking beer in our dining room. She went to the local dance hall to report to a group of Nazis that Kurt, their leader, was having supper and beer in Mr. Graumann's home. When the Nazis heard that Kurt and two other men were eating with a Jew, they rushed to my father's house and demanded that Kurt and his men come out. Kurt went out on our balcony and angrily ordered the men to leave, and they obeyed. Kurt reassured my father that he shouldn't worry about the incident because he had those men under his control. But the next morning the police came and took my father away. They told my mother that he was being placed in protective custody.

I tried to console my poor mother, but we were both at a

loss as to how to help him get out of prison. My mother could not even go and see him; she was physically unable. I immediately went to prison to see my father. Since his arrest, the night before, he had refused to eat, and drank only water. My poor father was humiliated and I felt sorry for him, and yet, he was utterly helpless. Daily I walked the long way to prison and brought him home-cooked kosher meals in casserole dishes.

Two weeks went by without a word from the authorities about his release. We did not know who to approach. In our despair we decided that I should see the local judge, who happened to be a tenant in one of our apartment houses, and ask him to use his influence to get my father released from prison. Late one evening, I gathered enough courage to walk up the stairs to his apartment, hoping that nobody would notice me. Frightened and uncomfortable in asking this judge for a favor, I knocked on his door. He looked through the peephole, and cautiously opened the door. "What do you want, Frieda?" he asked. I begged him to help us, because my father was wasting away in prison. He just nodded his head, saying, "I understand," and quickly closed the door.

In a few days my father was released from prison, depressed and haggard-looking, of course. It took him a while to recover from this ordeal. After his release my father was forced to sell his pastures and liquidate his business by selling his livestock, at a loss.

He did not allow me to go back to school. He felt it was senseless to finish my studies. He was certain there was not going to be any future for young Jews to study because they wouldn't be able to pursue their chosen professions. They would be unable to make a living. Thus, my life as a student at the Heinrich von Kleist Oberreal Gymnasium in Frankfurt an der Oder came to an abrupt end.

That same year my brother, Gerhard, had a traumatic experience at the Real Gymnasium for boys in Kuestrin. While Gerhard was sitting at his desk during class, an anti-Semitic student who was sitting behind him stabbed him between the ribs, piercing his lung. My brother was rushed to the hospital with a collapsed lung. Fortunately, he recovered. From then on, Gerhard was an ardent Zionist. He left school and enrolled in a newly opened Jewish agricultural school that prepared young people for immigration to Palestine.

Nine months later, Gerhard, while bicycling home from Agricultural school, was ambushed by three Nazi's in a nearby forest. Fortunately, Gerhard fought them off and rushed home. Immediately, my father contacted a Zionist organization in Berlin which advised Gerhard to leave town and take the next train to Berlin. When he arrived in Berlin, the organization arranged for Gerhard's departure from Germany within hours. Gerhard fled to Holland and was assigned to freighter where he supervised live stock destined for Palestine. For weeks, we had no word of his whereabouts but finally, he arrived safely in Palestine in the summer of 1935. He worked on a Kibutz for four years until my parents arrived in Palestine in June of 1938.

As for me, there was nothing to do in Kuestrin. My former school friends could not speak to me anymore; I felt like an outcast. They were not even allowed to greet me when we met on the street. My mother felt sorry for me and took me along to visit her sister, Olga, in Baden-Baden. It was good to get away. I had not seen my cousin Ruth for several years and we had a great time together. Sometimes we would go to five o'clock tea and dance. People did not know that we were Jewish. Jews were still allowed to eat in restaurants and go to all cultural events in Baden-Baden. It felt like old times, until we returned home and life again became unbearable.

My Au Pair Jobs

I finally decided to look for a job as an au pair in another city where nobody would know me. Through a weekly Jewish publication I found a job without pay. I was to take care of a six-year-old boy near Duesseldorf in the western part of Germany. His parents owned and worked in a shoe store, and they lived in a lovely old house. The housekeeper taught me to cook while the little boy was in school. It was a pleasant job. I had planned to stay there for a year, but the man of the house, a fat, disgusting-looking, baldheaded person, soon tried to make advances on me. He chased me around the dining room table until he cornered me and then tried to kiss me. After several such incidents, I quit, having spent barely three months there.

I immediately found another job, as a chambermaid at a bed-and-breakfast. I had to get up at six in the morning. to make coffee, help serve breakfast, and clean ten rooms. I was not used to such hard work. Every night I sank into bed exhausted. I lasted only one week and quit after I received my first paycheck.

It was carnival week in Duesseldorf at that time, and the mood was gay and festive. I decided to splurge and enjoy the merriment for just a little while before going home to my parents. I checked into a very nice hotel for just one night. In the lobby I happened to get acquainted with two young couples from Brazil who invited me to join them. We had a jolly good time singing in the streets of Duesseldorf until the wee hours of the morning. I forgot for a while all the trouble in Germany.

After a few hours of sleep, I took the train back to Kuestrin, where I relaxed for a few days before finding another au pair position in Berlin, again through the Jewish newspaper. The

children, an eleven-year-old boy and seven-year-old girl, lived
with their grandparents. The parents had immigrated to
England already, and wanted to get adjusted there before
bringing the children over. The grandparents and the children
were very nice people. They lived in a small apartment in an
old section of Berlin. I was put in a dark, gloomy maid's room.
The first night, after a few hours of sleep, I woke up itching,
with large welts all over my body. I turned on the light and saw
swarms of bedbugs on my white bed sheets, crawling up the
wallpaper and on the bare mattress. I was petrified and could
not sleep another minute in that room. I waited for the
grandmother to wake up to tell her I was leaving. The old lady
begged me to stay until she could get a replacement. She
promised to have the room fumigated immediately.

I felt sorry for her and agreed to stay as long I could take
the afternoon off while the fumigation was being taken care
of. She let me off until eight in the evening. I decided to go to
the Excelsior Hotel for five o'clock tea in the outdoor garden.
In good times, my parents used go there when they came to
Berlin. I had no intention of dancing; I just wanted to watch
other people. I still remember the outfit I wore. It was not at
all appropriate for dancing, but it was the only dress I had
brought from home. It was black satin with a wide, black, patent
leather belt and a black and white Scottish plaid bow tied at
my white collar. Because it was a cool day, I wore a bright red
knit-cardigan over the dress and beige cork-soled shoes. It was
not long before young men began to ask me to dance, but the
cork shoes made it awkward for me to move gracefully. None
of the men asked me for a second dance, except one young
man, who asked me twice. His table was at the other end of
the dance floor. He danced as poorly as I did, but he was witty,
amusing, and very good-looking. We both laughed about our
clumsiness. He asked me where I came from and knew
immediately that I was a country "bumpkin," because he grew
up in the city of Landsberg, not far from Kuestrin.

When the music stopped at seven o'clock and people

started to leave, he came over to my table, introduced himself, and asked me for a date. I could not understand his entire name clearly; all I heard was Doctor Hans. I agreed to meet him on Saturday at four o'clock at the Uhland Eck on Kurfuerstendam. He emphasized I must not stand him up, that I should rather tell him now if I didn't really mean to come. He said he was a very busy man and time was important to him. I promised I would keep the date.

This was exciting. No one had ever asked me for a date before. I was very happy when I returned to my au pair job at eight o'clock, but my room smelled so strongly from the fumigation that it gave me a headache. I couldn't sleep in that room and so I slept on an ottoman in the living room. I told the grandmother that I was definitely leaving on Saturday and she should get a replacement, which she did.

I could hardly wait for Saturday to come, when I left my job. I took the subway and left my small valise in a locker at the train station. I could not leave Berlin until after sundown, because my father would not allow me to take a train before the end of Shabbat.

Very excited, I proceeded to walk to my first rendezvous with Hans. On the way to my date I ran into my cousin Herman, who was studying for the Rabbinate in Berlin. He didn't approve at all of me going out with a stranger. "Have you gone mad?" he asked. "What you do is daring. Who knows whether this man is really a doctor and comes from Landsberg? Have some sense. Come with me and watch me play tennis." But no one could stop me from going to my first date and I left my cousin.

My First Date

It was May 5, 1934, a beautiful sunny day. I waited impatiently at Kurfurstendam and Uhland Eck for ten minutes before Hans finally arrived. He took me to an exclusive outdoor cafe and invited me to order anything I liked. His generosity impressed me. He was very easy to be with and constantly amused me with his great sense of humor. After we each had a fruit salad, we walked in the nearby Tiergarten.

There he told me about his family and himself. He and his ill father were living with his recently widowed sister, Margrit, and her nine-year-old son, Joachim.

Hans had passed the law exams, summa cum laude, in 1932 and had been appointed to the federal court in Berlin, Germany. He proudly revealed that, because of his outstanding scholastic achievements, he was the youngest judge ever to have received this nomination to the court. Unfortunately, this position lasted only half a year because of the new Nazi rules against Jews. Hans was forced to retire without pay. He was now employed as in-house council at a Jewish bank.

He spoke about how the relatives on his mother's side were mentally ill. His mother had died in a sanatorium of dementia at the age of fifty-seven, just two months earlier.

One of her brothers, Hans's uncle, jumped off the roof after the 1929 stock market crash in New York; others took overdoses of pills; one cousin hanged himself in Mississippi; and his grandmother ran in front of oncoming horses and died. All of his mother's five siblings had suffered from mental illness. I was puzzled why he told me all that. I wouldn't reveal that to someone I had just met. Why, he almost bragged about the mental illnesses of his relatives! This was not something to be proud of. In those days people would keep that secret. I was taken aback for a moment and thought to myself, *What a family! I had better stay away from him.* But he was so charming, amusing, and open, and I enjoyed his company. Before I returned to the train station, he took me to another restaurant for dinner, and again I was to order whatever I liked. After a meal of delicious calves' liver with red cabbage, it was time for me to take the train home. He offered to look in the Jewish newspaper for an au pair job for me and to write to me about it. I told him he would only be able to write to me through post office delivery because I knew my strict mother would not allow me to correspond with a stranger.

When saying goodbye, he embraced me and gave me a wet kiss; something I had never experienced before. I cannot say that I liked it. Somewhat disgusted, I closed my lips tight. I had the feeling that Hans sensed that I disliked this move. A boy had never kissed me before—not even on my cheek. Embarrassed, I said goodbye to Hans, stepped onto the train and sat in my compartment, happily reliving the exciting day. It had been such a wonderful feeling to be embraced. But then I thought about the wet kiss.

At the age of nineteen I had never been told about the facts of life. In those days, sex was not a topic to be discussed in the family or in school. My friend Dorothea had once told me that something wet gets into a woman and then she could become pregnant. But she did not explain any details and we didn't talk about that subject any more. When I first started to menstruate, I thought I was bleeding from the navel. Miss Gerson, our housekeeper, told me that the bleeding will occur every month, and that only when a woman is expecting a baby would menstruation stop. I had my own idea of how babies came into his world. I thought babies came out of the navel. The vagina and rectum were both just for elimination.

Could that wet kiss have made me pregnant? It started to worry me. It was on my mind a lot, but at home I had no one to tell my worries to. I was very happy when I got my period that month.

Every week Hans sent me charming notes and want ads for au pair jobs. I sent out applications but didn't ever get any response. Apparently, by the time my application arrived, the position was already filled.

Six weeks had passed since I had last seen Hans, when two of my brother's friends drove by one morning and asked me to go to Berlin with them for the day. My mother allowed me to go. This was an unexpected chance to see Hans again, and I called him as soon as I arrived. We met at a cafe on Kurfurstendam. We were very happy to see each other.

Hans had brought the weekly Jewish newspaper, and together we searched for an ad for an au pair. We found one and I called the number. The lady asked me to come for an interview right away. Since it was not too far to walk to the address, we strolled happily up Kurfurstendam. Hans waited outside while I was being interviewed. The lady had a beautiful face, bleached-blonde hair, and was fashionably dressed. She lived with her three-year-old son on the ground floor of a very elegant apartment house. She told me she conducted her business from her home and needed someone to take care of her adorable little boy. I accepted the position. However, I did have to ask my parents' permission, as I was only in Berlin for the day. I promised her I would return as soon as possible. Hans and I celebrated by eating in a very nice restaurant and then we went to the zoo park where we stayed until it was time to meet my brother's friends.

My parents allowed me take the job, and I returned to Berlin a few days later. I was happy to be in Berlin and was able to see Hans on my days off, which came twice a week. When we met on my first day off he wanted to give me a passionate kiss again, but I refused and told him the reason why. I let him know how I had worried about that wet kiss he had given me at the train station. He was amused, but thought it was irresponsible of my mother to send me out into the world without having told me the facts of life. He knew I was not ready to have sex and he was not asking for it. He taught me all about sex, though we did not engage in it until almost a year later. Hans was a person I could depend on and tell what was on my mind without being embarrassed. He was nine years older and so much wiser than I was and I learned a lot from him. In a way he was almost like a father figure and I looked up to him.

The new au pair job was enjoyable. I loved the little fellow and his mother was kind to me. Unfortunately, this job did not last very long. The mother of the little boy always had many guests until late at night. She may have had a dating service, but she also could have been a madame, because she rented out rooms to couples who were not married. Usually the guests came late in the evening after I had put the boy to sleep and retired to my room, at the far end of a long corridor. When I discovered what was going on I told Hans about it, and although I loved the job, he made me quit immediately. He was scared the police might raid the place, and I could easily get drawn into a scandal.

Fortunately, I found another job the day I left, taking care of two little boys. The parents were very wealthy and snobbish, especially the mother, who treated me more like a servant than as a member of the family. As was customary with au pair jobs, I had time off Wednesday afternoons and every other Sunday after ten in the morning. On those days I would meet Hans, who always showed me a great time, taking me swimming or boating on Stoelpchensee or Wannsee with some of his friends and their girlfriends. We ate in quaint pubs and went to movies or cabarets. Berlin was a vibrant, exciting city.

I had been there eight months when they fired me unexpectedly. The sister and brother-in-law had moved in with us, while the parents were on a trip to Palestine. During the parents' absence, the six-year-old boy developed a high fever on the day I was to have my afternoon off. It never occurred to me that I should stay home, since the boy's aunt was there too. When the parents came home from their trip and heard that I had taken time off while the boy was sick, they asked me to leave. Upset and crying, I packed my belongings and left.

Plans to Study Nursing

I called Hans, who consoled me and said that these au pair jobs were not for me. These positions had no future and were not challenging enough. He suggested that I should go into nurse's training at the Jewish hospital of Berlin. If Hitler should make it intolerable for Jews in Germany, I would at least have a profession, which would provide me with work wherever I might go in the world.

Hans knew about that profession because he had had a girlfriend named Jetty who had been an operating nurse at the hospital, and she had recently immigrated to England.

It seemed to me that Hans's suggestion made sense. Although I had never set foot in a hospital and had no idea what nursing involved, I followed his advice and requested for an interview with the directress of nurses at the Jewish hospital of Berlin. I told the secretary I was only in Berlin for the day and she gave me an interview that same afternoon. The directress (Frau Oberin as she was called) was an elderly, heavyset lady. She wore a black uniform and a starched nurse's cap on her silvery hair, and her collar was held together by a silver enameled brooch decorated with a red Jewish Star of David with the inscription, "The Jewish Hospital of Berlin." She looked like a nun. With a benevolent smile she asked me, "Tell me child, why do you want to become a nurse? It is a hard profession. Do you realize what you are getting into?" I was somewhat intimidated by her authoritative presence and answered in a low, hardly audible voice, "I want to help the sick, because I have a sick mother."

She paused for a moment and looked me over from head to foot and then said, "I am not sure whether you are strong enough for this very hard profession. I look at your hands and think you have never worked a day in your life. I advise you to go home and really think it over seriously. Find out more about nursing. And, if after two months, you still want to enter training, write to me and I will let you start in June."

Hans and I were happy that my prospects of becoming a nurse looked good, but it meant I would have to convince my parents. What if they wouldn't let me? For the next two months, I stayed in Kuestrin. My mother was very much against my plan. She had never heard of a Jewish girl becoming a nurse, although I had told her the hospital accepted only Jewish girls. She did not think I was suited for that profession but eventually she allowed me to go ahead. A week before I was to enter my training, Uncle Max had a car accident. I visited him in the local hospital. Walking the polished floors and smelling the chlorine-filled air, I was excited about becoming a nurse. But as soon as I saw his bandaged head, I fainted.

How could I think of becoming a nurse? My relatives begged me to back out, but I stayed steadfast in my resolve to go into training. Of course I never let them know that my real reason for going into nursing was to be able to live in Berlin and be near Hans. I was not concerned about dedication and love for the nursing profession. It didn't even enter my mind. All I knew was that Hans had given me the right advice, and I trusted his good judgment. It proved to be an invaluable decision, which has served me well for my whole life.

Student Years: 1935 to 1937

I had anxiously awaited the day I was to enter the nurse's training school, and it finally came. I had not seen Hans for a long time, and was looking forward to our reunion in Berlin.

I stepped off the train in Berlin early in the morning, and Hans greeted me with open arms. It was a joy to see him again, but I had little time to spend with him then because I had to report to nursing school by ten in the morning for orientation. He accompanied me to the Jewish hospital, kissed me goodbye, and wished me good luck. I told him I would call him later.

The directress of nurses, Frau Oberin, greeted the new students in her office at the nurse's residence, then orientation began. She showed us the large dining hall and the infirmary on the main floor, and then she took us to the main hospital and laboratory for blood tests. A doctor examined us and ordered chest x-rays. When it was time for lunch we all sat in the huge dining room and waitresses served us. Frau Oberin sat at the head of the long U-shaped table. The meal was simple but it was served with a certain elegance. After lunch we were sent to the sewing room where we were measured for our size. Each of us received a light-blue uniform, an apron, a student nurses' cap and brooch, a white starched collar, and warm black coats.

Frau Oberin then lectured us in an authoritative tone as to how to conduct ourselves on and off duty.

All nurses were called *Schwester* (or "sister"). Because there was already a nurse by the name of Frieda, I was given a new name. Frau Oberin gave me the name Friedericke, and from then on I was to be called Schwester Friedericke. I had no choice in that matter. Actually, I liked Friedericke better than my real name.

Finally we were escorted to our rooms. The first year students occupied the top floor of the three-story residence. I shared my room with three other students: Schwester Regina, Schwester Edith, and Schwester Trude. They hailed from other parts of Germany. In a very short time we became friends and got along well.

Our room was large but sparsely furnished. There was a bed, a nightstand, an armoire, and a desk for each student. Bathrooms had to be shared. A maid cleaned our room and bathroom and changed the linen twice a week. The place was spotless. The linoleum floor was sparkling clean and shined like a mirror. Our personal laundry was taken care of weekly. On our days off, we could even get our meals served in our rooms, just like in a hotel, by sending a request and filling out the menu the day before. Working hours were from seven in the morning until eight in the evening, with one and a half hours off for lunch. Then followed a one-hour lecture by a physician. We were permitted to be off duty every Wednesday afternoon and every other Sunday all day until ten in the evening. If we failed to come home in time, we had to report to Frau Oberin the next day. The punishment was that we could not go out on our next day off. There was only one phone on each floor. The line was so busy I could not even get in touch with Hans that first evening before I went to bed.

The next morning after breakfast, all first-year students received their assignments. I was to start on the male ward of internal medicine together with another student, Schwester Lea. We were both excited and walked across the beautiful hospital grounds to our assigned station. The head nurse, Schwester Ida, a tall, middle-aged woman, greeted us warmly. She spoke fast and had a slight lisp. It was often hard to follow her. She took us to the utility room, and demonstrated to us how to measure and record the urine of each patient. We had to clean the urinals and bedpans with Lysol and a brush, and then return them to their respective night stands. There were twenty of them. She told us we could join her for the second breakfast break in the nurse's lounge after we finished our assignment.

It took us forever. I was very clumsy and splashed water all over my shoes and white, starched apron. It was a disgusting job, but there was nothing I could do about it. I had chosen to become a nurse, and this cleaning job was apparently part of the training. Little did I know what else was in store for me. As I was about to return a urinal to the nightstand of a patient, he asked me, "Please place the urinal for me." Taken by surprise I asked, "What, why can't you do it yourself?" The patient took his bandaged hands from under the bedcover and showed them to me. I blushed from embarrassment and thought, *Oh, my God, how am I to handle this?*

I had never seen mature male genitals except on sculptures. The thought of having to touch them totally disgusted me, but I had to do it. Cautiously, I picked it up with his hospital shirt, looked under and wiggled a small something into the urinal, then quickly covered the patient and left the ward very ashamed. This was more than I was willing to handle. I ran into the utility room and told Lea, "If this is what nursing is about, I can't stand it. Please, tell the head nurse I quit." I quickly left the ward, returned to the nurses' residence, and soaked in a hot bath, brushing my fingers with a big brush that was supposed to be used for scrubbing the tub. After hurriedly packing my belongings, I sneaked out of the building unnoticed. I was unfortunately unable to reach Hans by phone and I felt terribly embarrassed. What could I tell him? God knows what he would think of me! As far as I was concerned, I was done with nursing. I took the next train home to Kuestrin.

One hour later I was home. My mother was sitting by the window doing her needlework as usual. She was not surprised when I entered the room. I told her that it was disgusting what I was asked to do and that I gave up the idea of becoming a nurse. She looked up from her work and replied with a strict tone, "Oh no, you are not going to do that. Tell me, you signed a contract when you entered nurse's training, didn't you?" I replied timidly, "Yes, but that does not mean anything."

"Oh yes it does, to me. I have talked with Frau Oberin, who called here. She is expecting you. You will take the very next train back. She will put you in the female ward. I want you to understand that when you have made a commitment you have to abide by it. This is not your home anymore. Do you understand? Goodbye." And she continued to work on her needlework.

Oh, did I cry! I knew once my mother had made up her mind, no pleading in the world would help to change it. I hated her, but I could not say a word. How cruel she was! I was all choked up inside. Sobbing, I left and went back to the train station.

When I arrived at the nurses' residence, Frau Oberin greeted me and put her arms around me and said, "My dear child, you will get used to your new environment here. I understand, it is hard for you." She exuded much more warmth than my own mother did. My roommates were happy to see me back, and the next day I started on the female ward. I, however, still resented the cruelty of my mother.

Years later, I realized what a great lesson she had taught me, for which I owe her my profound gratitude. Had I not finished my training as a nurse, I would never have had a chance to come to America. It is doubtful that even I would have been able to go to Palestine with my parents, since I was over eighteen. I would have had to initiate my own immigration, which was restricted for an unskilled person like me. It is dreadful to think that most likely I would have had to succumb to the same fate as the six million victims of the Holocaust.

Life was not easy for me as a student nurse. To be perfectly honest, I do not think that I had the appropriate qualities to become a nurse. I was squeamish and finicky and lacked the dedication of other nurses. But I enjoyed the camaraderie amongst the student nurses, and, above all, I wanted to stay to be near Hans. I was fascinated by the lectures in obstetrics that taught us all about the reproductive organs. When I had told Hans how worried I was about the wet kiss, he had explained that I couldn't get a baby from that, that it had to be a different kind of fluid, and he promised me he would never force himself on me. But still I didn't know the details about sex. I was only twenty years old and still very naive. I was under the impression that the male genitalia was a bone that would somehow retract after intercourse.

After my mother's cruel rejection, I was longing for Hans's love. Hans was the only man I had ever dated and the only man I had ever kissed. He was my first love, and our love grew as time went on.

Hans became my closest and most trusted friend. I knew that he genuinely cared for me. I clung to him like a child. He was nine years older than I was, and I respected him for his intellect and wisdom, and, above all, he was witty and made me laugh a lot. Besides, he was tall, dark, and handsome; the Gregory Peck type. At twenty-eight, his thick, wavy black hair had turned slightly gray already, which added to his distinguished appearance. He had clean-cut features and deep-set searching eyes. He always had an immaculate appearance. At twenty, I still did not have the maturity to judge a person by his character. So I was very lucky that I had found Hans. I easily could have fallen into the hands of someone who would have used and dropped me.

Meanwhile, I became accustomed to nursing. Life was not easy, but I was determined to prove to Hans that I could endure all the hardships of nursing, just like his former girlfriend Jetty had. The hours were long, but we received very good training, not only in nursing skills and medical education, but also in cleanliness and general hygiene.

I remember working at the tuberculosis station and learning all the special techniques used to avoid contaminating myself. Unfortunately, after a short while, I began to have nightmares wherein I woke up in a sweat, holding my hands up high, in fear I had been contaminated with something. I told Frau Oberin about my dreams. She was very kind to me and immediately transferred me to the ear, nose, and throat ward. The head nurse there, Schwester Helga, was known to be very strict. She did not like the way I cleaned bedpans and was determined to make a model nurse out of me. One day, she ordered me to take all bedpans and all urinals from the entire floor, submerge them into a deep bathtub filled with soap and Lysol, soak them for a while, and then scrub them until they were absolutely spotless. With great disgust I obeyed her orders and she personally spot-checked my work. Cleaning bedpans and urinals on the ward was my daily assignment for the next six weeks, and I gradually improved until I became a model student. Only then was I allowed to join the other students, whom she invited every afternoon for tea.

Soon thereafter, I was assigned for night duty on Schwester Helga's floor. I had never worked a night shift before. It started at seven in the evening and ended at eight in the morning. On my first night, I was the only nurse taking care of the twenty patients on the floor. I was very busy doing routine evening care and giving out medications. Some of the patients were post-operative and required special care, but by midnight everyone was taken care of and it became quiet. I made myself comfortable, with my legs up on the sofa in the nurses' station, as I read the paper. I must have fallen asleep. I woke up at six o'clock in the morning and opened my eyes to find Schwester Helga standing there staring at me, frowning. "Oh, my God! What happened?" I cried out. She pointed her finger at the light indicator panel and said, "Just look." Every sick room was lit. The patients needed me and I wasn't there for them. I was utterly embarrassed and apologized. She helped me answer all the bells and, as soon as day relief came at seven, she sent me over to Frau Oberin, who was very understanding. She arranged for a second nurse to work the night shift with me.

After that I liked night duty, mainly because it gave me a chance to sneak out of the nurses' residence for several hours during the day. I had come up with a great idea: Whenever I was out I carried a package of Modess (sanitary napkins) with me. That way, when I came home and was asked why I had left the residence without permission, I would have a valid excuse. This made it possible for me to see Hans every single day for the next two weeks that I was on night duty. Nobody ever caught me, and soon every student on night duty was copying my idea.

During my training I had to get used to a lot of things, like seeing blood in the operating room without passing out, and changing dressings on patients' wounds in spite of the odor. But one thing I never got used to was witnessing and assisting deliveries in obstetrics. We had to assist in thirty of them. Every time a baby slipped out of the birth canal into the obstetrician's hand or lap, my face turned white, I became light-headed, and my ears started ringing. I felt like I would faint any second, and I had to sit on a stepstool and lower my head below my knees. Everybody knew what was happening to me, including the chief obstetrician, Dr. Josef, who was also my mother's cousin. It was a fact which embarrassed me even more. That was one department I was glad to leave after fulfilling the requirement of thirty deliveries.

During my training years I sustained two injuries, both of which caused me a great deal of concern. One day an orderly and I were rushing a hospital-bed into the operating room. I was in front, at the head of the bed, and the orderly, by a freak accident, pushed the bed against the doorframe instead of through the open door, and the action crushed my head. I passed out and received a fractured nose and concussion. They taped my nose back in place right there in the operating room, but I had to stay flat in bed for twenty-four hours because of the head injury.

The other incident occurred while I was extracting fluid from a patient whose body was covered with pustules due to syphilis. I had to observe sterile techniques by using a gown and gloves and covering my face with a mask, with only my eyes exposed. I siphoned the fluid into the sterile syringe and then tapped it to get the air bubbles out. Suddenly, the needle that was attached to the syringe popped off and the fluid splashed over my covered face and into my eyes. Petrified, I ran out of the room, my eyelashes dripping with pus, and cried for help. One of the nurses tried to wipe my eyes with an alcohol swab, and I screamed with pain. As a result of this accident I was quarantined for two weeks, until my Wasserman came back negative. This was not only a tremendous scare, but, even worse, I was unable to see Hans for more than two weeks.

Frau Oberin had heard through the grapevine that I had a relationship with Hans. She knew him through Jetty, the former operating room nurse. Because Hans had not married Jetty, Frau Oberin despised him. She was a motherly figure and cared a lot for her nurses, and did not approve of my relationship with Hans. One particular incident almost caused my dismissal. After a severe cold, I suffered from an inflammation of both Achilles tendons. I could barely walk, and only with considerable discomfort. Frau Oberin was going to send me to the orthopedic staff doctor, but I insisted on seeing the head of the department, whose office was in the western part of Berlin, not far from Hans. The doctor put casts on both legs up to my calves, and ordered bed rest for two weeks. It was difficult to walk with my crutches, even just to get into a cab, but I had to see Hans. I returned to the nurses' residence four hours later. Frau Oberin was furious when I returned and ordered me to the infirmary. I asked her to have someone help me get my bedding and toiletries from my top floor room. She angrily refused and snapped back, "If you can manage to stay away for hours, you can handle your own bedding. No one is going to help you." I guess she knew where I was hanging out so long and was angry. Climbing the three flights of the highly polished, circular staircase was very difficult, but somehow I managed. However, I found it impossible to carry the heavy featherbed and two pillows down the stairs, so I decided to throw all of it over the banister from the third floor. As I watched with amusement from the top, it landed with a resounding thud in the vestibule, busting the bedding wide open just when Frau Oberin was passing by, engulfing her in feathers. She looked like a chicken that had lost its feathers all at once. At the same time, many nurses were descending the stairs to go to the dining hall for Shabbat dinner. They saw Frau Oberin submerged in all the feathers and they broke out into a roar of laughter. The poor woman must have been frightened, and I felt bad and utterly embarrassed. She was still agitated, trying to brush the feathers off of her black uniform and her white hair when I reached the vestibule. I knew she was angry and I apologized. At once she ordered me to go to the dispensary, but all beds were occupied there. I thought she would let me go back to my own room but she made me sleep on a cot that was too short for me. Both legs in their casts hung out at the end. She completely ignored me when she came in to visit the other sick nurses on Shabbat morning.

On Sunday morning she brought me a pail with raw potatoes and ordered me to peel them. I flatly refused, because I considered it an insult. I told her that if she was short of kitchen-help, I could get her a maid from home, and that I had not come there to learn to peel potatoes. She was furious and told me she would see to it that I be transferred to another Jewish hospital in another town. She would take it up with the chairman of the hospital, Dr. Lustig. One of his duties was to perform a chest-examination of every new student on arrival and periodically thereafter, and it was known that on some of the young students he took the liberty to become more personal than he should have. Frau Oberin didn't even look at me while I was on bed rest. After my casts came off, she promptly took me to Dr. Lustig. She didn't speak a word on the way to his office. All the while I worried about the outcome of this meeting with him. What if I were fired or transferred to another hospital? When we arrived at his office, he wanted to know the reason of our visit and let Frau Oberin speak. "I request that Schwester Fredericke be transferred to another Jewish hospital, Dr Lustig. She doesn't respect my orders [she mentioned the potato incident at this point] and besides, she is immoral. On my recent inspection of her room I found a huge photo of a man hanging over her bed." He paused for a while and touching his mustache in obvious embarrassment he responded with a smirking grin, "Frau Oberin, isn't it better to find a man over her bed than find him in her bed?" Even she had to grin, and I was relieved. He told her this was too trivial a matter to make an issue of. "We should forget what happened and shake hands," he added. We did shake hands and I was allowed to continue my studies in nursing.

I learned a lot in those years, not only professionally but also personally: how to endure hardships, how to be precise, how to have patience, how to have compassion, and above all, how to be caring. My studies trained me to be strong and to be able to face the difficult times that were to follow later in life.

Visit to America

In September 1937, after two and a half years of rigorous training, I graduated from the nursing school of the Jewish hospital of Berlin. In a solemn ceremony, Dr Lustig, a stocky, bald-headed man with a lusty smile, handed me my Registered Nurse Diploma, issued by the German Reich and sealed with a Swastika. (I still have it.)

Immediately thereafter, I started to work as a staff nurse at the Jewish hospital, and continued there until I left Germany in 1939. I was given a room of my own in the nurse's residence. Life as a graduate nurse was considerably easier than as a student. The work was administrative, no more cleaning bedpans or urinals, and I could stay out until midnight as often as I wanted. The salary was not great but I did not care as long as I had freedom in my private life.

At home, my father was in the process of liquidating his business. In September 1936, he had made an exploratory journey to Palestine after his release from prison, also visiting my brother, who was working there on a Kibbutz. While he was in Palestine my father was still able to transfer German money legally to a British bank. This money could only be used for purchasing land in Palestine, and not for any other purpose, such as food.

My father returned from his trip with his mind made up—to immigrate to Palestine—although he realized that life there would be extremely hard. Also, he was concerned about the warm climate. Would my mother be able to adjust to it with her asthma? Furthermore, my parents would have to learn a new language (Modern Hebrew) and adjust to a totally different lifestyle. It was not an easy decision, but he wanted to live among his "own" (Jewish) people, in the land that Britain had promised to give them as a homeland. He was willing to help build that new country.

My mother began shopping for all kinds of new household goods such as fine china, crystal glasses, embroidered bed linens, and rugs and clothes, all things which, she later found out, would be totally useless for the primitive life she would lead in Palestine.

My parents never encouraged me to join them and I had no desire to live a pioneer's life. My years away from home while I was in nurse's training had made me independent. I had not been homesick like some of the students. I kept in touch with my parents mostly through letters and occasional visits.

Hans never wanted to immigrate to Palestine, and I intended to follow him wherever he would go. Actually, Hans thought the Hitler regime would not last, and he would eventually regain his position as a judge. He lived comfortably with his sister, Margrit and nephew John (Joachim) on their parents' inheritance.

Unexpectedly, in 1936, Hans was named executor of his Aunt Gerda's estate in Germany by a German court, because the former executor had died. She had inherited great wealth from her father in Germany. She was married to Hans's Uncle Herman, who was the brother of Hans's deceased mother. Aunt Gerda and Uncle Herman lived in New York. He owned the largest pants manufacturing concern in the country and was a philanthropist. The oldest of five children, Uncle Herman had been sent to a relative in America in 1877 at the age of fourteen, following the death of his father. He learned pants manufacturing, and was a millionaire by the age of twenty-one. In 1912, at the age of forty-five, he married Aunt Gerda, who was eighteen years old. The couple was childless.

Uncle Hermann was very attached to all his family, and, until his sudden death in 1938, he and Aunt Gerda traveled to Switzerland every year to vacation with his three sisters and their spouses at the Suvretta House in St. Moritz. Aunt Gerda's money in Germany was used to support his relatives. Generous donations were also made to all Jewish charities in Germany. Uncle Herman's younger brother had also moved to America in the 1880s, but he had jumped off a roof to his death, in New York, during the 1929 bank crash. Hans, as the newly appointed executor, had to come to America once a year to confer with Aunt Gerda. He was very excited when he left on the SS *Europa* for the United States of America in the summer of 1936 to confer with his relatives for the first time.

Hans had not learned English in school; he had attended a humanistic gymnasium where Greek and Latin were taught. But since the Nazis had started making life unpleasant for us Jews, he had taken English lessons at the Berlitz School, just in case he had to leave Germany at some time. Like every foreigner, he had trouble with the language, and he often misused words. The day Hans arrived in New York for the first time, his relatives and Uncle Herman's business partners greeted him at the pier. They asked him, "How was your trip and the weather?" Hans replied in a typical German accent, "Se trip was fine, but it was very *fucky*." Everybody burst out in laughter. Poor Hans couldn't understand why they were laughing until he was corrected, but it was quite embarrassing for his first appearance there.

Like all proud naturalized Americans, his uncle and aunt only conversed in English, although both had a slight accent. They made life very pleasant for Hans when he came to New York. They arranged for him to stay at the fashionable Barbizon Plaza Hotel and he had dinner with them every night at their posh duplex apartment on Central Park West. Both became very fond of Hans. While he was in America in 1937, conditions for Jews worsened and the thread of war hung heavily over Europe. His uncle and aunt urged him to remain there for good. But Hans had many reasons not to stay. He would never leave without his widowed sister and his nephew Joachim (Johnny). Also, he and his sister had considerable wealth, which they couldn't take out of Germany anymore. So the prospect of joining his uncle's business was not inviting enough for Hans to leave Germany at the time. He didn't have the foresight that my father had as early as 1936, when, understanding that there was no future for Jews in Germany, he initiated his immigration to Palestine. Hans believed that Hitler wasn't going to stay in power much longer. He was certain that one day he was going to get his position back as a judge, and he didn't have the courage to face an uncertain financial future. He was used to a very sheltered life, living in great comfort with his sister, where meals were served on a beautiful balcony in Berlin. Besides, life in New York was not comfortable (*gemuetlich*), and it was much too hurried for him. He said only if Hitler made life intolerable for Jews would he leave Germany for America. Uncle Hermann phoned Hans after he returned from his trip to the United States in 1937. He pleaded with Hans to reconsider and get out of Germany.

But Hans didn't heed his uncle's advice. This was unfortunate. Had Hans moved when his uncle wanted him to, he would have avoided much mental anguish and would have fared immeasurably better financially. This was a mistake, which Hans regretted for the rest of his life.

Because Hans might live in New York one day, I decided to try to find a relative in America who would vouch for me. At that time, American immigration laws were very strict. Only a relative could vouch for an immigrant. This person had to show proof of his yearly tax return and guarantee that the immigrant wouldn't become a financial burden to the government. Such a document was called an affidavit. It was also possible to obtain a working affidavit from any stranger, if they would guarantee permanent employment, so that the immigrant would never become a public charge. America had a quota system; only a certain number of immigrants from each country were permitted to enter each year. It took fifteen months until I finally was allowed to immigrate.

My parents were very pleased with my decision to seek a

relative in the United States. My grandfather's brother, who had immigrated to the United States around the turn of the century, lived in New York, and I intended to approach him. As a reward for my graduation from nursing, my parents had given me a generous check, which I used to buy a ticket to go to America on a visitor's visa. I even had enough money left to buy a Leica, a fine, German-made camera. I was to stay in New York with my Uncle Leo's sister-in-law, Ann. She worked as a cook in New York and she was able to get me a low rent room in the apartment building where she lived in Manhattan.

On the 26th of December in 1937, I started my journey to America. It was a very exciting, but also frightening experience. It was my first visit alone to a foreign country. I took a train from Berlin to Bremen and from there traveled on a ferry to London. I stayed in a small hotel in London for one night. I had forgotten a lot of the English I had learned in a two-year's course in high school, and I found myself in embarrassing situations at times, from using a word improperly. At a restaurant I tried to read the menu and ordered "roast beef," which is similar to the German name, but porridge I didn't know. It sounded like "cabbage" and I thought I would try it. When the waitress came I said, "Please bring me roast beef and porridge." She looked puzzled, "Porridge?" Very certain of what I wanted, I answered, "Yes, porridge." She said something, which I could not understand. When she finally brought the food, I was disappointed and pointed to the porridge disgustedly. She asked, "What's the matter?" I questioned her, "What is this? I thought this would be some kind of garbage." I meant cabbage but used the wrong word. The waitress broke out in loud laughter. "You don't want garbage. What do you want?" Now I remembered the word cabbage, but she didn't have any cabbage on the menu, so she brought another vegetable, which I had never eaten before. It was green squash.

Another embarrassing incident occurred when I wanted the bellhop to knock at my door to awaken me the next morning. I wanted to say to him, "Please wake me in the morning at such time—", but I couldn't think of the word "wake." So for lack of the word "wake," I winked at a bellhop and asked politely, "Would you like to come to my room?" "Surely, in a moment," he replied and I proceeded to go to my room. When he showed up I demonstrated by knocking at the door what I wanted him to do at six o'clock the next morning. The young man, obviously full of expectations, was disappointed and said, "Okay, but is that all?" And with a grin said again, "Are you sure, nothing else?" I told him, "No, thank you," and he went away.

The SS *Empress* of Briton sailed from Plymouth the next morning with me on board. It was a huge ocean liner, the proudest luxury ship of the British Empire. I had a beautiful cabin on the second highest deck. But when the ship left the harbor, I suddenly was gripped by fear. I had never sailed on an ocean liner before. I did not expect the North Atlantic would be so choppy and soon I became seasick. I had to stay in bed the entire trip, with nurses looking after me. I was so miserable and felt ready to die. More than once I lay in my own feces because I had no control of my bowels. I could not even hold down water and had to be fed intravenously. It made the trip unbearable and later caused a medical problem. Almost immediately after arriving at New York Harbor, I felt 100 percent better.

I knew Ann had a day job as a cook and was therefore unable to pick me up from the pier. She lived on 137th Street and Amsterdam Avenue in a rooming house. When I got off the ship, I hailed a cab. While the driver was putting my suitcase in the trunk of the car, I slumped into the backseat, exhausted from the ordeal of the sea voyage. The driver asked for my destination. I handed him a piece of paper with the address, but was shocked and scared when I saw he was a Negro, (as one would call a black man in those days), and only hoped he would bring me unharmed to the right address. I thought Negroes only lived in Africa, and I had only seen one black man in my whole life, one day in Berlin on a fashionable street, the Tauentzin, where curious onlookers had surrounded the man. We had been amazed to see such a novelty.

It was a bright, sunny day. The taxi drove along beautiful Riverside Drive, with the Hudson River on one side and elegant high-rise apartment houses on the other. I was relieved when the driver stopped at the right address. He even helped me bring my suitcase to the elevator of the rooming house. A friendly, bleach-blonde landlady showed me my small, sparsely furnished room in her dreary, dark-looking railroad flat. It was dark even on a bright day. The window of my room opened into a main shaft, facing a concrete wall. A lone light bulb hung from the ceiling and a small washbasin was set in one corner of the room. Every so often, the radiator would make banging noises. There was only one bathroom for the entire apartment. I ended up spending three and a half weeks in that dismal place.

At six o'clock, Ann, a chubby, plain-looking woman with a friendly smile, and her Italian boyfriend came home from work. Apparently, they lived together. I thought it was odd that they were sleeping together so openly and unashamedly. They could not have legally done so in Germany. She looked different from her younger sister, my chic and slim Aunt Kate from Berlin, who was Uncle Leo's third wife. However, the couple was very kind to me, and we became good friends. They gave me a map of Manhattan and explained the New York transportation system, so I could explore the city while they were at work. I had a few contacts to make, including a Dr. Brown, a gynecologist, whom I visited soon after my arrival, to report greetings from a friend. He told me how hard it was for him to get his license. Because of hard times in America, nurses could not easily find jobs in their own profession.

But all the discouraging news I got from Dr Brown did not stop me from seeking an affidavit from my eighty-four-year-old great-uncle. He lived with his daughter, a Mrs. Birnbaum, in a poor neighborhood in the Bronx. He was unable to help me, but he advised me to approach his well-to-do son, Fred Salomon, who owned an advertising and printing business.

One evening Ann took me to the Cameron Hotel on 86th Street, to which we had been invited by Fred Salomon and his wife Gertrude. I was anxious to meet my new relatives, but a little nervous. I hoped they wouldn't refuse my request for an affidavit.

Fred, a short man in his early fifties, dressed in a dark silk jacket, opened the door to his tastefully furnished apartment and ushered us to sit down. He only spoke English, so I was glad I had Ann with me to assist me in the conversation. Soon his wife Gertrude appeared, dressed in an elegant robe. She looked like a model; her dark, well-coiffed hair framed her beautiful face. She was much taller than Fred and at least twenty-five years younger. Both were interested to hear about conditions in Germany and about my family.

I told them the purpose of my visit to America and I asked Fred whether he would give me an affidavit. When he told me he was willing, I was delighted and thanked him many times. I felt my mission was already accomplished by getting the promise of the affidavit. Little did I know how much Fred would disappoint me later. Gertrude was about my age, and I had the feeling she liked me. We had difficulty communicating at times, but it was a very pleasant evening and she promised me she would show me around New York. She was very kind to me during my stay in New York and spent a lot of time with me, almost daily, and my English improved a lot. She showed me Manhattan and took me out for lunch to posh restaurants and on shopping sprees to elegant department stores like Bergdorf Goodman and Saks Fifth Ave. She gave me three of her very stylish dresses, because she was tired of wearing them. They fit me perfectly and I felt very American in them. Twice she invited me for dinner, which was served by her colored cook. Fred was not very talkative. I had the feeling something was wrong in their marriage. Each time I saw him, I reminded him of his promise to sign an affidavit for me, but he told me he could not yet find the time for it.

I met Gertrude's friend Sally Ferguson, who spoke German. She offered to stay in correspondence with me after I returned to Germany to help me brush up my English. Sally turned out to be a godsend to me when I finally was able to come to the United States in 1939.

One evening, Ann and her boyfriend took me by taxi to Radio City Music Hall. As we were driving along Central Park, I noticed a huge neon sign on the dark horizon, displaying the words SEX HOUSE. I could not imagine that there was such a thing here in America. It took a while before I had the courage to ask, "Is there really such a thing as a big sex house?" They burst out laughing. They explained that the two first letters, the E and S, must have failed to illuminate. It should have read ESSEX HOUSE, which is a well-known hotel on Central Park South.

We arrived at Radio City, and I was overwhelmed by the beauty and size of the theater. I had never seen anything like it before. I admired the spectacular Christmas show with the dancing Rockettes. A movie was playing on a large screen, and an actress was singing, "*Bei mere bist du shane*," which translates, "in my mind you are beautiful." It was a hit song at the time. And when I heard Al Johnson's "Yes we have no bananas" I felt as if I were in a dreamland.

In no time, I had fallen in love with New York. It was a huge city with a pulse of its own. There was so much to see and the skyscrapers were so tall. It didn't take me long to get familiar with the transit system, and soon I was able to explore the great city by myself.

But above all I loved the American people who were very friendly and easy to be with; so free and uninhibited. There was no bowing and kowtowing, no formalities or etiquette to observe, like there was in Germany. I felt I could easily get accustomed to the American way of life and couldn't understand why Hans didn't feel the same way.

Unfortunately, my visit was marred by an ugly episode. Soon after my arrival I noticed a vaginal discharge, which I attributed to the time I lay in my dirty linen on board the ship. At first, I hardly paid any attention to it, but it got worse. I decided to consult a doctor. I was too embarrassed to go to Dr. Brown, whom I had just met. On Park Avenue and 86th Street I spotted a shingle that read: Dr. Robert Schwartz, Gynecologist. The name sounded German, and I walked in without an appointment. He examined me alone, without a nurse, and then ushered me into his consultation room. He told me, "This is not from you being sick on ship, young lady. You have an infectious disease. It is gonorrhea." I could not believe what I had just heard. I was terrified and questioned him, "How is this possible, when the only relationship I have had was with Hans?" He said, "Well, you know, men are not always faithful." He then gave me specific orders to take nightly douches and return to his office to get a suppository inserted daily. With a stern look he warned me, "If you fail to come, I will have to report you to the Department of Health." I was devastated. I told him I would not have enough money to pay him. I suggested I could insert the suppositories myself, being a nurse. "No you can't." He spotted my Leica hanging from my shoulder and said, "I will take that as a payment." In my distress, I gave it to him. After I left his office I bought a rubber douche in a drugstore and went to my room and cried. I sat down and wrote an angry letter to Hans, asking him how he could have done that to me. That he had ruined my vacation. How could he have deceived me? I had always believed that he was faithful. I would never forgive him because I had lost faith in him. In this letter I never mentioned the word gonorrhea, because I was afraid that the Nazis might censor this letter and I would have trouble on my return. In my excitement I forgot that this letter probably would arrive around the time of my return, since it took two to three weeks for overseas delivery in those days.

As it was, Hans got my letter just a few days before I was to return to Germany. He told me later, that the letter didn't make sense to him. He thought the trip must have been too much for me and it must have affected me mentally.

All that time I felt unclean and disgusted with myself, and I didn't share my problem with anybody. The washbasin in my room came in very handy. It was necessary for my personal hygiene and comfort.

I was so depressed that I was in no mood to go out with Gertrude anymore. Ann had lost her job as a cook and she asked Fred for a job in his business. He needed workers to stuff envelopes. I thought perhaps he would give me the affidavit sooner if I worked there too. Every day we both worked in his office doing piecework, but I was too slow and after ten days he let me go. He kept Ann though, who was happy to have a job. Fred never made any attempt to give me the affidavit, and I finally realized that I could not count on him. I was unhappy about my lack of success in securing an affidavit and was very depressed about my condition.

After going to Dr. Schwartz's office daily for more than a week, and treating myself with douches, I didn't notice any more discharge. He reduced the visits to three times a week, but still insisted on me coming to his office. I must have seen him ten times. One day, while I was sitting in the waiting room, I heard a woman moaning and groaning very loudly in one of his treatment rooms. Now I knew for sure that Dr. Schwartz was an abortionist. All along I had felt uneasy about him. There was never a patient in his office when I came, nor was there a nurse or a receptionist there. As soon as I heard the sound of moaning, I ran out of his office and immediately called Dr. Brown, who saw me the same day. He took a smear and examined it and said, "You never had gonorrhea. It is a different bacillus. It probably stemmed from the problem you had while you were seasick. What a shame, you have been taken." But, oh, was I relieved to hear that it was just a simple infection! Many years later, when I was already a citizen, I read on the front page of the *New York Times*: "Abortionist gets 15 years." It was Dr. Robert Schwartz.

After my visit with Dr. Brown, I was in good spirits again and contacted Gertrude and Florence. With all my troubles, I had completely forgotten to get in touch with Cantor Levy, my former cantor, who had immigrated from Kuestrin to Scarsdale, New York in 1934. He was happy to hear from me and invited me to a Purim party (a Jewish holiday) out in Scarsdale the following Sunday, just four days before my departure. Little did I know that this call would determine my destiny.

That Sunday was a cold and snowy day. I wished I hadn't committed myself to go, but I didn't want to disappoint Cantor Levy. It was difficult for me to deal with the complicated IRT subway system, and I had trouble getting to Grand Central Railroad Station and finding the right track, but I finally made it to Scarsdale. Cantor Levy was delighted to see me. At the party he introduced me to a lady, Mrs. Gillis, and her two children. Mrs. Gillis' mother happened to sail on the same ship as I, the SS *Bremen*, in four days. She told me she would be greatly relieved if I could look after the old lady, and she would gladly pay me for it. I did not want to accept any money, but decided to ask her instead for a working affidavit as a nurse-governess to her children. She said she would be glad to do that for me before our sailing date, and she did. This was my lucky day! Some angel must have been watching over me. Had I not gone to that party and met Mrs. Gillis, I might never have had another chance to immigrate to America, since Fred never sent me the affidavit he had promised.

I never heard from Gertrude again. Maybe she was embarrassed at Fred's behavior. But Sally and I became pen pals, and kept in contact after I had returned to Germany.

The SS *Bremen* sailed on Thursday. Mrs. Gillis had been able to switch her mother's cabin so that we roomed opposite each other. Her mother, Mrs. Simon, was a spry and delightful old lady. It was fun to be with her. She also became my chaperone when I went dancing, as I did almost every night.

One man seemed to pursue me wherever he could. He was a nice person, but I was not interested in him. He was short, bald, and, at thirty-six, he was too old for me. He told me he was a doctor and a widower. His wife had died of cancer. They had adopted a child, and he and his six-year-old daughter lived with his mother. His name was Bill Landfather. He was on his way to Budapest to study hospital administration. His grandfather, who had immigrated from Hungary, owned a hospital in Maryville, Missouri, which Bill was to take over. My "chaperone," Mrs. Simon, kept Bill entertained by playing cards, while I was dancing elsewhere. Just before landing at Bremerhaven, he asked me for my address and phone number because he intended to visit Berlin before returning home. Later, he sent me postcards from Budapest.

Mrs. Simon and I parted upon landing. Her other daughter expected her at the pier, and I took the train to Berlin.

When I met Hans I explained to him my dreadful experience with Dr. Schwartz and he felt sorry for what I had gone through. I was happy to see Hans again. I told him how great life in America was. I urged him not to hesitate any longer and to immigrate as soon as possible. He agreed and said he would ask his uncle to send him an affidavit. I met Hans for just a few hours, and then spent the weekend with my parents in Kuestrin, before going back to work at the hospital.

When I returned to Berlin, Hans had some very disturbing news for me: His Uncle Herman in New York had committed suicide. He had suffered a heart attack several months ago, and although he had been making a good recovery, he was depressed. Hans had received several phone calls while Uncle Herman was recuperating, urging him to come to America.

Just a few weeks earlier, while strolling along Central Park in New York, I had passed his uncle's apartment building and seen Aunt Gerda and Uncle Herman leaving their chauffeured limousine. I had been tempted to approach them and introduce myself as Hans's friend, but hadn't dared, as I was unsure whether Hans would have approved of it. Perhaps, if I had told them that I might be able to convince Hans to come to America soon, Uncle Herman wouldn't have killed himself. Who knows?

Hans was very upset and worried about his future. Now that he finally had made up his mind to ask his uncle for an affidavit, Uncle Herman was gone. He was not sure whether Aunt Gerda would give him an affidavit, now that she was a widow.

Hans left for New York the following day, to visit the distraught widow. While visiting and consoling Aunt Gernda, he told her that he had decided that he would definitely be moving to America with his sister and her son. Aunt Gerda willingly filled out the affidavits.

Because of the quota system, it took Hans more than a year to be permitted to enter the United States. However, in May 1939, with the help of Aunt Gerda and various Jewish organizations, Hans, his sister, and her son Johnny fled to Stockholm, Sweden, where Aunt Gerda generously supported them while they waited to be allowed entry into the United States.

Soon after I had returned from America, I received a summons to appear at Nazi headquarters for questioning. Needless to say, I was nervous. I thought perhaps Dr. Schwartz might have been a Nazi and had informed them about my condition. When I got there, two tall Nazis in black S.S. uniforms were waiting for me in a large, dimly lit room. They ordered me to sit and questioned me. "Why did you go to America and what did you do there? Where did you stay? Who paid for you while you were there? Did you take pictures? Where are they? Where is your camera? Was it a Leica?" Now I realized the salesman at the camera shop must have reported me to the Nazis. I told them that I had not taken any pictures because I had to give the camera to a doctor as payment for treatment. They wanted to know the name and address of the doctor, and the illness I had. I told a lie; I said I was bleeding. They asked me if he was a Jew like me. "I didn't know," I said. They drilled me with questions, often repetitious, and then let me go. I was called back two weeks later and was asked the same questions by different Nazi officers. Again, I was frightened and felt very drained from the ordeal.

I continued to work at the hospital until I was permitted to emigrate from Germany fourteen months later, on the 26th of March 1939.

Kristallnacht

Every November 9, since 1938, I am reminded with chilling pain of the horrendous persecution of Jews that took place that day in Germany. I experienced the ordeal of the *Kristallnacht*, ("the night of broken glass") and the turbulent months that followed, while working as a nurse of the Jewish hospital in Berlin.

Images of brutality are so deeply carved in my mind that I remember that terrible episode as vividly as if it had happened yesterday. It is hard to describe the horrors, fears, and worries that overwhelmed and shocked all Jews living in Germany at the time. What brought on this infamous pogrom?

On November 7, 1938, shocking news came over the radio that a deranged Jew, by the name of Greenspan, had shot and killed the German ambassador to France in the streets of Paris. The newspapers showed gruesome pictures of the crime, and retaliation was predicted. We feared the serious repercussions this senseless act might bring, and anticipated some form of punishment. But no one imagined the scope of the swift reprisal that ensued. The Nazis must have been planning this for a long time before then.

During the night of November 9, 1938, the Nazis rounded up every Jewish male over the age of fourteen. All people living in Germany had to be registered with their particular religion, and they had to carry that registration with them, making it easy to find Jews in their homes, in the streets, and in restaurants. Wherever they could be found they were arrested, loaded onto trucks, and transported to labor-detention camps, most of which were quarries. There they had to stand in the freezing cold or snow for hours until they were processed and given work assignments, which usually consisted of filling sacks with sand, and then carrying those heavy loads on their backs to the silos. If they broke down they were severely beaten. The round-up of all male Jews began simultaneously over the entire German Reich, by the order of the Fuehrer, Adolf Hitler, and it lasted several days.

I was employed as a graduate floor nurse at a hospital staffed exclusively by Jewish doctors and nurses. I had worked there in that capacity since February 1938, after I had returned from my visit to America. Since my return, conditions had steadily worsened in Germany, and I was anxiously awaiting permission to immigrate to the United States. Many arrests were made and more restrictions were imposed in the months that followed.

When my parents had left in June 1938, immigrating to Palestine, they were still able to take out some valuables. But shortly thereafter, all Jews were ordered to give up all jewelry and silver to Nazi depots. It was painful for me to give up the few possessions I owned (an Aquamarine ring, my birthstone, which my parents had given me for my tenth birthday; a bracelet, which I had inherited from my beloved Miss Gerson; and a golden watch.) Ironically, a Nazi gave me a receipt and then threw my belongings into a huge barrel, while I watched with tear-filled eyes.

Late in June 1938, massive arrests occurred of Jewish men who were known to have had longtime relationships with "Aryan" German women. Severe financial restrictions were imposed upon all Jews. They were not allowed to withdraw more than one thousand marks from their bank accounts per month. In addition to this harassment, the imminent threat of war loomed heavily over Germany, making the urgency of an escape from Germany even more pressing. I was glad my family had been lucky enough to find a safe haven in Palestine, but I was alone in the menacing turmoil of Nazi Germany, and I was scared. I restlessly hoped to receive my permission to enter America. Every night, I prayed that God would let me out before it was too late. I wished I had never returned from my visit to America that year. I felt trapped.

At seven o'clock in the morning on that cold day of November 9, I entered our nurses' stations completely ignorant of what had happened during the night. After the patients had received their breakfast, the nurses usually sat in the nurses' lounge and ate some of the leftovers from the food truck. I was eating my favorite farina with raspberry syrup when we heard over the radio the incredible news that Hitler had ordered the arrest of all male Jews across the entire country. My first thoughts concerned about where Hans, friends, and relatives might be. I was terribly frightened. Soon we heard that synagogues were burning. From our hospital windows we looked out in the direction of the Grand Synagogue in the Oranienburger Strasse, where my Great Uncle Lembke officiated as chief-cantor and resided with his wife. We were petrified to see the flames and billowing smoke shooting into the gray sky.

Soon news circulated that our hospital and the nurses' residence might become a target, and we were not permitted to leave the hospital compound.

All of us were frightened, but tended to our chores as best we could. It was evident that Hitler really meant what he had written in his book, *Mein Kampf,* that he truly intended to make Germany *Juden rein* ("free of Jews").

We received orders from the hospital administration to admit any Jewish male who wished to seek refuge and to write out charts with fictitious complaints. Soon, frightened men of all ages began to arrive at the hospital. These were the lucky ones, who were fortunate to have not been caught yet. The chief rabbi of the Great Synagogue, Dr. Warshauer was one of the men hiding in our ward. Every one of these men brought with them new horror stories. Berlin was burning. Every Jewish business had been broken into and plundered, and store windows were smashed. The streets, smattered with heaps of glass, made walking hazardous. Painted slogans like *Juden raus!*

("Jews get out") were visible on Jewish-owned properties. Fire engines were forbidden to come to the rescue of synagogues and Jewish-owned stores. It was absolute chaos.

By noon the hospital was swarming with men seeking asylum, and we admitted everyone and made out fake charts. Not only was every hospital bed occupied, but also bare mattresses that had been stored in the basement were brought up to line the long corridors. Patients rested on them with just blankets or sheets.

Nazis gradually infiltrated our hospital. Some of them stood in corridors and on the hospital grounds in full uniform; others were disguised in hospital garb, working as janitors or window cleaners, mopping floors on the wards and in the long corridors. Each patient was given strict orders for absolute bed rest, no bathroom privileges; they were not even allowed to sit up in bed. Those who did not heed our instructions paid dearly. They were mercilessly seized by the Nazi spies and forcefully removed from the ward. One could hear the screams for help, which we were unable to answer. God knows whatever happened to those poor men.

All nurses were asked to work on sixteen-hour shifts and remain in uniform at all times, on high alert, in case of fire. Once during the night I heard the fire engine next to our residence. From my window I saw smoke coming from the adjacent building, which housed nuns who worked at a Catholic geriatric center further down the street. Apparently the Nazis had mistakenly set the nun's home on fire instead of ours.

All day I could not get Hans out of my mind. Where could he be? Several times I tried to call him but it was impossible to get an answer. I was so worried about him, and I had to find out where he was. Although we had strict orders not to leave the hospital grounds, I dared to sneak out. I had a plan all worked out. The morgue was located in the basement of the pathology building, quite a distance from the main building which was connected by a subterranean a corridor. The morgue had a big iron door leading to the street, through which coffins were generally transported out of the morgue. It could be opened from both the inside and the outside.

As soon as it got dark I put on my black coat and wrote out a fictitious ID card for a patient who had expired that day. The tag was always placed on the dead patient before he was removed from the ward, so, if anyone stopped me on the way to the morgue, I would be able to say that I had forgotten to put on the tag. Unnoticed, I walked down the long, cold underground corridor. I left my nurse's cap, apron, and the hospital brooch, with the Star of David, under the stretcher of the dead patient. In my coat, which covered my uniform, I walked up the few steps, and cautiously opened half of the iron door. Luckily, no one was on the street. It was dark and silent. I stepped out and closed the door quietly behind me.

At the corner, I boarded an almost empty trolley car, which took me to the western part of Berlin, where Hans lived, about half an hour away. The fashionable Kurfuerstendam, usually full of shoppers, was deserted. Most of the elegant boutiques and the big department stores were owned by Jews. These stores had been looted and all of the display windows were smashed. The streetlights reflected off the glistening glass that covered the sidewalks, giving the street a surreal appearance, like an ice skating rink with nobody on it.

Soon I reached the street where Hans lived, which was not in the business section. It was a quiet street, and I felt safe walking there. Looking up at Hans's apartment I didn't see a light in his room. But where was Margrit, his sister? There was no answer when I rang the doorbell, and I feared the worst. In my despair I rang the bell of a neighbor. Two Jewish ladies lived there. I cried for joy when they told me Hans was safe and hiding with his two old aunts. Thank God for that! But Margrit, his sister, had been called to S.S. Headquarters for questioning. It was possible that she was not answering her doorbell because she was shaken up from the ordeal. The ladies allowed me to call Julian, Hans's best friend, who had recently been married. I hoped Hans and Julian were hiding together.

His wife, Ilse, answered and was crying bitterly. The Nazis had come during the night and forced him out of their apartment. I felt very sorry for her.

It had been a horrible day and no one knew what else was to come. Tired but relieved that at least my Hans was safe, I returned to the hospital. I slipped back into the morgue, put on the rest of my nurses' attire, and walked out into the poorly lit, cold underground of the hospital, feeling relieved at not having been detected. Suddenly an S.S. man (Hitler's Elite Guard) in his black uniform with a swastika on his helmet and armband stood in front of me and asked me with staring eyes, "What are you doing here?" I felt my knees were sinking. I explained that I had to put an ID on a corpse. With searching eyes he looked me over and asked, "Do you know where Dr. Knopf is?" Too scared to open my mouth I shook my head. "Are you his girlfriend?" he asked. Again, I shook my head saying, "No." I was still trembling when he allowed me to move on. With great relief, but exhausted, I returned to my ward and told my colleagues what I just had experienced.

After long, tiring hours of work, I slumped onto my bed in full uniform as we were ordered. I fell into a deep sleep, but was awakened to answer a phone call from my cousin Brunhilde in Kuestrin, who desperately needed my help. Nazis had broken into my Aunt Kate's apartment while she was sleeping alone in her bedroom. Her husband, Max, had been arrested earlier in the day. These Nazis had come into her bedroom, beat her, tortured her, and left her. Her daughter found her unconscious and brought her by ambulance to the local hospital in Kuestrin, but Aunt Kate was refused admission because she was Jewish. Immediately our admissions office made arrangements for my aunt to be transported to our hospital. I rushed over when she arrived a few hours later. She was semi-conscious and in critical condition, with a fractured skull and fractured bones in both arms. I felt faint when I saw my poor Aunt Kate. When I eventually returned to my room, I could not fall asleep and just rested there reliving this infamous day, until it was time to go back to work.

The next day was not any better. As soon as a bed was vacated, a new patient was admitted. Aside from taking care of the real patients, all we did all day was hand out and collect urinals and bedpans. The morning newspapers showed pictures of destroyed Jewish stores and houses, on which large swastikas and the words *Juden Raus*, meaning "Jews get out," were painted. The pictures showed the heaps of shattered glass on Kurfurstendam Street, just as I had seen the evening before. Orders came from Nazi headquarters that Jewish owners were responsible for cleaning up their own property and their sidewalk within twenty-four hours.

Luckily, our hospital was not set afire and none of our doctors were arrested.

Later in the day I received a most unexpected phone call from Budapest. It was Dr. Bill Landfather, the man I had met on the S.S. *Bremen* on my return from the United States. Bill had heard what was going on in Germany and was worried. He wanted to know whether I was all right and if there was anything he could do for me. I was surprised that he cared. I told him that if he could speak with the American Consul here in Berlin, perhaps he could expedite my immigration. I begged him to try to get me out of this "hellhole." He promised to call the American Consulate immediately for an appointment and said he would take me there. I couldn't get over his generosity and thanked him ever so much. What a great guy! Now I had a glimmer of hope. He might be able to speed up the processing of my affidavit.

I was excited when he arrived the following day in Berlin. He took me to the American Consulate, on Tiergarten Street. People were standing in line that was many blocks long, waiting desperately to get their papers processed, in order to leave Germany. Since Bill was a U.S. citizen, we were ushered in immediately to speak to the consul. Both men spoke English so fast that I understood very little. I thought I heard Bill say something about a bond of fifty thousand dollars and marriage, but I wasn't sure. The visit was short. When we left, the consul wished us good luck.

We walked in the park and sat on a bench. "Did you understand what the consul had suggested we should do?" Bill asked me with a smile on his face, and added, "Get married." Then there was a pause and he looked straight into my eyes and asked, "Would you marry me?" I was stunned. I couldn't believe he really meant it. Then he explained what had been said. He would not be permitted to set a bond for me as he had hoped to do. The only way he could get me out of Germany within twenty-four hours was if he married me. I still could not believe what I had just heard. How could I possibly make up my mind? I did not even know him well, but I was overwhelmed by his desire to help me and by the goodness of his character. He tried to convince me that the marriage would not necessarily have to be binding. If it didn't work out we could get an annulment, if I wished. My head was spinning. How could I leave Hans, who was in hiding from the Nazis? I could not just vanish! But I could not tell Bill these thoughts. Trying to find a way out without hurting his feelings, I told Bill that I had doubts whether my parents would ever permit me to marry out of my faith, because they were conservative Jews. He insisted that I give him their address, saying he would write to them. He wanted to leave Berlin before dark and my special permission for leaving the hospital to go to the consulate was almost over. With tears in my eyes I kissed him goodbye. He gave me a snapshot of himself, which I have kept to this day.

My parents cabled their consent for me to marry Bill, explaining that according to Jewish law, in order to save a life, intermarriage would be permissible. But by the time my parents' cable arrived, the arrests, the looting, and the fires had subsided. Slowly Jewish stores were allowed to reopen, after the owners had replaced the store windows. When Bill called, I told him I'd rather not make a hasty decision and would wait for my visa, which I expected soon. I thanked him for all he was willing to do for me and said that I hoped to see him again one day. Shortly after, Bill left Budapest to return to America, and wrote me a beautiful letter about how much he had enjoyed meeting me and how he wished, from the "bottom of his heart," that he could have helped me. He wished me good luck, "*Auf Wiedersehen*, lots of love, Bill." It was beautifully written and I should have saved it.

Hans came out of hiding two weeks after Kristallnacht, when things were quiet again. I was very happy to see him, but all my uncles and their sons, except one cousin, were sent to labor camps. They were only released if seriously ill, or with proof of a one-way ticket to another country, which had been obtained by their wives or mothers while the men were detained. Those families who were fortunate enough to leave found refuge in Cuba, South America, or China, where they were allowed entry in return for substantial bribes.

The overflow of male patients in our hospital had subsided, but new patients arrived daily with severe injuries inflicted from brutal beatings by Nazis in labor camps. In some cases gangrene had set in, and partial amputations were performed. Among these amputees was a distant cousin of my mother. He begged me to visit his brother, Erich, in New York, so that his brother could help him get out of Germany. This I did as soon as I arrived. The poor patient was willing to go anywhere in the world, but I doubt that he ever made it out of Germany.

The pogrom on Kristallnacht was the reason for the mass immigration of Jews out of Germany. All hurried to escape Hitler's claws. Nine months later, with the start of World War II, it was no longer possible. As a result of Hitler's subsequent invasion of many European and North African countries, further Jewish lives were imperiled, and approximately 6,000,000 Jews died in the Holocaust.

My Family's Exodus and its Aftermath

After the pogrom of Kristallnacht, my relatives were dispersed all over the world, to whatever country allowed them refuge. Unfortunately, many did not make it out of Germany in time. My six years of enduring the Hitler regime paled in comparison to what some of my family members and millions of other Jews had to suffer. They were transported to labor camps where they either died of diseases or were gassed. I lost fifteen close relatives. Others, including myself, were fortunate and escaped Hitler's claws, and settled in distant countries. The close ties we used to cherish were broken, but their memories are forever with me. Having my family dispersed all over the world, and being unable to even communicate with some of them, left a deep void in my life. I feel great pain for those who perished. I would like to remember them by recording briefly the lives they lived, the friendships that bound us, and what happened to them.

My father had one brother, Jacob, and three sisters. Unfortunately, he had had no contact with them since his marriage. Until I was eleven I had never heard my parents mention my father's siblings. His older brother, Jacob, reconciled and congratulated us by phone when my brother, Gerhard, became a Bar Mitzvah in 1926. He and his wife, Frieda, visited us soon after that. Jacob, his wife, and two daughters immigrated to Palestine before Kristallnacht, and he worked there as a glazier.

On the occasion of Gerhard's Bar Mitzvah, Aunt Else

reconciled too, and came to the celebration. She was a widow and had two children, Manfred and Recha. Soon after the Bar Mitzvah, during summer vacation, Recha visited us. I liked her, although she was much older than me. She later married and was able to escape to Brazil. She and her husband both struggled at first to make a living by working in factories, but later she became very successful in the catering business. She visited us in New York whenever they came to purchase goods and machinery that she was unable to buy in Brazil. At first we communicated once a year, by sending greetings on the High Holidays, but later on I did not hear from her for a long time.

In 1976, while spending a one-week vacation in Rio de Janeiro, I flew to Sao Paolo for the day to see her. Her husband had died. She lived alone in a villa surrounded by a huge stone wall, in the midst of modern skyscrapers in downtown Sao Paolo. I was shocked at her appearance. I remembered her as an elegantly dressed, vibrant person. She apologized for the way her house looked because she did not have servants anymore. She claimed they stole her belongings. The meal she served me was barely edible (a salty beef-bullion and undercooked beef brisket). I had the impression she had the beginnings of Alzheimer's. When I inquired what happened to the rest of the relatives on my father's side, she told me her mother, Aunt Else, and her brother, Manfred, died in Auschwitz, and my father's two younger sisters, the ones I never met, also died with their families in concentration camps.

My mother's siblings always held close ties. They had great love for each other. We spent vacations together in resorts on the Baltic Sea or in the Black Forest, or we vacationed at each other's homes. My mother had three sisters, Ella, Kate, and Olga, and four brothers, Adolf, Leo, Max, and Hugo. All of these relatives hailed from the part of Germany that was annexed to Poland after World War I. They did not want to live under Polish rule and migrated into Germany after 1918.

My mother's sister Kate, her husband Max Wiersch, and their two children, Brunhilde and Berthold, and her brother

Adolf, his wife Bertha, and their two children, Hertha and
Herman, were the first to leave the newly annexed Polish
territory and settled in Kuestrin, a small town about sixty miles
east of Berlin. I saw these relatives almost daily when I was
growing up.

My Uncle Max had served in the medical corps in the war.
He used to tell us children gruesome war stories. In Kuestrin
he dealt in scrap metal and traded in horses. The family lived
in a beautiful ten-room apartment in a luxury building that
they owned. Aunt Kate was my favorite aunt. She always
consoled me when my mother mistreated me. I would run
over to her home and she would say lovingly, "Go, my sweet,
pick anything you like out of the storage bin," and I would
indulge. They lived a comfortable and peaceful life until
Kristallnacht, when Aunt Kate was brutally beaten by the Nazis
in her own home, and remained hospitalized for months before
her eventual release.

Uncle Max, his son Berthold, and son-in-law Arthur were
sent to labor camp but were freed as soon as Brunhilde was
able to purchase visas for all of them to immigrate to Cuba.
Brunhilde, Arthur, their two-year-old daughter Mirjam, and
Berthold left immediately, leaving all of their possessions
behind, except their personal belongings and four dollars each.
But Aunt Kate and Uncle Max needed time to recover from
their ordeal before undertaking the journey on the stormy
sea. It was June 1939 when they finally sailed for Cuba with just
their suitcases and four dollars in cash. When the ship reached
its destination in Havana, Cuba, it was not allowed to dock.
They experienced the most painful disappointment in their
already troubled lives. Their hopes of joining their family were
shattered when the Cuban authorities suddenly decided to
stop immigration, and did not allow the passengers to
disembark. Their despair and heartache were unimaginable.
They saw their family standing and waving at the pier, while
anxiously still hoping for their release. For days Jewish world
organizations pleaded with the Cuban government to allow

these passengers to land, but to no avail. With more than nine hundred passengers on board, the captain was ordered to leave the harbor. The ship sailed to Miami, Florida, in a last effort to find refuge there, but President Roosevelt refused to give these poor people asylum. It was a cruelty for which he was severely criticized here in the United States, as well as by most European nations. The ship had no choice but to return to Hamburg, Germany, the place of its origin, with all its frightened passengers aboard. Now penniless and homeless, my aunt and uncle were supported by the Jewish World Congress in Hamburg until Aunt Kate's older sister, Ella, heard about Aunt Kate's misfortune and came to her rescue by purchasing visas for them to find refuge in China.

Aunt Ella herself had experienced great tragedy. Her husband, Samuel, and son, Joachim, were taken to a labor camp during Kristallnacht. Both had been standing for hours in deep snow in northern Germany when Uncle Sam suddenly collapsed and died; his twenty-one-year-old son stood by, helpless, seeing his father dead in the snow. Aunt Ella, Joachim's mother, grieved over her husband's demise, but was able to get Joachim out of the labor camp with tickets to China for her and her two children, for which she paid enormous bribes.

When she heard about her sister Kate's misfortune, she was able to obtain two more visas for Kate and Max. All five of them left Germany together, herded with many refugees in one cattle car. (One corner of the boxcar served as a toilet.) They traveled for days under the most unsanitary of conditions over Poland, Russia, and Manchuria, until they finally reached Shanghai, China. There they were forced to live in a Jewish ghetto, which consisted of primitive houses with thatched roofs, no windows, and poor sanitary conditions. They were supported by the World Jewish Congress.

They lived there for seven years. Even though Aunt Kate was always the strongest and the healthiest of the sisters, she contracted dysentery, and lost more than fifty pounds. When she finally arrived in America in 1946, she weighed ninety-eight pounds. Finally, they were united with their children here in the United States. Brunhilde, her husband Arthur, their daughter Mirjam, and Berthold had left Cuba in 1941 and settled in Vineland, New Jersey. With financial aid from Jewish organizations, Arthur and Bert bought a chicken farm. When Aunt Kate and Uncle Max arrived, they were of great help to their children. I loved my Aunt Kate and visited her every year in Vineland on her birthday, until she died many years later, at the age of 97.

Before the Holocaust, Aunt Ella, her husband Samuel Reich, and their children, Rosel and Joachim, lived in a northern German border town of Schneidemuehl. Uncle Samuel dealt in scrap metal. We all spent several vacations at the Baltic shore. I liked Rosel a lot. She was three years older than I was; she was my role model.

At first Aunt Ella, Rosel, and Joachim lived in the same ghetto in Shanghai as her sister Kate, but soon their lives changed. Rosel, who was a beautiful girl, had fallen in love with a French Legionnaire (a high-ranking officer) and married him. The couple moved into the elegant section of the city, and enjoyed a good life. Rosel and her husband Andre made sure all relatives received adequate food and medicine during their exile in China.

After the war, Rosel and Andre lived in France for a while, and then, in 1947, they immigrated to Cleveland, Ohio, where Uncle Max and son Alfred had settled after leaving Cuba. Rosel became very successful in the costume jewelry business. Aunt Ella and Joachim left China in1946 and immigrated to Naharya, Israel, where they lived in a bungalow that my father had built in his backyard. My mother, however, made life miserable for her sister. Ella was very unhappy there, but, because of the housing shortage, was unable to leave. As soon as Joachim finished his training as a dental technician, Aunt Ella and Joachim left Israel and were reunited with Rosel in Cleveland. Joachim was able to make a good living as a dental technician.

Aunt Olga, the youngest sister of my mother, had lost her first husband in the early months of World War I, while expecting her first child, Ruth. Olga remarried, to Ernst Mainzer, and they had twin boys, Herbert and Alfred. They lived in Wissek across the big market square from us, and owned a piece-goods store. Ruth was one year older than me, and was my constant playmate. The day the twins Herbert and Alfred were born, Ruth and I were playing in the courtyard of her house. A stork nestled on its red roof, and we were told the stork had just brought them.

The Mainzer family had emigrated from Wissek in 1919 and settled in Baden-Baden, in the beautiful Black Forest region of Germany, where they opened another piece-goods store and made a very comfortable living. I have very pleasant memories of vacationing with them. At five o'clock every morning, Uncle Ernst would take us on a hike up the Fremersberg, which is five hundred meters high. On top was a restaurant with a magnificent view where we would consume a hearty breakfast and eat the blueberries we had picked on the way. In 1934, I saw Uncle Ernst and Aunt Olga for the last time, when I visited them with my mother. Ruth married very young and immigrated to America, and the boys were shipped to England on a children's transport.

During Kristallnacht, Uncle Ernst was dragged to a labor camp. It was a while before Aunt Olga was able to buy visas for Cuba and he was released. They were able to book a passage on the ill-fated American liner, S.S. *Saint Louis*, which sailed just a few days after Aunt Kate's ship had departed for Cuba. Their ship, with nine hundred passengers on board, was also refused entry into Cuba and the United States and was forced to return to Germany. But due to public outcry, Holland, Belgium, and France granted asylum to a small number of passengers. Aunt Olga and Uncle Ernst found refuge in Holland. They thought they were safe there, but when the German Army invaded Holland, Jews were rounded up and shipped to the infamous Auschwitz concentration camp, where they perished.

As for Ruth Mainzer, after her divorce from her first husband, with whom she had a son, she married an American soldier during the war and had a daughter. Unfortunately, he abused her, so she divorced him too. She had a hard life. I saw her once shortly after she came back from England, where her husband was stationed, and again in 1980, when she already had signs of Alzheimer's.

During the war, her twin half-brothers joined the British Armed Forces. Later, Herbert settled in Australia and I never saw him again. Alfred married a girl, Norma, from San Antonio, Texas, and they settled there. He and his wife visited me unexpectedly on my seventieth birthday in 1985. Both brothers have since passed away.

Uncle Leo, my mother's oldest brother, and his third wife, Kate, lived in Berlin above their furniture store. When I studied nursing in Berlin, I visited Aunt Kate and Uncle Leo often. Aunt Kate had a beautiful home, was a great hostess and a fabulous cook. Every time I was hungry for a home-cooked meal, I just had to call her and she would invite me. I have very fond memories of them. Unfortunately, they were not able to get out of Germany in time and were transported to Auschwitz.

Uncle Leo's only daughter, Friedel, was married to Arnold Jacobson, an optometrist. Friedel spent many vacations in my parent's house. My mother always invited all my cousins during the summer. Friedel, Arnold, and their son Alfred left Germany for Shanghai after Kristallnacht. They booked passage on a ship to Bombay, India and then took another boat to China. Arnold was able to work as an optometrist there and lived comfortably in Shanghai. Their son, Alfred, grew up in China, attending a school that refugees had founded. Twenty-five thousand refugees from Germany had sought refuge in Shanghai.

The Jacobsons arrived in the United States in 1946, and settled in New York on West 84th Street and Amsterdam Avenue; they lived in a dreary low-priced tenement walkup, a far cry from the way they lived in Germany and Shanghai.

Arnold could not practice optometry in the United States without lengthy additional study, but he found a job as an optician. Friedel, who suffered from asthma and had never worked in her life, worked as a saleslady. She had a hard time adjusting.

Alfred, who was twelve when he came to this country, was an excellent student. He went to City College and later became a successful businessman.

My mother's brother, Adolf, who lived in Kuestrin, had a haberdashery and piece-goods store. He was prosperous. His wife, Bertha, baked delicious croissants every Friday. I always made sure to go over to their house so I could taste at least one each week. When my mother took her daily walk, she never failed to stop and chat with her brother in his store.

On Kristallnacht, Uncle Adolf and his son, Herman, a rabbi, were forced into a labor camp. I don't know when they were released. I heard later that Uncle Adolf suffered a nervous breakdown from which he never recovered. He, Aunt Bertha, Herman and his fiancée were deported to Auschwitz, where they perished.

Their daughter Hertha married an orthodox Jew, Sam Oppenheim, in Berlin in 1932, and we all attended the elaborate wedding celebration. Sam was an executive in a metal concern. The year Hitler came to power, he was transferred to Sydney, Australia, where they had two children. Their son, Jehuda, a psychiatrist at Hadassah Hospital, lives in Jerusalem; and their daughter Hannah, lives in Sydney.

My mother's brother, Max, and his wife, Cilla, lived with their two children, Alfred and Hilda, in Schneidemuehl, the same town where Aunt Ella and Uncle Samuel lived. Max owned a houseware and fine china store. I used to vacation with both families.

On Kristallnacht, Uncle Max had just arrived by train from Berlin when he was accosted by Nazis at the train station and dragged to his store. They forced him to walk over the rubble of glass and broken furniture, and tortured him while his wife,

Cilla, looked on in horror. He was then loaded onto a truck and taken away. Uncle Max, Uncle Sam Reich, and Joachim Reich were taken together with many other Jewish males to the same labor camp where Uncle Samuel collapsed and died.

But Uncle Max's son, Alfred, was very fortunate. He was the only one of all my uncles and cousins who was not arrested during Kristallnacht. At the time of the turmoil, he happened to be in America on a visitor's visa. He too was looking for a relative who would give him an affidavit, just as I had ten months earlier.

Aunt Cilla called Alfred in the United States, and with the help of Jewish organizations, he was able to secure a passage for his father to Cuba. Uncle Max was released from camp as soon as he could show proof of immigration, and left for Cuba when it was still possible to bribe one's way into that country. Aunt Cilla, however, did not want to leave, because her daughter, Hilda, was still unsettled, nor could Alfred find a relative in America who would vouch for him. When his visitor's visa expired he was taken to Ellis Island and detained there for weeks. After many threats of deporting him, a Jewish organization in New York stepped in and secured an affidavit for him and his father. As a formality, in order to enter America legally, Alfred had to leave the country for three days. Alfred went to Cuba and from there, he and his father finally legally immigrated to the United States and settled in Miami, Florida. Alfred married a girl from Cleveland, where he and his father later manufactured leather goods.

Uncle Max's daughter, Hilde, was able to immigrate to England in 1939. After the war she moved to America, where she married a distant cousin in Vineland, New Jersey.

Soon after Hilde left Germany, Aunt Cilla became ill. She was unable to leave the country and died alone in her home in Schneidemuehl.

My mother's youngest brother, Uncle Hugo, a widower, lived with his daughter, Rita, above one of his furniture stores in Potsdam. Rita was my age and we saw each other many times during vacations. Uncle Hugo was well-respected and trusted by all his siblings. He was a successful businessman. Because of the devaluation of the German mark after World War I, all brothers and sisters bought large amounts of twenty mark gold coins. They put their gold coins in marked, leather bags and hid them deep underground in Hugo's cellar. A tremendous fortune was hidden there. All my relatives hoped to reclaim their signed sacks after the Hitler regime ended. Unfortunately, Uncle Hugo and Rita never made it out of Germany. When the Gestapo came to their house to transport them to Auschwitz, they took cyanide pills, killing themselves instantly. During the war, the house in Potsdam was demolished and later the land was converted into a parking lot. No one knows whether the money was ever discovered.

Nineteen members of my close family survived, but fifteen lost their lives in the Holocaust.

My Final Journey

Ever since Kristallnacht, our lives had changed and we didn't dare to go to public places anymore. We were filled with fear of what might still be in store for us. I was working on the surgical floor taking care of brutally beaten men who had been sent to us from the notorious Sachsenhausen concentration camp near Berlin. The threat of war hung heavily over us, and everybody was hoping to be able to get out of Germany in time.

I finally received my visa to enter the United States in March 1939, thirteen months after my return from America in February 1938. The last five months, after November 9, were the most dreadful I had ever experienced. Although I was anxious to leave, I didn't have enough money to pay for the fare. My parents had given me money for it before they left for Palestine but I had used most of it already, having stayed longer in Germany than I anticipated. As a graduate nurse the salary I received was a meager forty marks per month, which was not enough to live on. Hans was unable to give me the money for a ticket because he was allotted only one thousand marks per month. I approached my Uncles Leo and Hugo, but they too were unable to spare the money for the ticket. Fortunately, a friend of my father was able to help me, and I was able to purchase the cheapest possible fare to the United States, a third class ticket for six hundred Deutsche mark, or about two hundred forty dollars. I was to sail on the S.S. *Pennland*, a small 14,000-ton ship belonging to the Holland-America line, which sailed from Scheviningen, Holland.

On March 26, 1939 I was finally able to leave Germany, a country that I once loved, where my family had lived since the seventeenth century, which my grandfather and father had proudly served, and which now, under a Fascist regime hostile to Jews, made it intolerable for us to live there any longer.

Leaving Berlin

It was a bitter cold night when Hans and I stood on the poorly lit platform of the train station in Berlin, waiting for the train to come and take me out of Nazi Germany forever. I held the beautiful red roses Hans had brought me. There was not much to say. With every warm embrace tears ran down my cheeks. The thought of separation was unbearable. How long would it be before we would see each other again? Or even worse, would I ever see him again? My heart was heavy, and yet I was anxious to escape that horrible place. The train would take me to Holland, where I would board the S.S. *Pennland.*

While waiting for it to arrive, I saw my old friend Dorothea waving her handkerchief a few yards away. How daring of her to come! Although it was forbidden, we always had kept in touch. She too had become a nurse in Berlin, at the Countess Rittberg Hospital. Just a few days before I left she had dared to visit me in our nurses' residence. The evening of my departure was the last time I ever saw or heard from her. After World War II I searched for her through the Red Cross, but they couldn't find any trace of her or her family.

It was eight o'clock when the conductor called out, "All aboard!" After one last embrace and with tear-filled eyes, I boarded the train. Slowly it left the station. I stood by the open window waving with my roses until Hans and Dorothea vanished in the distance. Exhausted, I slumped into my seat, looking at my beautiful flowers, and finding comfort in the thought that, at last, I wouldn't be harassed by anyone anymore. I felt sorry for my poor Aunt Kate, who was still recuperating, and for all the relatives I left behind. I began to worry about my new life. I wondered whether I would be able to adjust, to learn a new language, to live alone in a strange country. It suddenly overwhelmed me. But my trust in God's guidance comforted me, and I fell into a deep sleep.

Suddenly, I was awakened by the German border patrol. A man in Nazi uniform stood before me and greeted me with, "*Heil* Hitler!" Of course I didn't respond. He asked me for my passport and when he saw the big letter J and the surname Sarah, which had been added to all Jewish-owned documents, he gave me a nasty look. Then he fixed his eyes on the fake diamond and emerald ring that I had purchased that afternoon with my last thirty-five marks, not wanting to leave a penny behind. "Don't you know Jews are not allowed to leave the country with jewelry? Come with me." I pleaded with him, "This is a fake ring. I paid thirty-five marks for it, trust me." "Get out," he ordered, and I followed him to the station. There I was given a body search while someone tested my ring. At first I was not worried; I had nothing to hide. My conscience was clear. But after a while I became restless. What on earth took them so long? What if they detained me and I miss the train? I was beside myself. I begged them, "Please, let me go. You can keep the ring. I can't miss that train." But the Nazi officer stood there stone-faced. I waited what seemed to be eternity. I heard the train's whistle and the conductor calling out, "All aboard!" I pleaded, "Please let me not miss that train. Please."

Finally a Nazi officer appeared, handed me the ring, and permitted me to leave. I dashed out to the platform. The train was already moving slowly, and I ran as fast as I could to catch it. I leaped onto the steps while the smiling Dutch conductor held out his hand. I grabbed it tightly and he pulled me to safety. Breathless, I stood there and let out a sigh of relief, crying for joy. Germany was left behind, and I was free at last!

Several hours after the incident at the German border, I arrived in Scheveningen, a coastal town in Holland, from which the ship was to set sail. The shipping company had invited its passengers to a luncheon at an inn by the harbor. Prince Bernard of the Netherlands was scheduled to christen a ship there that day. Just as we were about to sit down at the table, a parade passed by the inn. At the sound of the music everyone rushed to the open window to get a glimpse of the prince; everyone except me. I had my eyes fixed on a small glass bowl of butterballs on my table. In Germany we had not had any butter in one year. The temptation to eat it was too great. While the others were stretching their necks to get a glimpse of the prince, I savored one butterball after another until they were all devoured. Then I quietly joined the crowd at the window, so nobody would suspect me. The waitress was perplexed when she saw that the butter dish was empty.

After lunch we boarded the ship. It was not a luxury liner like the S.S. *Empress of Britain* or the S.S. *Bremen*, on which I had sailed on my previous visit to the United States in 1937. Women and men slept in separate wards; there were no private cabins in third class. In the mess hall we were served sitting on benches at long tables. Luckily I did not become seasick, although the sea was very rough. I did not dare move around too much, for fear I might get ill, and I ate very little. Finally, early in the morning of April 4, 1939, the ship sailed into New York harbor. I had hardly slept that night and stood on deck and watched as we passed Ellis Island, feeling sorry for the poor people who were detained there. But when I saw the Statue of Liberty, the symbol of freedom for all, cold shivers trickled down my spine, and I was jubilant. This was going to be my country! Here I would finally be free of any harassment. The ship docked at a pier in Manhattan and everybody left, but no one had claimed me yet. I had to wait for my sponsor, to be able to leave. I sat with my small trunk on deck near the entrance, eagerly awaiting Mrs. Gillis, the lady who had vouched for me and engaged me as an au pair for her two children. As time passed I became increasingly worried. What on earth had happened to Mrs. Gillis? She was the only person who could get me released from the ship. I was told that if she did not show up before five in the afternoon, I would be transported to Ellis

Island. I sat there on my trunk crying for fear of what might happen to me.

At last, after two and a half hours, I spotted her coming up the gangplank. Was I relieved! Thank God she was here! She apologized but I did not understand why she was late as she spoke too fast. After being processed by the naturalization authorities, we were finally allowed to leave. Her car was parked right at the dock, and a porter helped put my trunk into her car. Finally we were ready to go, but then she dropped the "bombshell." She informed me her husband had financial difficulties on account of the Depression and would not allow her to take me to their home. She wanted to know where she could "drop me off." I had never heard this "slang" before, and I took it literally. I thought, *Oh my God, she will just abandon me at some corner in this big city?* I was so confused and helpless and I cried again. I had already shed so many tears waiting for her, my eyes were still burning. She asked me, "Don't you have any friends here where you could stay?" I was thinking I couldn't possibly ask Gertrude Salomon, whose husband Fred never sent me the affidavit he had promised. But then I remembered my pen pal Sally Ferguson. I opened my address book and pointed out Sally's address. "Oh," she said. "That's where I will drop you off." Now I understood what "drop you off" meant, and she quickly drove me to 151 West 86th Street. The doorman informed us that Miss Ferguson would not be back from work before six o'clock, but he permitted me to wait for her in the lobby. Mrs. Gillis got me a bottle of Coca-Cola from the stand on the next corner, and the doorman helped me carry my trunk inside. I thanked Mrs. Gillis for getting me off the ship and for the drink. Then she said goodbye and wished me luck, but I never heard from her again.

I waited patiently, slowly sipping the delicious Coca-Cola, a drink I had never tasted before. Finally, Sally arrived. She was of course surprised to see me in the lobby. I explained to her why Mrs. Gillis could not take me to her home and that I had no place to go. "Oh, but Frieda, I have no space! What about your relative, Fred Solomon?" "I never heard from them. They had let me down. He never sent the affidavit he had promised. How could I possibly ask them to help me now?" Reluctantly, she took me up to her apartment, and showed me how cramped she was. "You see, I sleep in the living room. My twin sisters who live with me are studying at New York University. They are occupying my bedroom. Where can I possibly put you? I don't even have a blanket or pillow." I begged her to let me sleep on the carpeted floor in her foyer. She agreed, and I was relieved. Because it was Passover week the Jewish charities were closed, or else they would be able to find me a better place to stay. Obviously, she felt bad that I had to sleep on the floor, but I didn't mind. After dinner her sisters came home and we talked a while and then we got ready for the night. Totally exhausted, but content that I had made it through this eventful but trying day, I fell asleep covered in my winter coat, with a rolled-up Turkish towel as a pillow.

New Life in New York

I slept soundly and woke the next morning refreshed and happy that I had finally made it to America. I felt safe here. We had an early breakfast together before everybody left home, and I savored the buttered Matzos with jam and the delicious coffee.

It was a bright April morning when I went out to look for a job. I knew the prospects for foreign nurses were bleak, and I wouldn't be allowed to work in a hospital without a New York license. First, one would have to complete the fourth year of high school requirements, followed by additional nurse's training, and then a four-day-long board examination. I was unable to do this because of my lack of money and familiarity with the English language. I would, however, be allowed to work as a private duty nurse in a home, but I had heard such jobs were hard to get, due to the bad financial times.

I walked briskly over Central Park to Park Avenue and stopped at doctors' offices that had street entrances displaying a Jewish name. With few words I explained to them my situation, that I had just arrived from Germany with four dollars in my possession and needed a private nursing duty job desperately. Most of them told me that they would keep me in mind, but were doubtful that they could provide work for me with such a bad economy, but I was not discouraged. Most of them were very understanding and wished me good luck. I walked for hours every day. When I was tired of walking, I returned to the apartment and listened to the radio, hoping to understand the American English. I was used to British English, which was quite different.

On the ninth day, my luck changed! I was standing on Park

Avenue and 70th Street in front of a sign that read: Dr. Hans Lehfeld, Gynecologist. I did not know if he was Jewish, but, since he had a German name, I walked in anyway. He was very friendly and spoke German. He had no need for private duty nurses at the present time, but he referred to a colleague who had a big international clientele who might be able to help me. He picked up the telephone and talked to this doctor, who agreed to interview me as soon as I could come to his office.

Hopeful and excited, I walked the twenty-four blocks to Dr. Max Jacobson's office as fast as I could and explained to the doctor, a very handsome, middle-aged man with searching eyes, my urgent need for a job. He had very little to say, but told me, "Go home. By the time the night is over, I will have a job for you." I left very excited and hoped he wouldn't forget.

Sure enough, at eight in the evening, his secretary called. She gave me orders to take a patient home from the hospital, with specific instructions as to how to administer the patient's medication. The patient had an incurable lung disease. I was to do twenty-hour duty at five dollars a day.

I was very happy that now I would be able to support myself. All along I had felt bad to impose on Sally. She had only limited means herself, but she was very kind to me, and allowed me to leave my valise with her while I was on this case.

The next morning I brought the patient home from the hospital. He was a kind but very sick old man and was not expected to live very long. He too was a refugee, a banker from Hamburg, Germany. I had to stay in his room at night because he needed attention. During the day I caught up on my sleep while his wife and daughter took care of him. Because of his wasting lungs, the room had a terrible stench. In those days air purifiers didn't exist yet, or if they did, I was not aware of it. I stretched a clothesline from door to door and hung strips of cloth dipped in turpentine, in order to alleviate the terrible odor.

After six weeks the patient died. The last few days I did not get any sleep. When I left, the family paid me with a check of two hundred eighty dollars and gave me a present, a beautiful Rosenthal figurine of a huge owl.

This was my first earned money in America. I felt really proud! Now I could get my own place to live. I was grateful and thanked Sally for having given me shelter and food, and, to show my appreciation, I gave her that beautiful owl.

I found a suitable room on the fourth floor of an old walk-up tenement building on 100th Street and Broadway. Two classmates from my nursing school in Germany, Edith Lyon and Gertrude Lyon (they were not related), also roomed there. The landlady, Mrs. Lange, was a refugee herself. I was lucky she had a room available, but I had to share it with a stranger. The rent was three dollars a week. Her top floor apartment was very hot and sparsely furnished, but clean. The windows faced Broadway, and I had to get used to the street noise and sirens from the fire engines and police cars. But, it was a shelter and I was living with friends. Mrs. Lange always invited us to Shabbat dinner, where she served homemade chicken noodle soup with big chunks of chicken in it. During the week, we could purchase the soup for fifteen cents a bowl. Exhausted from my last case, I rested for four days.

But then I received a pitiful letter from my parents in Palestine, in which my mother wrote about how hard my father had to work as a laborer, building the road between Haifa and Acre, where he was in constant danger of attacks by Arabs. Everyday she prayed that he would come home alive. I was deeply moved and concerned. I kept forty dollars for myself and immediately wired them two hundred forty dollars through the Barclay Bank in New York. (I still have the receipt.) I was so glad I was able to help my parents.

They sent me a letter back thanking me for the Mitzvah ("good deed") I had done. "God will reward you a thousand fold," they wrote. They also wrote that my father had quit this job and that they could live a whole year on the two hundred forty dollars. It relieved my worries about them and made me feel really good. I decided to support them as much as I could from then on, in the hope that they would one day be able to build a house on the land my father had bought with the money he had transferred from Germany on his visit to Palestine in 1936. Between 1939 and 1953 I was able to send them close to six thousand dollars. Eventually, my father built a nice ranch house and gave me credit for having contributed towards it.

After four days' rest, Dr. Lehfeld gave me another case. I was to take care of a newborn at his home, but it lasted less than twenty-four hours. The job also involved house chores like cleaning up after dinner, and washing the dishes and pots, for which I used a steel Brillo Pad. Right away I felt a slight sting on my finger but paid no attention to it. When I woke up to give the baby her bottle, I felt ill and the finger ached. I noticed a red streak going up the forearm. I knew I had blood poisoning and so I left the job. By the time I reached home the arm was swollen to the armpit and the redness had reached the upper arm. I felt faint and feverish. Luckily, Edith Lyon was home. She elevated the arm and put me to bed. Edith must have realized I was seriously ill because she called Dr. Rosenstein, who used to be chief of surgery at the Jewish hospital in Berlin and now lived just a few blocks away. He came over immediately and started a continuous intravenous with a strong sulfa drug, Prontosil, added to it. (Penicillin was not yet available.) He came every day and watched over me while Edith stayed in my room at night. Because of the high fever, I was delirious at times. Luckily, it broke on the fourth day and I recovered. I don't know why Dr. Rosenstein did not send me to the hospital. Perhaps because I didn't have insurance, or perhaps it was too dangerous for me to be transported.

On the fourth day, I received from Hans in Sweden, where he had been living with Margrit and Johnny since May 1939, my first letter after a long hiatus. He wrote that he had been granted permission to enter the United States, and it wouldn't be much longer before we would be able to see each other.

Because of the war between England and Germany, not many passenger ships were sailing the North Atlantic (transatlantic flights and air mail didn't exist yet), so he couldn't give me a definite date when he could book passage. I was still weak and lying in bed when the good news reached me, and it surely aided my recovery.

As soon as I felt well enough to work, I spoke with Dr. Jacobson's secretary about taking on another case. She offered me an easy night duty with an elderly lady, Mrs. Prohaska, who lived at the Grosvenor Hotel on 5th Avenue and 10th Street. The patient suffered from occasional lightheadedness. It was the easiest possible case, and paid five dollars for a twelve-hour duty. The patient slept all night and so did I. She was in her late seventies, a widow, and apparently in good financial circumstances. Her husband was the chemist who had invented the color for margarine. Her unmarried daughter had an apartment in the same hotel and was very devoted to her mother. After a while, the patient asked me to take the day shift. It was more of a companion job. Sometimes, all three of us would go to the movies. We ate in fine restaurants or just went for rides in her chauffeured car. One time we traveled to the Williamstown Inn in Massachusetts and watched the Yale/ Harvard regatta in which her grandsons participated. It was a very relaxing and well-paying job; I had no overhead except my three dollars rent, and was therefore able to continue to support my family in Palestine generously, allowing me great satisfaction and peace of mind.

I eagerly awaited Hans's arrival in New York, which came finally, after many months of separation, on December 4, 1939. He came without his sister and nephew, whose papers for entry in the United States were not yet ready. (Margrit and Johnny arrived in the summer of 1940.)

I would have liked to greet and embrace him at the pier, but Hans did not want me to come because he knew Aunt Gerda would be there to release him from the immigration authorities. After his debarkation, she drove him in her

chauffeured limousine to the Hotel Barbizon, where she had
rented a room for him until he was able to find a suitable,
furnished room.

Aunt Gerda had quite generously supported Hans and his
family in Sweden, ever since their departure from Germany
with only four dollars in their possesion. Now that he had arrived
alone, she invited him for dinner almost nightly and provided
him with pocket money.

I hardly could wait to see Hans, but when I met him the
next day, my disappointment was tremendous. He had gained
thirty pounds from the rich diet of smorgasbord, and he looked
like a big, fat slob. His appearance and his whole demeanor
were different. We had grown apart in those nine months of
separation, and I wondered, had I become so Americanized
that I didn't like him anymore? He spoke with a distinct guttural
German accent and looked outlandish in the German suits
that no longer fit him. He did not seem overjoyed to see me
either, which I didn't mind. Later he told me that he had met
a nice girl (also a refugee) in Stockholm and apparently had a
great time with her. I wondered why I had stayed faithful to
him all this time.

He was always sad, not the jolly man that I had once known.
But I felt sorry for him. He felt degraded to be dependent
upon Aunt Gerda's support. The greatest disappointment for
him came with Aunt Gerda's news that she had sold her
deceased husband's business to his junior partners for three-
and-a-half-million dollars, an enormous amount in those days.
Aunt Gerda had made an agreement with the new owners to
employ Hans in the firm upon his arrival, but Hans had hoped
to take over the business one day. Instead, the new owners
hired him as a shipping clerk. He had to take orders from a
black man, and his starting salary was fifty dollars a week. This
was more money than was paid for such a menial job elsewhere,
but it was, nevertheless, quite a change from the prestigious
position he had held in Germany. He had to carry heavy

packages to the post office daily and developed a double hernia, which later helped him get deferred from the army.

Hans deeply regretted that he had not come to America earlier, when his uncle and aunt had begged him to come. If he had done so, Uncle Herman most likely would have given him partial ownership of the company. However, now that he had missed that chance, he realized that he had to accept what was offered to him and be content that at least he was safe in America.

It was pitiful to see him so down and out; and I therefore stood by him and tried to encourage him. Unfortunately, Aunt Gerda did not have any influence in her former company anymore, and Hans had to endure these hardships. Slowly he became accustomed to hard work, and, in the process, lost at least twenty pounds. Hans rented a room, with a beautiful view of the Hudson River, in an apartment building at 202 Riverside Drive, which was owned by an elderly lady. In his spare time he took evening courses in accounting at City College.

Every Sunday he was invited for lunch at Aunt Gerda's, and then was expected to spend a few hours with her old mother, Mrs. Karger, who lived with her in her twenty-one room duplex at 88 Central Park West. Aunt Gerda's mother had sheltered Hans for two weeks during *Kristallnacht* in November 1938, and soon after that pogrom had immigrated to New York to live with her daughter. She was an old lady who had never learned to speak English, and was very lonely. So she enjoyed Hans's company and looked forward to his weekly visits.

At a German-Jewish club, Hans and I met and befriended other German refugees. Weather permitting, we spent a few hours each evening with them on Riverside Park, discussing the current world events or reminiscing about our past life in the old country. At a certain time during the evening, the Good Humor Ice Cream man would pass by, and Hans would treat me to a five-cent cone. We always spoke German because it was much easier for us, especially after being tired from a hard day's work.

Soon after Hans came to New York, I gave up my job with Mrs. Prohaska. I was tired of the good life with her. It was not challenging enough, and staying with her twelve hours a day, without a day off in nine months, was draining. My friend, Trudy Lyon, took my case with Mrs. Prohaska, who was very pleased with her.

Now that Hans was here, I wanted a nine-to-five job, with Sundays off like other people, but it was impossible to get that in nursing. I found a temporary sales job at Ovington's in Fifth Avenue at the time Fortieth Street, a large store specializing in fine china, gifts, antiques, and jewelry. It did not pay well, but I guess I liked the novelty. I had learned a lot from my mother about fine china and antique porcelain. My customers liked it when I suggested that they not buy an article that I felt wasn't worth the price. One day I helped a well-dressed gentleman purchase a lot of gifts for his family for Christmas presents. He introduced himself and I learned he was related to the owner of the well-known Schrafft's restaurant chain. He was a professor of English at Columbia University and, curious about my accent, asked, "Where do you come from?" I never liked it when people detected my accent and first I let him guess. He tried several countries and I finally had to tell him that I came from Germany, and wished I could get rid of my guttural German accent. I asked him whether there was a way to lose it, and he replied, "Yes, there is. But, if I were you, I would just leave it as it is." However, I was determined to lose my accent as much as possible, and over the years I would sometimes speak into a recorder and listen to my own voice, which helped a great deal.

While I was working at Ovington's, I bought myself a beautiful, old eighteen-carat hand-carved ring with one fine pearl and two rubies for thirty-nine dollars and a string of cultured pearls for nineteen dollars. I was told the ring was an antique Hungarian wedding band. I cherished that ring. It was the only jewelry I owned for many years.

But my job at Ovingtons didn't last very long. I needed to earn more money, so I went back to nursing. Dr. Jacobson' s office supplied me with a variety of cases. I worked for quite a few celebrities, among them: Elizabeth Bergner, a famous German actress; Enzio Pinza, who sang in *South Pacific*; and Mr. Bonwit from the fashionable department store, Bonwit Teller. He lived at the Blakstone Hotel, and at times suffered from dementia. One day he became so violent that he attempted to push me out the window. Petrified, I called security for help. They came to my rescue just in time. Of course, I never went back to him.

Another well-known patient was Madame Molotov, the wife of the Russian ambassador to the United States during the Stalin regime. And I was once called to take care of a patient by the name of Thom Mansville, the heir to the asbestos fortune. I did not know who he was at that time. When I arrived at his home on Park Avenue, a beautiful young lady ushered me into a huge living room and asked me to sit down in a comfortable chair. She introduced herself as his nurse but she did not wear a uniform and was fashionably dressed. I complimented her on her beautiful red hair. She informed me, "Mr. Mansville likes nurses with red hair and he doesn't want nurses to wear uniforms. I have been with him for two weeks and he has taken me out to fashionable restaurants. It isn't really a nursing job. I hate to leave, but he never keeps nurses longer than two weeks." When I asked her why he changed nurses all the time, she said, "He is a lonely man, somewhat odd, who needs companionship." Then she excused herself to let him know that I had arrived. A short while later, Mr. Mansville, a good-looking man in his forties appeared in a dark, silk robe. He looked me over from top to toe and then said, "I am sorry, you won't do. You see, I am looking for a certain type." I was stunned and embarrassed, I said, "Are you sure you are looking for just a nurse?" His answer was, "Yes, because nurses are always so clean." I realized the man was weird and said, "But sir, I have lost a day's work!" He answered,

"Oh don't worry about that. How much do I owe you?" When I told him five dollars, he took out his wallet and asked, "Did you come by cab?" I said, "No." With that he pulled out ten dollars, handed it to me, and said, "And this is for taking a taxi back home." That was the strangest case Dr. Jacobson's office ever assigned to me.

Dr. Jacobson had become well known in America. Despite his odd bedside manner, patients flocked to him. He took care of the most prominent people in the world, including Stalin, playwright Alan Lerner, and many others. Later he was the personal physician to President Kennedy and his wife, Jackie. He accompanied the president and his wife on their trip to France and Germany in the early 'sixties.

He was the most dedicated doctor I ever knew. It was not unusual for him to make house calls at all hours of the night. One evening, Hans had suddenly developed a severe back pain (lumbago). He was crouched over and in terrible discomfort. I called Dr. Jacobson for help. He said that he would get there as soon as he could. It was late that night when he arrived. Without asking any questions he drew up some fluid in a big syringe and injected it into Hans's buttocks. Miraculously, Hans was able to stand up straight almost instantly, and the doctor left without saying a word. There was something very secretive about him. He was a man of few words. The office had a strong smell from vitamins that were mixed in with the secret medication from his injections. Whatever it was that he treated the patients with, it showed excellent results. He never disclosed the content with his patients or with his staff. When he held office hours, his wife was his constant companion, a beautiful, young German socialite. He had met her in Paris, where he had practiced prior to coming to the United States. His office on 79th and Lexington was always crowded with patients, ready to receive the "miracle injection."

When he asked me to assist him from five to seven in the afternoon, I gladly accepted the job. It meant additional income for me; besides, I felt I owed it to him because I received private duty almost exclusively from him.

My work in his office was to inject patients intravenously with fluid that I extracted from three numbered vials. I was told the bottles contained certain vitamins. My patients were more or less ordinary working people who came after work. It was a very gratifying job, since patients showed almost instant improvement.

Many years later, Dr. Jacobson was accused of having treated his patients with amphetamines. The newspapers reported it and labeled him, "Dr. Feelgood." I still wonder whether the injections I had given when I worked for him had contained this drug. Nevertheless, I am forever grateful to Dr. Jacobson for having helped me so much when I was in dire need.

After twenty months of doing private duty and helping Dr. Jacobson in his office, I decided to attend one semester of evening classes at Rhodes High School in order to attain my high school equivalency. I found studying for exams here much easier than in Germany, but, because of my lack of language skills, I only received a passing minimum grade of 65 in English. However, in American history, I scored 85, in civics 95, and in economics 95. After completing the semester, I applied to Mount Sinai School of Nursing, but the tuition was too high and I couldn't afford it. I became discouraged and thought that maybe I should try something other than nursing.

A friend of mine was a masseuse. She had an office on West 86th Street and made a good living. She advised me to take the course at the massage school located in the St. Moritz Hotel. The day I started, I paid the full tuition of one hundred and twenty dollars, which was a lot of money. After a few hours of lectures on anatomy, we were permitted to practice on clients. But very soon I realized that I did not have sufficient strength in my fingers and hands. I was sorry that I had paid all that money in advance, but was too shy to ask for a refund. I finished the course in three months and received my New York

State Massage License. I never practiced on anyone except Hans, but I still have the license certificate.

A nursing shortage existed in 1941 and small hospitals permitted foreign nurses to join the staff as undergraduate nurses at a lesser salary than RNs. I found a job at Knickerbocker Hospital on 131st Street and Convent Avenue, in the midst of Harlem, at a salary of sixty-five dollars a month with room and board. It was not a lot, but I still managed to send my parents some money. I liked working in an American hospital; it was much easier than in Germany. First of all, floor duty was only eight hours, not twelve. Nurses did not have to scrub beds, nightstands, and mattresses after each patient's discharge; nurse's aides were assigned to that work. And the utility room was equipped with an automatic waste disposal, which facilitated emptying and sterilizing bedpans.

I clearly remember when, on Sunday, December 7, 1941, we heard that Japan had viciously attacked America at Pearl Harbor. I was sitting in the nurses' dining room having ice cream when we heard the terrible news of the attack on the radio which destroyed the entire U.S. fleet and killed many of our servicemen. In a moving speech to the nation, we heard President Roosevelt declare war on Japan and call December 7 a day of infamy. "We had nothing to fear but fear itself." It gave me the chills. We spent the rest of the day glued to the radio, listening for more news.

Since many registered nurses joined the armed forces immediately, positions in hospitals were easily available and I decided, after nine months, to leave Knickerbocker Hospital.

Another reason for wanting to leave was that Hans never escorted me home after a date, and it was always scary to walk the lonely streets of Harlem late at night, from the bus station at 125th Street to the nurses' residence five blocks away.

I found a position through the *New York Times* as a graduate nurse at Sloan Kettering Cancer Hospital, for eighty-five dollars a month with room and board. I was assigned to the evening shift, from three to eleven, as a head nurse on the private pavilion of the newly built hospital on East 69th Street. The old hospital had become the nurses' residence, located on 106th Street and Central Park West. It was more convenient and safer for me to come home at night.

I took care of some very interesting patients, such as Mr. Woolworth, founder of the Woolworth chain, and Mrs. George Kaufman, wife of the famous playwright, who always had well-known visitors like Moss Hart and many other celebrities.

My job consisted of making rounds with doctors, assigning nurses to do evening care, and giving out medication. At twenty-seven years old I looked very young. Patients thought that I was a student nurse. They could not believe that I was in charge. I liked my work, but, after over a year on the job, five of our nurses, including my supervisor and one doctor, were diagnosed with cancer. The doctor was the famous Dr. Ewing. (A brain tumor is named after him.) He was an old man and somewhat eccentric. I liked to give him special attention. One day I asked him whether cancer could be contagious, since we had so many nurses with this disease. His answer was, "I have devoted my whole life to the study of cancer. For all I know, it could be contagious."

That was enough for me to quit my job at Sloan Kettering, and since jobs were easy to get, I started a new position at Woman's Hospital on 110th Street and Amsterdam Avenue. I liked the location and the accommodations for nurses, but I did not like to work in gynecology, and stayed only a few months.

Finally, in 1943, I made up my mind to study for the registered nurse license examination. I was worried that, when the war ended, there would be an abundance of registered nurses returning, and I might not be able to get work so easily. The New York State Department of Licensing evaluated my foreign credentials and asked me to do additional training in Pediatric and Psychiatric Nursing, for a total of six months, at an accredited school. I searched and found Bellevue Hospital, which offered to pay student nurses twenty dollars a month with room and board.

Bellevue was an experience. It was best known for its Psychiatric Division, which was located in a new building. Every so often we found mice in the kitchen on Pediatrics. The wards were inadequately equipped with linen and other supplies. At all hours, fifty children would be screaming or crying in chorus, "I want to go home." Often we had no linen for them, and the kids would have to lie on the bare rubber sheets. One of the nurseries had all the unknown, abandoned infants. Since they had no names we identified the babies alphabetically: baby A, B, C, and so on. The nurses' residence was overcrowded, and a group of us were placed in rooms down the hall from the screaming children. It took a while to get accustomed to the noise, especially when we could only sleep with open doors because of the sweltering heat. Underneath us was the TB ward. One night I was awakened by a TB patient, dressed in his hospital gown, who had found his way to our floor. He stood in my doorway mumbling incoherent words and staring at me deliriously. I screamed so loudly that my colleagues came running to my rescue and transported him back to his floor.

While in training we had weekends off. Often I spent my free time at the shore in Far Rockaway with Hans, staying overnight and relaxing from the hard work at Bellevue. On one of those weekends at the beach, Hans had to work on Saturday and was only able to join me on Sunday morning. I waited for him on the boardwalk for more than half an hour, dressed in a two-piece bathing suit, with the hazy morning sun shining on my back. It was shortly before noon when Hans arrived, and we went to Nathan's famous frankfurter stand for a bite to eat. While waiting for our order, I suddenly collapsed. When I regained consciousness, a large crowd had gathered around me. I felt sick and couldn't stand up. I had come down with sunstroke. Hans called the Bellevue ambulance but was not permitted to come with me. I was admitted to the surgical ward and was given a continuous intravenous. The diagnosis was first and second degree burns on the back and severe dehydration. I had to lie on my stomach and had constant chills, but could not tolerate any covers, not even a sheet. I was given sedation for the pain from the blistering wounds, and was hospitalized for over a week before being sent back to the nurses' residence to recuperate.

All this time I did not hear from Hans. I was very upset; there was no excuse for it. While on the ward I could not be reached by phone, but he could have sent me a card or flowers. He was just very negligent and did not care. I was so disappointed and angry that I wrote him a nasty letter in which I told him I was through with him and that as soon as I was finished with my studies I would leave New York. I told him he was the biggest disappointment in my life. He responded by sending me a letter postmarked from Lake Placid, begging me to forgive him. He had not realized that I was so sick. His reason for being in Lake Placid was that he had been asked to bring Aunt Gerda's mother there and would return the following Sunday. He hoped I would forgive his negligence and that he would see me at Grand Central Train Station when he arrived back in New York. He asked me to please give him another chance.

While I was recuperating and was angry with Hans, I regretted that I had not married Bill Landfather, who was so caring during my most troubling days in Berlin. Since I had never let him know that I had arrived safely in America, I wrote him a letter and told him about my life here in New York. Immediately, I received a special delivery letter from him. He was so happy to hear from me. He was running his grandfather's hospital and lived with his mother and daughter on a 450-acre farm. He had told his mother a lot about me, and they would love for me to come out to Maryville, Missouri. He would be happy to send me the ticket. I was surprised when I got his letter, and felt uneasy about such a swift invitation. Even though I was upset over Hans's behavior, I was not ready for a new relationship, and I never responded to Bill's invitation.

When Hans returned from Lake Placid, I forgave him. For the first time he told me that he realized how much I meant to

him, that life without me would not be worthwhile. He promised
that he would marry me, but he felt morally obliged to care for
his sister Margrit and her fourteen-year-old son, Johnny, and I
had to be patient until he could support all of us.

I trusted him. Never before had he even mentioned
marriage. Some years ago, when I was impatient with our long,
drawn-out relationship, he had advised me to look for someone
else who wanted to get married. I answered an ad in the Jewish
paper, the *Aufbau*, and had a date with someone who didn't
interest me at all. After that I made up my mind then that if I
couldn't have Hans, I would never get married. I always tried
to be understanding about his reasons for not committing
himself. As long as he was dependent on Gerda's support, he
could not possibly think of marriage. She supplemented his
income with two hundred fifty dollars a month, and gradually
decreased the amount whenever Hans received an increase in
his salary. Hans was living with Margrit in a very nice apartment,
and she waited on her brother hand and foot. Long before
they left Germany, when they still could, they had sent
beautifully carved furniture for four rooms, rugs, china, and
even a refrigerator, washer and dryer, and clothing to
America in a large container, and it had been stored in a
warehouse until they moved into 215 West 91st Street. So
he was comfortable living where he was, and was in no hurry
to make a commitment.

Margrit, however, could hardly cope with the housework
without help. She was not accustomed to do those chores and
was very disgruntled about life here in a country where she
had to learn a new language. She had an especially hard time
adjusting and was lonely. In time she got acquainted with
German refugees—women who met with her every afternoon
at Schrafft's ice cream parlor. She was eighteen years older
than me, and wanted always to be with us. But I knew she
didn't approve of my relationship with Hans, solely because I
was poor. She often quarreled with Hans when he refused to
take her along, and I did not enjoy her company. Basically, she

was depressed about having lost her husband when she was only thirty years old. Now she was in her early fifties, and was heavy and short. Although she had a pretty face, the prospects of finding a meaningful relationship were dim. Financially, she was solely dependent upon Hans and was afraid she might lose his support if he married me.

After I had finished the required six months training at Bellevue and passed my four-day registered nurse examinations I was able to work in all the major hospitals such as Columbia-Presbyterian, Mount Sinai, New York-Cornell, and Roosevelt, which paid much better salaries. I signed up with the New York Labor Department Nurses' Registry, which sent nurses to the major hospitals, wherever they were needed. This had great advantages, and I could choose not to work on weekends. I requested day-duty only. The registry also did not charge the usual ten percent fee, so I liked the set up.

I found a cozy little place in a brownstone at 108 West 91st Street, down the street from Hans. It had a spacious living room. In an alcove stood a bathtub, which had a hinged metal cover. When I was preparing food, I let the cover down, and the bathtub became my working table. The alcove also had a gas stove with two burners and a small (non-electric) wooden icebox. Twice a week the iceman came to bring a block of ice. It was a great location, convenient to transportation, and also near Hans's apartment. I was able to have my hot lunch in the hospital, but I prepared my own supper, the same meal every night: a bowl of hot milk with a chunk of butter and bits of a Kaiser roll dunked in it, and an apple for dessert. Having this meal five times a week was most economical and nutritious, and I did not mind eating the same food every evening. This way I was able to afford to send money to my family weekly, as well as food packages and some clothing. They suffered from a great food and clothing shortage in Palestine. It was amazing that in all the years I sent them a twenty-dollar bill and letter every week, in addition to packages, only once did a letter with the money get lost.

Once a week Hans took me out for dinner, and every Saturday I prepared a scrumptious meal and dessert in my small kitchen, which we enjoyed by candlelight. During the week we often met with other refugee friends on Riverside Park for an hour or two, or we went to the movies, which featured newsreels showing the latest war events. The bitter battles that were fought on both fronts were reported daily in the *New York Times* and every evening we listened anxiously to the radio news reports and hoped that the end of the war would come soon.

Draping and Dressmaking

It was 1945, and I had not had a vacation since I had come to America. I considered perhaps taking a much-needed rest in the Catskills that summer. But one Sunday morning, as I was leisurely looking through the *New York Times*, an ad in the magazine section under Summer Schools, caught my eye. The ad showed a slender woman with a flowing garment draped on her figure. It read: MISS TRAPHAGEN'S SCHOOL OF DESIGN. Learn to drape the French way without a pattern in just six weeks.

That looked like fun to me. Why not try Miss Traphagen's School, instead of going to the Catskills? Staying in a small hotel there for two weeks would cost about the same as the dress design course, and by attending the school instead, I could learn something really useful. I had always had an interest in clothes.

When the war began in 1941, I worried clothes might get rationed. My mother told me that this happened in Germany during the First World War. When Macy's had their after-Christmas fabric sale, I bought quite a lot of material and put it away for a "rainy" day, which never came. Years ago, my mother's seamstress had shown me how to use the sewing machine, but I had forgotten most of it. Now I had all that material, but I had no machine. I decided to sew a dress from a *Vogue* pattern by hand and I got a lot of compliments whenever I wore it.

I could hardly wait until Monday morning to go to Miss Traphagen's School of Design on 52nd Street and Broadway. It was a very prestigious art school, had a four-year program, and also offered summer courses. I signed up for the French Draping Class that started that very day.

First, we were required to make a quick sketch of the dress

we intended to drape. Then they showed us the basics of how to drape muslin fabric on a dummy. After that they taught us to mark and baste the fabric. I learned a lot in a very short time, and enjoyed the course immensely.

Toward the end of the course, we were asked to bring in a striped material. Since I did not want to spend a lot of money, I bought four yards of a pink, candy-striped seersucker fabric from Woolworth for thirty-five cents a yard. I made a quick sketch of a two-piece suit and applied the fabric to the dress form. I decided to make double lapels, cuffs, and pockets, having the stripes going in opposite directions. It had an interesting effect.

While my striped dress was still draped on the dummy, Miss Traphagen and a group of French-speaking people came into the classroom and made the rounds. When they came to me they nodded approvingly and uttered something in French to Miss Traphagen, which I could not understand. A little while later I was called to Miss Traphagen's office. I had never met her before. She had a matronly appearance and greeted me with a warm smile. She asked me about myself and what I had been doing in the past. I told her I had been a nurse, and, instead of taking a vacation, I had chosen to take her course for fun, and that I enjoyed it a lot. She paused a while and then said, "I think you have talent. Would you consider doing this professionally? I think you should give it a try." I was amazed and flattered, but I told her that I had financial obligations toward my parents, who needed my support desperately. She asked me how much I was earning in nursing. I told her seven dollars a day and she replied, "The starting salary as a draper would be that much. Later on you could earn much more. I can get you a job right away. You should really give it a try." I could hardly believe that after six weeks in this field, I would be earning as much salary as it had taken me three hard years to earn in nursing. But I thought, what have I got to lose? So I told Miss Traphagen I would like to try it. She then picked up the phone and called Florence Lustig, a very fashionable haute couture house at that time, on 57th Street off Park Avenue. Miss Traphagen told her that she had a student who would do well as a draper in her atelier and asked if Miss Lustig would give her a chance. When she hung up, she smiled and told me to go on Saturday morning for a try out. If I qualified, the job would be mine for seven dollars a day. I thanked Miss Traphagan and she told me to keep in touch.

Very excited, I went to the very posh Florence Lustig Salon on Saturday morning. There, I was given a bag containing a black, hand-beaded fabric weighing about ten pounds or more with instructions and a sketch of the dress that I was to drape, pin, and baste on a form to certain exact measurements. I was nervous and shaking inside. How would I ever be able to tackle this? These dresses sold for five hundred to eight hundred dollars.

I was instructed to go to the drapery department on the third floor, where a young woman greeted me with a friendly smile. "Hello, Frieda! What are you doing here?" I recognized her immediately. It was Edith Loeb, Hans's sister Margrit's seamstress. She was surprised to see me. I told her that I was totally inexperienced in draping and was only here for a tryout and terribly nervous that I might mess up this expensive dress. She told me I shouldn't worry, and assured me she would assist me. She was the head of the drapery department on that floor. Was I lucky! Of course, I was hired at the end of the day. Without Edith's help I doubt that I would have made it. I enjoyed my new job and she taught me a lot over the next four months. Occasionally, I was called in to the designing department, where I also learned a lot. It was very creative work and not nearly as strenuous as nursing.

But, unfortunately, this job came to an abrupt end. One day, the fire department came and declared the premises a fire hazard and said that until major renovations were completed, all workrooms had to close.

I went back to Miss Traphagen and told her about my misfortune. I discussed with her the possibility of learning to sew on an electric sewing machine, because I wanted to sew dresses for myself from the fabric I had bought from Macy's a few years earlier. I could not afford to be without a job for any length of time and intended to go back to nursing. Miss Traphagen suggested I get a job as a learner for $16.50 a week. It would take me about three months to become proficient in it. She called Bergdorf Goodman and I was hired as a learner.

My first assignment was to sew hand-stitched buttonholes on the cuffs of a white silk blouse for the famous actress Vivian Leigh. Oh, was I clumsy and slow! I ruined the cuffs and had to rip them off the blouse. They showed me how to thread the needle into an electric machine but did not let me sew anything anymore. For the rest of the week I was only allowed to baste, and on Friday I was told I was not experienced enough and was fired.

Again, I went to Miss Traphagen, since I knew she liked me, and I told her what happened. She offered to call another fine establishment, Jay Thorpe on 57th Street. They needed help in their custom dressmaking department for the Christmas season, and they wanted me to come over right away for an interview.

The woman in charge was from Vienna, and she detected a familiar accent. Soon we started to talk in our native language and became instant friends. I told her about my adventures in sewing. She said that I shouldn't worry, that she would teach me in three months all there is to learn about constructing a couture garment. The rest was skill, which would take years. She took a special interest in teaching me step by step. By Christmas time I had learned how to construct a beautiful dress, intricate in design, with lining and interlining. We celebrated my last day at Jay Thorpe's. She said she was proud of me. In appreciation for the special interest she had shown in me, I gave her a jade Chinese figurine.

Now I was feeling pretty courageous. In the *New York Times* I found a new job as a draper for seven dollars a day in a negligee salon. It was early in January of 1946 when I started there. Most of the garments looked like evening gowns with matching cover-ups. The cheapest sold for one hundred dollars. However, it was not as creative or fascinating as Florence Lustig's salon. The owners of the negligee salon were foreigners and spoke Syrian all the time. I was the only draper and felt lonely. In June it was so stifling hot in that place that I quit my job and went back to nursing.

Now I took time to do some sewing for myself. I bought an electric sewing machine and a dummy on credit, and, in my spare time, I made my own clothes from the Macy's fabrics I had bought. It became my hobby. I even made Margrit a dress, which was extremely difficult because she had scoliosis and she didn't have a well-proportioned figure. I did it in the hope she would stop being so nasty towards me, and offer me occasional invitations to a home-cooked meal. I did get some invitations, and her attitude towards me improved somewhat, but not for long.

Much later, when I was married, I made all my slipcovers and drapes and I sewed all the dresses and coats for my daughter, Hope, and me. I even made matching coats for our little dachshund Schatzi to wear in cold weather. People often stopped us on the street to comment. When Hope was three years old she wanted to learn how to sew. She started to sew simple dresses for dolls by hand. For her birthday she wanted to have a sewing machine of her own. The Singer Sewing Company had little, hand-operated machines for children, and on her fourth birthday she received her desired present, wrapped in colorful birthday paper. But when she unwrapped the paper she broke into tears. I could not understand what was wrong. She had thought she would get a real sewing machine. I had to return her gift. She insisted that I teach her how to operate my sewing machine. I allowed her to work on it but only in my presence. At thirteen she was able to cut dresses from a pattern and sew her own clothes beautifully.

That six-week summer course at the Traphagen School was an excellent investment and a rewarding experience. It most certainly paid off in many ways.

Ship Nurse

As the years went by, Hans slowly advanced in business and continued taking courses in accounting at City College. Although his salary increased every year, he thought it still was not enough to support two families. Whenever I pressured him about marriage, he always succeeded in making me understand how much it would complicate our situation. I knew he would never renege on his promise to marry me, but sometimes I became impatient because our relationship was not going anywhere.

Twelve years had passed since I had first met Hans, and as time went by, I became more and more disillusioned with him. I wished I had someone from my family to talk to. I did have relatives in Vineland, New Jersey and in Cleveland, Ohio, but like me they were refugees and had enough problems of their own. In my unhappiness I felt utterly homesick. I longed to see my family. I had not seen my parents in eight years, and my brother in twelve. Unfortunately, the British authorities had clamped down on visitor visas to Palestine for U.S. citizens; even the prominent Rabbi Wise was denied a visa, so it was impossible for me to get there.

With all that trouble about our relationship, I still did not have the strength to break up with Hans. Every so often my patients asked me whether they could arrange a blind date for me with their sons, but I had no desire to meet anyone else.

Years earlier, while I was working at Doctor's Hospital, the grateful husband of one of my patients, who happened to be the president of American Express Co., offered to help me if I ever wanted to become a stewardess on a plane (in those days one had to be an RN) or a ship nurse. His name was James

Crowley. Unfortunately, his young and beautiful wife had died of TB in the hospital.

One very hot summer day at the end of August, I decided to seek Mr. Crowley's help in securing a position as a ship's nurse. I went to his office on Fifth Avenue and 51st Street. He remembered me and greeted me warmly. On a business card he wrote:

> *To whom it may concern:*
>   *Anything you can do for Miss Frieda Graumann, RN will be greatly appreciated.*
>
> *James Crowley.*

He told me my best chance would be to apply to the American Export Lines because their ships went all over the world. When I thanked him, he asked me to join him one day for dinner. I felt he was interested in me and told him I would let him know when I could possibly make it, but I never did.

Clutching the introductory note from Mr. Crowley, I immediately took the IRT subway downtown to Battery Place, the large headquarters of the American Export Lines. I was sent to the employment department where I had to fill out an application. The man in charge looked at the form briefly and said, "Lady, you and a thousand other nurses." But when I handed him Mr. Crowley's note, he looked at me astounded and said, "Oh, that's different. You will hear from us." I did not put too much hope into it but I thanked him and left.

That night, as usual, Hans and I sat with our friends in Riverside Park on 96th Street, discussing the latest world events and cooling off in the breeze from the Hudson River. At ten o'clock everybody went home. No sooner did I arrive home when the doorbell rang. To my surprise it was a Western Union messenger with a telegram from the American Export Line. It read: "You are offered a position as a ship's nurse. Please report to our office at 8:00 A.M. After a medical examination you will be sworn into the U.S. Coast Guard. Further instructions will be given to you. The ship you will be assigned to will leave tomorrow at 5:00 P.M."

What a shock this was! I could not believe I would be hired so soon. To what part of the world would this ship be sailing? It was late, about eleven o'clock, but I quickly ran to the nearest newsstand, on Broadway, and purchased the early edition of the *New York Times* to find in the daily shipping news toward which port the ship belonging to the American Export Line was going to set sail the following day. I could hardly believe my eyes! I read: "The S.S. *Carp*, departure 8/28/46, destination: HAIFA." I was in total disbelief. How could I be so lucky? It was destiny!

I hurried into the local drugstore, which was luckily still open, and quickly bought some toys for my nephews and some chocolate for my family. At home I wrote a letter to my parents announcing my arrival in the "near future," since I was unable to give them a definite date, and then I tried unsuccessfully to sleep. First thing in the morning I called Hans and let him know that I was leaving and was sorry not to be able to kiss him goodbye. He was stunned but wished me bon voyage. At eight o'clock sharp, I reported to the American Export Company, where I was told the necessary steps to take before boarding the S.S. *Carp* at five o'clock. First, the medical examiner, Dr Kimball, whom I had coincidentally worked for at Cornell Hospital, performed the physical exam and took a blood sample for a Wasserman test, which I then brought downtown to the Public Health Station on Worth Street. Then I proceeded to the United States Coast Guard headquarters where I was sworn in and given my ID. I just barely made it back to the ship by five in the afternoon.

The S.S. *Carp* was a converted warship, which was now carrying about one thousand five hundred soldiers and their families overseas to various military bases. Two doctors, five nurses, and a crew of a few hundred were assigned to the ship. Nurses had their own private cabins and shower adjacent to the sick bay. Upon arrival at the dispensary, I was greeted by the head nurse, introduced to the rest of the medical staff, and informed of my duties. If I had any problems, I was to report them to the head nurse or the first officer. There would be extra pay of two dollars and fifty cents a day for going through dangerous waters in the Mediterranean, which was still mined. I felt uneasy when I heard that. I doubt I would have taken the position had I known, but it was too late to back out now.

After settling into my cabin and changing into a uniform, I went with the other nurses to the mess hall. We were introduced to the first, second, and third officers and ate with them. I was so excited I could hardly eat. I was the only newcomer, so the head nurse suggested I should take the seven to eleven evening shift, because it was usually the easiest. The ship was now sailing and, as ordered, I was alone on duty and started my assignment in the sick bay at seven in the evening. Everything was fine until we reached Ambrose Light. There the sea became so rough that I got violently seasick. Every few minutes I ran over to the basin to vomit. In those days, the only remedy for seasickness was Phenobarbital. It did not help too much but I took it anyway. The first steward came into the bay to offer me some refreshment, which I had to decline because of my nausea. I told him how sick I was.

Soon some soldiers came in who were just as sick as I was. I would rush with them to the sink and we would gag together. For relief, I offered them Phenobarbital, knowing it wouldn't do much for them. At eleven o'clock the relief nurse came. I worried about what I should do if this didn't stop. I lay down exhausted on my bunk and fell into a deep sleep.

The next morning the medical staff was ordered to report to the captain's bridge. I was still terribly seasick. I dragged myself up to the bridge. It was a miracle that I made it. The captain, a very nice, elderly man, had already been informed of my condition. He handed me a ten-ounce tumbler of straight whiskey and told me not to drink it, but to sip it slowly all day. If I needed more, I was to contact the second steward, who had already been ordered to bring one full tumbler to my cabin every morning. The drink worked like magic! By evening I had stopped vomiting, although I was still not able to eat anything. It took three days and three tumblers of whiskey for my seasickness to disappear.

The food on ship was plentiful. Unlike at home, where meat, butter, and many other goods still required food stamps, nothing on board the S.S. *Carp* was rationed. We enjoyed huge, juicy steaks and strong coffee and cream. The work was easy, just taking care of some minor accidents and anyone who suffered from seasickness, many of whom I told about my own experience with whiskey.

During the day I usually went on deck and read a book or talked to passengers. It was very relaxing. The weather was perfect. I enjoyed the ocean breeze and the deep blue sky. I will never forget the breathtaking view when we reached the Rock of Gibraltar at sunrise. On one side you could see Europe and on the other Africa. The ship stopped in every major port along the coastline of Africa: Tangiers, Morocco, Algiers, Tunis, and Alexandria, Egypt, where military personnel and their families got off and heavy boxes were unloaded. Nobody was permitted shore leave in Egypt because of bubonic plague. On the pier, merchants traded fine leather goods, embroidered tunics, and fezzes. They would send up the merchandise on a pulley. I bought a fine leather duffel bag, which I enjoyed for many years, and a fez, which I wore on deck during my time off. We had a lot of fun dancing and playing cards and games with the stewards.

We arrived in Haifa on the seventeenth day, a Friday, September 13, 1946. Because of shallow waters, the ship docked outside the harbor. It was a while before we were permitted to leave the ship. At first, the British authorities did not want to let us off the ship, because there had been a bank robbery. The crew became restless and threatened mutiny. After long negotiations between the captain and the British, we were permitted shore leave for five hours only. Incredibly excited and dressed up in a thin, flaring dress, I was the first one to step off the ship, carrying my presents. But there was another hurdle to overcome. Since the ship was docked outside the shallow harbor, a small boat manned by Arab laborers was to transport us to the shore. In order to get to that tiny boat I had to descend a straight rope ladder from our tall warship. Clutching my handbag and presents and holding on for dear life, I ever so cautiously descended, step by step, my flaring dress exposing my entire legs, much to the delight of the whistling workers below. I finally made it ashore and ran to the nearby bus that was to take me to Naharya, the town where my family lived. The bus driver knew my father and pointed out historic sights such as old Roman water aqueducts along the way. Suddenly the bus was stopped by three British soldiers with machine guns, looking for contraband. Everybody had to exit the bus. I was the first one out, and when I saw a gun pointing at me, I shouted, "Don't shoot! I am an American!" The soldiers searched everyone and the inside of the bus and then let us leave.

Every so often, wandering Arabs blocked the narrow, dusty road. The driver had to honk the horn at them. They would cover their faces, but still would not budge. He had to open the window and scream at them in Arabic before they would move.

At last I arrived at my parents' house. It was a modern ranch house surrounded by a fenced in garden with magnificent flowers. I opened the gate and stepped into a lovely garden. There was a terrace the length of the ranch house with three entrance doors and many windows, with flower boxes. I looked in all the glass doors and windows on the terrace, and I called out, "*Mutti*!" (the German word for "mother"), but there was no answer. Finally I saw an old woman in the last room, sitting on a sofa bed. It was my mother. I opened the door and said, "*Mutti*!" She looked at me in disbelief and answered, "*Nein, bist Du das*, Friedel?" ("No, is that you, Frieda?") I embraced her. The shock was apparently too much for her; she closed her eyes and fell back onto the bed in a faint. I took her pulse and fanned her until she regained consciousness.

Of course they had not yet received the letter that I had sent them before my departure. I told her that I had only about five hours shore leave, so she immediately took me to see my sister-in-law, Judy, who lived just around the corner. It was the first time I had met Judy and her sons. Judy was a pretty woman, and she and her children all had beautiful blond hair and blue eyes. Uri was four years old and Dan was just six weeks old. We were all happy and excited. My brother, Gerhard, was expected to come home for lunch at any moment. Judy and her family lived together with her sister Ella in a large, Spanish-style villa. Judy prepared delicious Wiener schnitzel for all of us. Soon Gerhard arrived home, and was he surprised to see me! We embraced with tears of joy. Gerhard rushed out to fetch my father from work. It was wonderful and unforgettable to see my family again after so many years. I can't describe the happiness I felt at being united with them. It was certainly worth the effort and the danger of sailing through mined waters. My mother had aged tremendously and, like usual, was disgruntled about everything: the climate, the hardships, and the influx of Jews from neighboring Middle Eastern countries into her neighborhood who also had escaped tyranny, but came from different cultures. My father and brother did not complain. On the contrary, they were content to be amongst Jews. At last they did not have to be humiliated by anti-Semites.

They wanted to know about Hans and whether I was in contact with my cousins and aunts and uncles in America. We also talked about the relatives that had perished in the Holocaust.

The time went by much too fast and soon I had to leave. The farewell was not too sad because I was sure I would return to see them again on my next voyage to Palestine. My brother, little Uri, and a friend, drove me back to the ship. My father could not come because Shabbat would begin while he was still on the road coming home.

To my surprise, when I came back to the pier, the captain told me I could stay until twelve o'clock the next day because the stay in Haifa had been extended. They had tried to reach me by phone in Naharya, but could not get any connection. I was lucky my brother had not yet left. Happily we drove back.

My mother had not expected me for dinner and just when I returned she was serving a dish of tasteless, salty noodle soup she had prepared. What had become of her good cooking? It did not matter to me, since all of the excitement had left me with little appetite. She told me about the terrible food shortages and complained bitterly about her Polish daughter-in-law, Judy. My mother couldn't stand her, but she liked her grandchildren, Uri and the new baby.

After dinner Gerhard and Judy picked me up to show me Naharya by night. It is a beautiful resort on the Mediterranean Sea with lots of restaurants and music everywhere. We enjoyed delicious ice cream and dancing at an outdoor dance cafe. Both Gerhard and Judy complained about my mother, how poorly she had adjusted to life in Palestine and how difficult it was for my father to deal with her. She was making life miserable for the whole family. They wished they could live far away from her.

It was getting late and I wanted to spend some time with my parents, but Judy and Gerhard would not listen. When they finally brought me back to my parents' house, my father had already gone to bed. My mother was very upset and felt insulted. I said I was sorry but I had to depend on Gerhard to bring me back. She handed me the bed linen to make my bed on the living room sofa and without another word walked out of the room and went to bed. I felt bad but helpless. I had not meant to create any bad feelings and felt guilty to have caused her to be upset. I was too wound up to fall asleep. Instead, I relived the exciting day. It was like a dream. Finally I dozed off for a few hours but was awakened by howling sounds of what I thought might be wolves, but the next day learned they were jackals.

In the morning my mother was not angry with me anymore. While having breakfast, we talked again about our relatives: Who was alive and who had perished in camps. I am sure the tragedy of having lost three brothers (Leo, Adolf, and Hugo) and one sister (Olga), two brothers-in-law, two sisters-in-law, and some of their children must have affected my mother mentally. There was a sadness about her. She was not the well-dressed and beautifully coiffed woman I had known. My family was happy that I had come, but my mother continued to complain bitterly about the shortage of food. I promised them I would send them more food packages, and as much money as I could spare. I told them again and again that I would be back. Then I embraced them and kissed them goodbye, and returned to Haifa.

Again I had to climb the straight rope ladder up to the S.S. *Carp*, with my dress fluttering in the wind, much to the amusement of everyone who watched from the boat below, but I did not care. It was wonderful to have seen my family again and the prospect of seeing them periodically was most satisfying to me. I also hoped that because of my travels, my relationship with Hans would come to a final resolution.

Everybody, including the captain, wanted to hear about my reunion with my family, and I told them how wonderful it was to have seen them but how little food they had and how hard the struggle was in Palestine. I told them of the skimpy meal my mother served for Shabbat dinner and how much their lifestyle had changed since they had left Germany.

The ship finally left for Beirut, Lebanon. I did not get shore leave there, but when we arrived in Piraeus, Greece, the captain invited me to lunch at an outdoor cafe at the harbor with a magnificent view of the Acropolis. He informed me that he had ordered a shipment of food to be sent to my parents from the military base in Athens, and I was extremely touched by his generous gesture. My parents were surprised and very grateful when they confirmed the arrival of a huge wooden crate with all kinds of food, such as condensed milk, coffee, and even canned kosher goods, all sent by the U.S. Army Depot in Greece.

The return to New York took another twelve days. Upon arrival, I was ordered to report to headquarters immediately, and I had no idea why. There, I was informed that I would not be sent on that route again, because of the political situation. The management feared I might one day decide to join my family, and they wanted to avoid any problem with the British. Instead they offered me a head nurse position on one of the many ships sailing to Germany. Needless to say I was disappointed and very upset. How could I ever set foot on German soil again? I felt too hurt by what the Germans had done to us Jews. I could not possibly accept that position and I was discharged from the U.S. Coast Guard. But I was content, having fulfilled my desire to see my family again. It had been one of the most memorable incidents of my life. Another twenty years would go by before I could return.

Years Before My Marriage

It took a while to accept the fact that I would not soon have another chance to see my family. Our twenty-two-hour reunion had been wonderful and most memorable, but it was not enough. Besides, I had liked life as a ship's nurse. It was exciting seeing different parts of the world. I was sorry to have been forced to give up such a perfect job, but, as always, when things didn't turn out my way, I said to myself, *God must have another plan for me.*

Of course, Hans was happy to have me back. Shortly after I returned from overseas, I was fortunate enough to find another very pleasant job. My friend from nursing school, Ilse Beck, offered me a position as a supervising nurse in Eunice Skelly's famous reducing spa at 5 East 57th Street, where Ilse also worked. The hours were great, as was the seven dollar-a-day salary, and the work was not as tiring as hospital nursing. All we had to do was monitor electric machines that had wide rubber bands, which were strapped around the patient's hips and thighs. These bands electrically circulated around those areas. When Miss Skelly, a former showgirl, heard that I could do massaging, she engaged me to administer all the facials. The cubicle for facials was a darkened room with a very pleasant fragrance circulated by an electric vapor machine. Relaxing music filled the entire spa. I took care of many celebrities such as Lilly Palmer and Gloria Swanson, also a well-known actress at the time, and many others.

Every so often, while I was giving facials to the patients, they would fall into a deep sleep minutes after I had started. What was I to do then? It did not make sense to continue to work on them, and I didn't think I should wake them up. Since

I sat on a chair behind the client's massage table, I would put my head down almost next to theirs and also doze off until the attendant came in to tell us that time was up. The clients loved my facials. They praised me and felt great afterwards, even though I had hardly done anything to them. I kept this job until Miss Skelly decided to move to the West Coast.

My relationship with Hans dragged on. I became discouraged and frustrated, but did not have the strength to break up with him. By June 1947, I needed a vacation and decided I would visit my Aunt Kate and Uncle Max. After having lived seven years in Shanghai, China, they had settled in Vineland, New Jersey, to be near their children, who worked in chicken farming. I stayed with my cousin Brunhilde and her husband, Arthur, and their adorable little girl, Mirjam, who had a doll face and was nicknamed "Puppi." My relatives were happy to see me. We had not seen each other since the pogrom in 1938.

I enjoyed my visit to Vineland. It was so good to see my aunt and uncle and the many other relatives who had settled there. Aunt Kate had recovered and had gained her weight back. I seriously contemplated moving to Vineland. At least, I would have some family to belong to. I considered opening a children's day care center for working mothers. I was interested in a house for sale down the road from my cousin. The cost was twelve thousand dollars, but I did not have enough money for a downpayment, so I gave up my plan.

By the end of 1947, Hans had succeeded in business. His many years of studying accounting had finally paid off. He had become familiar with the latest tax laws and suggested changes to his bosses, Mr. Frank and Mr. Levy, which saved the business enormous amounts of money in taxes. As a result, he received a junior partnership and a yearly profit-sharing bonus, and was named executive vice president and treasurer of that multi-million dollar concern. He finally had achieved his American dream. I was proud of him. He no longer was that struggling refugee, lost in a foreign country. Now he was upbeat and self-assured. He had lost all the weight he had gained in Sweden, and wore stylish American suits. He looked handsome. Even Aunt Gerda was impressed with his success and, when he was asked to buy into the company, she gave him a substantial loan without interest payments.

Christmas 1947 came and went, and he still had not said a word about marriage. I waited for him to pop the question. Just a few days before New Year's, I had an argument with him not only about marriage, but also about how he was neglecting me. His excuse always was that he had to entertain a lot. I spent New Year's Eve at Ilse and Walter Beck's house, crying about that jerk, Hans. He knew that I was celebrating with the Becks and called me there at midnight to wish me a Happy New Year. Hans always had charm, and his warm personality always won me back.

Shortly before my birthday in March 1948, he asked me what I would like for a present, and I said just one word, "marriage." He smiled and embraced me. He realized it was time and that now he could easily afford to marry. Finally, my greatest wish was going to be fulfilled, and I was thrilled. We made plans about our future together. We knew, of course, that there were hurdles to overcome. First of all, he would always have to support his sister. Her son, Johnny, who had worked for a while in Hans's business but was terribly unhappy there, was still unsettled. On Hans's advice, he left the business to study optometry at Columbia, for which Hans had to pay tuition.

With my impending marriage, I worried about how I would be able to help my parents. Hans did not want me to continue working as a nurse for "peanuts," once I was married. How would it look, if a man in his position allowed his wife to work? What would people think? That was unheard of in those days.

Another problem was the acute housing shortage in New York. Hans was too spoiled to live in my little brownstone apartment. We agreed that he should stay with his sister until we could find a suitable place for us to live. But his greatest fear was how the all-important and influential Aunt Gerda would react to his decision to marry a poor girl (an *arme medubbe* in Hebrew, as Margrit would call me). And what would his bosses say if they heard he was marrying a girl without money? Hans was a very insecure man. Money was his greatest obsession. Too many times in his life he had experienced financial losses. In his youth, when he was twelve years of age, his parents suffered financial losses during the hard times in Germany following the First World War. He was old enough to understand and share his parents' problems. They later became prosperous and left him a sizable fortune when they died. Again, not long after Hans had reached the height of his career as a judge, he lost his position and faced an uncertain future. When he left Germany in 1939, he was forced to leave his parent's inheritance behind and arrived here, like all refugees, with only four dollars. All these factors contributed to his insecurity. Despite having advanced from office boy to executive vice president since his arrival in America, his worries of losing his position remained. I could well understand his fears.

One Sunday morning in May, he gathered enough courage to go to Aunt Gerda and let her know about his intention to marry me. Apparently she was happy at the news and anxious to meet me at tea the following Sunday. I still remember the beautiful navy blue dress I wore, which I had made myself. It had a matching blue satin collar, cuffs, and a wide, blue satin belt around my narrow waist. I had also treated myself to an expensive navy blue handbag and high-heeled platform shoes at Henri Bendel's.

I was excited and yet quite confident that she would have no objection to our marriage. But when we were ushered into her twenty-eight-foot long carpeted drawing room, my knees were shaking. Aunt Gerda and her constant companion, concert singer Mary Bothwell, were sitting on a sofa by the fireplace at the other end of the room, watching us enter. They invited us to sit down on a comfortable sofa opposite them. Aunt Gerda wanted to know about my family. I had to tell her that I was very worried about them and had not heard from them in months because of the war in the Middle East (the War of Independence), which was raging between Jews and Arabs. She was also interested to hear about my work and how long I had lived in America. Then she popped the question, "When do you plan to get married?" Hans and I looked at each other and just smiled. He said, "We have not made any definite plans yet." "What are you waiting for?" she asked. Hans had an excuse. He first needed a hernia operation. She urged him to have this done as soon as possible. After about an hour we said goodbye. I could tell she was pleased.

We were both excited, and strolled happily along sunny Central Park West. Now he was going to tell Margrit the news right away. He thought it would be best to tell her alone without me, and to assure her that he would provide for her always.

Soon after I came home, the telephone rang. It was Aunt Gerda and she told me how delighted she was to have met me. She said she would again urge Hans to have the operation done immediately and then plan a wedding date. I was so happy. I only wished I could have shared it with my family.

Aunt Gerda and her companion, Mary, were ready to leave for Europe, where she spent three months of every year in her suite at the Suvretta House in St. Moritz, Switzerland. Before she left, she told Hans that if he was not married by Thanksgiving, she would not attend our wedding—and she was very serious about that.

It was an exciting time in my life; I was introduced to his bosses and business associates, and we were invited to their homes.

In the summer Hans had his hernia operation at Mount Sinai Hospital, and I was his nurse. I must say he was not the easiest patient I had ever taken care of; on the contrary, he was most impatient and sometimes even nasty. But I attributed his behavior to the sedation he got for his discomfort. After the operation, we went to Atlantic City, where he spent two weeks recuperating. We stayed at a very nice hotel on the Boardwalk—

in separate rooms, of course. In those days it was illegal to register for just one room if the couple were not married. Hans still had a lot of pain, but he enjoyed going to the auction houses along the Boardwalk, which were plentiful, while I just loved to take long walks on the then snowy white sand at the beach or take a dip in the ocean.

One day he returned with a small jewelry box and proudly presented me with a diamond ring he had just got at an auction. I took a good look. I hated to disappoint him, but the ring had no luster and it had many visible imperfections. When I asked how much he paid for it—I knew he had been taken. I told him to go back and ask for his money back, which he did. He did the same foolish thing a few days later. This time the ring was bigger and it had more dark spots in it. I made him understand that these so-called auctions were rigged, that they have shills sitting there hyping the price for the audience to bid. I told him that I didn't want a ring now. Later, when he could well afford it, he should buy one at a reputable firm. He argued that it was important for me to have a ring because everybody would want to see the ring he gave me. I suggested getting a Zircon stone for the time being, and he agreed. So again he went to return the black coal diamond ring. But this time the owner refused to give him his money back.

Disappointed, poor Hans came back to me. I immediately went to the Better Business Bureau. The person in charge called the store and negotiated with the owner. He was told Hans should go back to the jeweler, who had agreed to exchange the ring for other purchases in the store. We returned the ring and bought a chest of silver-plated cutlery instead. Hans had learned a good lesson. He was never again tempted to go to another auction house.

By the end of our vacation, Hans was able to take long walks. One sunny day we were strolling on the Boardwalk looking into jewelry window displays. One owner was standing outside his store observing us, and asked whether he could assist us. I had spotted a set for twelve of fine sterling silver cutlery in the

Royal Danish design for two hundred forty dollars. I really liked it and thought this was a much better value than what we had paid for the silver plated set. I told the gentleman about our experience with the auction house, and he suggested that I should bring him the silver plated set and he might be able to trade it in. It was not far from the hotel so I rushed back and returned with the silver plated Reed and Barton set. We gladly paid the difference of fifty dollars, and acquired something that I really enjoyed and used every day of our married life. We liked the man and also bought a two-carat Zircon ring from him for fifty dollars. Of course everybody thought it was a real diamond, but after a while the ring yellowed, and I stopped wearing it.

In September, Aunt Gerda and Mary came back from Europe. They were happy to hear that we planned to get married the evening before Thanksgiving. Aunt Gerda offered to arrange a celebration at the prestigious St. Regis Hotel for us, but I could not accept her offer, as much as I would have liked to. I could not imagine dancing in a big ballroom and enjoying an elaborate festivity while my family was lying in trenches in the midst of an ugly war. Aunt Gerda understood my point and offered to give dinner in her home just for the immediate family. I found that much more fitting.

Every year, when Aunt Gerda returned from Europe, she arranged for Mary Bothwell to sing at Carnegie Hall or Town Hall and all her friends, the "Jewish crowd," as well as other prominent people were invited. This particular year Lotte Lehmann and Lawrence Melchior, both famous Metropolitan opera stars, attended. After the concert, everybody was invited to Aunt Gerda's apartment for a catered cocktail party. Now I was introduced to everybody as Hans's fiancée.

On that evening, Aunt Gerda's close friends teased Hans in Margrit's presence, asking him how on earth he was able to catch a "jewel" like me? Margrit interrupted, bursting out in her heavy German accent and rolling her eyes angrily, "No, no, he could have done much better than that." Everybody looked at each other with astonishment at this unfitting remark. Hans, somewhat embarrassed, smilingly brushed it off by saying, "You know, it's just jealousy." I tried to avoid Margrit as much as possible after that.

One day Hans asked me how much money I had saved in my bank account. I had one thousand four hundred dollars. He said, "Go and buy yourself a decent Persian lamb coat." Years earlier I had bought one for one hundred dollars; it was of poor quality, but warm. With the last one thousand four hundred dollars I had saved, I bought a beautiful coat imported from France and Hans jokingly said, "This is my dowry."

I designed and made my own wedding dress, of a light, blue wool. Heavy shoulder pads and wide raglan sleeves were in style. It had a deep, V-neckline. I hand-crocheted imported copper-toned tinsel thread into loops. I hand-stitched these hundreds of yards of loops into a scroll design all over the flared skirt and over a matching ascot. A milliner made a hat to match the dress. I thought it looked stunning. (For sentimental reasons, I still have the dress.)

Hans and I were looking forward to our life together and were very happy.

My Wedding and Married Life

Finally, after fourteen years of waiting, the day of our wedding arrived. The ceremony was scheduled to take place in the evening on Wednesday, November 24, 1948, at seven o'clock at a Temple on 79th Street off Columbus Avenue. In Jewish tradition it is said to be a bad omen to see each other before the wedding, so I didn't see Hans all day until we met at the sanctuary. Early in the morning, I woke up full of joy and excitement, and waited impatiently for the hour to arrive. It seemed to take forever. It was a sunny, but very cold and windy day. As I sat all by myself in my apartment, reliving the last fourteen years and contemplating what my life would be like, I suddenly felt overwhelmed and scared of the responsibilities I would have to face as a wife. I wished my family were here to give me encouragement and to share this joyous occasion. How happy I would have been! In those days, telephone communication to Israel had not yet been established.

Often weeks went by without receiving any mail. Sporadic fighting was still going on in the newly established State of Israel in 1948. I was constantly worried about Gerhard, who was still on patrol duty in his hometown of Naharya. My parents and Judy, Gerhard's wife, kept the news from me that he had been shot in the face by an Arab. Not until years later, in 1958, after Gerhard had immigrated to America, did Judy tell me what really had happened to Gerhard.

I had not received any congratulatory note from my parents, even on my wedding day. Naturally, I worried about them and wondered whether they even received my letters and my weekly support. I was glad that the wedding was not going to be a big social affair, as Aunt Gerda first had suggested. My heart wouldn't have been in it.

Seven o'clock drew closer and it was time to put on my pretty blue wedding dress and matching hat. I wore high-heeled shoes and carried a copper-colored, sequined evening bag. It was a bitter-cold evening but I felt warm in my chic, new Persian broadtail coat as I waited for a cab to take me to the synagogue. There, Hans and I met in the sanctuary. How handsome he looked in his navy-blue suit! Margrit, Johnny, Aunt Gerda and her companion, Mary, had already gathered. Soon the rabbi called us into his study and asked us to sign the marriage certificate, for which Hans paid thirty-five dollars. Aunt Gerda and Johnny were our witnesses.

Then the ceremony began. Hans and I stood in the sanctuary, under the *chupah* ("a canopy"), and the rabbi blessed us in English and Hebrew and we repeated our vows. As is customary in the Jewish tradition, Hans broke a glass by stamping on it with his foot, then placed a platinum wedding band on my finger, and the rabbi pronounced us husband and wife. We kissed and everyone congratulated us. The ceremony took less than ten minutes, but I was happy; I was now Hans's s wife, until death would us part.

Aunt Gerda invited us to her home for a lovely dinner of shrimp, rib roast, and plum pudding, and the next two nights we spent happily at the Greystone Hotel on 91st and Broadway. Hans could not take time off for a lengthy honeymoon; we just had Thanksgiving weekend to relax. We had decided to postpone our honeymoon until the summer, and spend it at Fish Rock Lodge on Lake George, which we loved.

The day after the ceremony was a day of partying. First we visited Hans's boss, Mr. Frank, who had invited us to a cocktail party at his Drake Hotel apartment, and then we all drove out for a Thanksgiving dinner with Mr. Levy, his other boss, who lived in Woodmere, Long Island. We were tired from all the partying but very happy and came back early to our hotel.

Friday morning a limousine service drove us to the Ulman Farm, a charming and popular inn, near Brewster, New York, where we stayed until Sunday. That weekend it did not just rain, it poured. We didn't leave our cottage until we went home at noon, on Sunday. In spite of the bad weather, we were happy. When we came back to the city we separated as we had planned. I went back to my little studio apartment and Hans continued to live with Margrit, until we were able to find a suitable place to live, but we saw each other every evening for dinner.

The First Years of Marriage

The following morning Margrit paid me an unannounced visit. I wondered why she came, and had an uneasy feeling as she entered my modest abode. She had never seen it before. I couldn't imagine that the reason for her visit was just curiosity, to inquire about our weekend as newlyweds. When I told her that in spite of the downpour, we were extremely happy. Her answer was, "Surely, you should be, because you know you have hit the jackpot by marrying Hans." Angrily and with a quivering voice she said, "But for Johnny and me, I want you to know you are our misfortune (*Unglueck*). I am very unhappy that Hans had married you." I was shocked. "Is this why you came here? Get out," I angrily replied. When she got up from her chair, she repeated again and pointed her finger at me, "You are the *Unglueck* of my family." With that, I took her by the collar of her coat and shoved her out the door. She yelled obscene words at me from the staircase. I felt so hurt, and I began to cry. I couldn't believe that she hated me just because I was poor. Basically she didn't trust that Hans would support her and Johnny after we were married. When I told Hans about it in the evening he assured me that it wouldn't happen again, and that he would have a talk with Margrit.

For Hans and me, living apart was not ideal, but there was a housing shortage in New York, and we just had to wait for an opportunity to get an apartment. It was impossible for Hans to move in with me. My studio was small, and I couldn't sleep with Hans in just a double bed, because he was too restless. There wasn't enough closet space and the bathtub was one of those old-fashioned short and narrow ones. I don't think Hans would have been able to fit in it with his big frame.

Finally, in February 1949, after three months of waiting and through pull, we were lucky and found a beautiful apartment at 308 East 79th Street, in a fashionable neighborhood, with a doorman and an elevator man. It was large and airy with three exposures on the twelfth floor, overlooking downtown Manhattan. I felt in heaven.

We immediately ordered furniture through a decorator, who had the cabinets made by French artisans. It took three months until we could move in. Hans asked me to give up my place and move in with him and Margrit, for the meantime, because he did not want to pay for all three apartments. I reluctantly agreed, but that turned out to be a major mistake. First of all, her place was dirty and the kitchen full of roaches. Hans's room was narrow; two beds did not fit in there, so I was bedded down on a mattress on the dining room floor. Soon, I suffered a severe sinus infection and could not shake it without medical help. The doctor advised me to get out of that environment as soon as possible, which I couldn't do. I decided to take twelve-hour private duty cases and not see Margrit all day long. She did not dare to be too obnoxious when Hans was around. I remember one Sunday morning I had joined Hans in his bed. We were cuddling when all of a sudden Margrit pranced in mumbling, "How disgusting!" Hans jumped out of his bed cursing and throwing his slipper at her as she ran out of the room.

At another time Margrit used abusive language and I lost my temper. I had been taking care of a forty-year-old patient who was recuperating at home from a heart attack, on constant bed rest. One day he showed me his art collection of fine etchings and asked me to select one for myself. I chose the *Wailing Wall* in Jerusalem by the well-known artist Gross, because my family was living in Israel. I appreciated his thoughtfulness. After lunch he fell asleep as usual. I was sitting in an easy chair next to his bed when I suddenly heard a loud rattling noise coming from his chest and seconds later he died. It was a terrible experience losing a patient so young and so suddenly.

Seeing his young wife and his child screaming was very
emotional for me.

After the patient was taken out of the home, and members
of the family had arrived, I left, still very shaken up. All I wanted
was to go home and rest. But Margrit wanted me to help her
prepare hors d'oeuvres for Johnny, who was going to give a
party. She was incapable of doing things like that. I told her I
was exhausted and needed to rest. She burst out, "You lazy
good-for-nothing." Well, I lost my cool. I shouldn't have done
it, but I lashed out and gave her a slap in the face. She screamed
into the telephone ordering Hans to come home immediately
and he did. I had to apologize to her.

The three months I endured at my sister-in-law were ugly.
Often I just went to visit my empty new apartment and brought
all our many wedding gifts over there. Our wedding gift from
Aunt Gerda was very generous. She gave us a complete set of
Rosenthal china with cobalt blue and gold rim for eighteen
people, with large platters and bowls, a five-piece sterling coffee
and tea set, as well as a set of Baccarat crystal wineglasses.

Finally, early in June, the beige carpet was laid wall to wall,
and the draperies were hung. The mattresses were delivered
before the rest of the furniture arrived and I immediately
moved out of Margrit's place. I slept on the bare mattress until
the cabinets, sofas, and chairs were delivered. Our little paradise
looked absolutely gorgeous to me.

I will never forget the day we moved in. It was a sweltering
hot day. Hans had worked all day, and when he arrived in the
new apartment with flowers and a bottle of champagne, he
picked me up and carried me over the threshold. I was
sublimely happy, and a little tipsy from the champagne, as I lay
on the new carpet. At last we had a place of our own!

The first night we were not used to the street noise, but
also we were both too excited to fall asleep. Our bedroom
windows faced Second Avenue, which still had cobblestones,
and room air conditioners were not yet available. Luckily, it
was a weekend, and we could sleep late. But what a great feeling

it was to wake up in our beautiful new home with the man I loved!

We had slept with the windows opened all night, and a lot of dust had blown in. I had never vacuumed a carpet before. After breakfast, I was eager to use my newly purchased upright Hoover vacuum, which moved so easily on the linoleum floor in the store. But I was greatly disappointed when I found out how hard it was to move it at home. At first, I thought there must be something wrong with this model, and I asked Hans to check what's wrong. First he tried the machine on the bare floor. There he found nothing wrong with it. But when he pushed it on the carpet he realized how hard it was to move. He immediately told me, "Get someone to do this job. I don't want you to do such heavy work." He didn't have to say it twice. I asked the elevator man and before long he found me a wonderful, elderly Hungarian woman. Her name was Gina, she had been a cook for a banking family for years and now did hourly housework. She stayed with us for seven years. She cleaned, cooked, baked, and helped serve whenever we had parties.

The first week we moved in, Aunt Gerda and Mary wanted to see our new home and, of course, I invited them for my first dinner. Naturally, I was eager to make a good impression. Gina did not work for me yet, so I cleaned and dusted the place for hours before they came. The dining table was decorated with a pretty flower arrangement and set with Aunt Gerda's fine china and stemware, as well as my freshly polished cutlery and silverware. It looked festive. I was very excited but also quite exhausted already before the two guests arrived.

Of course, they admired our lovely apartment, and we sat down for our meal. While we ate a fresh fruit salad as an appetizer, the chicken breasts, which I had prepared exactly after a recipe in a cookbook, were simmering in fine herbs and white wine on the stove, or so I thought. But suddenly I sighted billowing smoke coming out from the kitchen window. I rushed into the smoke-filled kitchen and found a mess. I opened the lid and found the charcoaled chicken breasts pitifully lying there, all of gravy evaporated and my new skillet covered with a black crust, completely ruined. Instead of turning the gas on low, I had switched it on high. Oh was I embarrassed! I had wanted to make a good impression as a cook with my first dinner and now it turned out to be a disaster. But my guests didn't think anything of it. They even insisted that I bring the burnt chicken to the table. But, when they saw the charcoaled food, they realized it was not edible. I felt terrible.

But Hans, with his usual charm, made very little out of it. He seemed to be amused about my failed attempt, and invited us to Longchamps, a very nice French restaurant, on 79th Street and Madison Avenue. We spent the rest of the evening there, eating a well-prepared meal.

Soon, with Gina's help, I became very skilled in giving parties and I loved to entertain. Aunt Gerda was a frequent guest in our house.

Those first six years of marriage were exciting and wonderful. We had many friends, attended social functions, and traveled to beautiful places. It felt great not to have to work for a living anymore. My parents no longer required my support. My father was able to find work, though there was still a great shortage of food and clothing in Israel. My mother wrote in every letter how difficult it was to get food, so I continued to send, through a kosher food-packing company all kinds of groceries, meats, and chocolates. At my mother's request, I even sent a refrigerator.

Hans felt she was taking advantage of my good nature, but how could I possibly enjoy my good life knowing my parents were in need? Since Hans didn't approve of my supporting them, I continued to work floor duty two days a week at nearby New York Cornell Hospital, without Hans ever finding out. As soon as he would leave for work at seven-thirty I would get into my uniform, and arrive for floor duty at the hospital in time. Even during the summer months when we stayed in Long Beach, Long Island, I found work at the local hospital for one day a week.

The summer of 1950 we spent in Long Beach and Hans commuted daily to New York. We shared the upper floor of a large house with an elderly couple, Emily and Jules Cherof. They were great company, and they became our closest friends. Emily loved to cook and bake. She was sixteen years older than I was. To me she was the mother I had always longed for.

We spent the next summer with them again in the same place. It was in 1951, and I was already in my third month of pregnancy. We were very happy but didn't tell anyone yet, except Emily and Julie. Unfortunately, I woke up with cramps one night. I didn't want to wake up Hans although, I knew I was in trouble. While I was sitting on the toilet with excruciating pain a big blood clot fell into the toilet bowl. I must have fainted and fallen to the floor. When I woke up I was lying in a pool of blood. Hans, his face white like a sheet, had summoned the doctor from the ground floor apartment. Both men were standing over me, trying to carry me into my bed. The doctor told me I had just lost a three-month-old fetus. It was a boy. We were sad, but not discouraged.

The following year I was pregnant again, and in my third month I started to stain. My obstetrician was Dr. Aldridge from Woman's Hospital, where I had worked before I was married. As a precaution, he ordered strict bed rest for two months. I was glad to have Gina to help me. It was not easy to stay in bed for so long. We did not have television yet and it was awfully boring, but I was determined to be good and follow doctor's orders. At the end of my fourth month, I noticed an offensive odor and the doctor examined me. He gave me bad news, the fetus had dissolved and I now needed an abortion. It had to be done soon because of the danger of infection. I was utterly disappointed and cried uncontrollably. Hans came home from the office immediately and I was taken to the hospital by ambulance.

The doctor thought I might have a low thyroid. The test was a lengthy procedure. I had to lie for one hour in a dark room and breathe into a long hose, which was connected to a machine. They found I did have a low thyroid, and I was put on medication. By fall of 1953 I had not become pregnant again, and I became very concerned. Hans's sperm was tested, and was found to be okay. As a last resort, Dr. Aldridge advised me to have a Rubin's Test done. It was a most painful procedure, where the fallopian tubes were blown with air in order to clear them. I later found out that this test could be dangerous and even fatal. I had promised myself that if I didn't conceive by the end of that year, I would give up trying to get pregnant. I felt that at forty I would have been too old to have a child. At the end of October 1953, right after the test, we spent a lovely weekend at the Ritz Hotel in Atlantic City and that's when I conceived.

I Am Pregnant

On November 28, 1953, I missed my period. When I had the pregnancy test, it was positive and we were thrilled. I stayed in bed for most of the first three months. As a precaution Dr. Aldridge gave me one single injection of Des (a medication to prevent miscarriage, which years later was found to cause problems for the offspring). But we were lucky Hope was not too adversely affected by it. Most likely, the one single dose I had received had not caused the severe damage that it caused in a great number of cases, in which the patients had received large amounts.

Being pregnant made me feel complete as a woman, wonderfully happy and full of energy. I had so much fun sewing my own maternity clothes, which I started to wear in my fifth month. I ordered a layette and the biggest baby carriage from Best and Co., and hired a baby nurse for a month. We looked for a larger apartment at the newly built Manhattan House on 66th Street and 3rd Avenue.

One day Aunt Gerda called me to tell me there was an apartment available on her floor, would that not be lovely? It showed that she was really fond of us and wanted us to live so close by. I immediately went to see the apartment, but it was too small. When I told Hans that Gerda wanted us to live right next door to her, he said, "Oh sure, that's all we need." He did not want to be under her scrutiny every single day. The anticipation of becoming a mother and sharing this much-wanted child with the man I truly loved brought me indescribable joy. How happy we were during those first six months of my pregnancy! Those were the greatest moments in my married life. Unfortunately, unforeseen circumstances brought all this to an abrupt end.

Hans's Illness

I will never forget when Hans came home from work on April 14, 1954, nervous and distraught.

Mr. Frank, a widower, had recently married his manicurist and wanted to retire from business. Negotiations with lawyers and accountants for selling the company to his young executives had been going on for several months. But on April 14 Mr. Frank suddenly announced that he was selling his multi-million dollar concern to the McGregor Sportswear Company, who had offered him a handsome price for his business. All five young executives who were counting on taking over the business were shocked to hear about the sudden change of plans.

The probability of losing his position as treasurer and executive vice-president was high and Hans was terribly upset and frightened. What were we going to do now that we were expecting a child? I tried to calm him as best I could, but to no avail. He paced the floor all night, smoking one cigarette after another. I had never seen him that way before.

Just two days earlier, we had celebrated Aunt Gerda's birthday. She was going to be the godmother of the baby. I was in my sixth month and we discussed a possible name. If it were a boy it would be Henry in honor of her late husband Herman, and if a girl it would be Hope. I liked the name Hope because I was not so young anymore, and having a child later in life can be risky, and I hoped for the best. Everyone was looking forward to the happy event, even my nasty sister-in-law, Margrit. (At least she said so.) How life could change so suddenly!

Hans's anxiety increased day by day. I became worried he might have a heart attack, and advised him to consult a doctor to prescribe something for his nerves. He saw our Dr. Gabrilove, who sent him to a psychiatrist, Dr. Kallmann, originally from Vienna, who was the doctor who introduced shock therapy to this country. After Hans consulted with him, the doctor called me and told me that Hans was in a deep depression and warned me, "Watch for a possible suicide." I could hardly believe that, but from that moment on, I was on alert as much as I could be. Hans had sleepless nights and I stayed up with him and tried to catch up on my sleep during the day while he was at work. The medication did not help at all. As time went by his condition worsened. He lost a lot of weight, at least thirty pounds. He had always had a neat appearance, but not anymore. He was restless, pacing the floor with constant and profuse perspiration for hours at a time. When he came home from work he hardly ate, and then he wanted to go to Central Park where we walked for hours. I always went with him. Unbeknownst to me, these walks were good exercise for my pregnancy. However, what Hans was telling me was often too painful to hear. He told me that he never really wanted a child and blamed me for being so stupid in talking him into it. Even to have married me was a mistake. "Why did you want to have a baby?" Knowing how ill he was, I kept silent, though with choking pain in my throat; I never argued. Sometimes, I couldn't control myself and burst into tears. Even the crying annoyed him and he would yell at me, "Why did you want to have a baby? Answer me." But soon after, he would feel sorry to have hurt my feelings. I always tried to reassure him. Aunt Gerda would never let us down. I reminded him what she had told me some time ago, while I was taking care of her when she was sick; she had said, "You are my daughter, don't you know?"

Aunt Gerda was about to go to Europe again and she asked us to come to her house for tea. Hans was a changed person. He was tense, haggard-looking, and very serious. Gerda sensed something was wrong. She talked to Hans alone. When she came out of the room, I heard her saying to him, "Don't worry, Hans, there will always be a breadcrumb for you and milk and honey for Frieda and the baby." On our way home he was angry with Gerda that she had not given him any concrete reassurance about what exactly she was going to do to help.

Hans did not want to see any of our friends anymore. Sometimes, Emily and Jules Cherof from Long Beach would drop in. They couldn't get over how Hans had changed. Nobody could drum any sense into his head. Often he preferred to be alone with his sister or with his best friend, Julian. Every weekend, he would meet them and pour his heart out. The closer it came to my delivery date, the nastier he became. He was very secretive and confided in his sister, who gave him bad ideas. One day he came home and told me in a rather suggestive way that Margrit had had an abortion in her sixth-month of pregnancy. I didn't react to that hint and he again asked his usual questions about why I wanted to have a baby. It was torture, but I knew this was a very sick man. I had to be strong and had to treat him as I would have any other patient.

Hope's Birth

My due date came closer and closer, and I had to make arrangements with Margrit for Hans to stay in her apartment while I was in the hospital. It was not safe for him to be left alone. When my water broke on the morning of July 19, 1954, Dr. Aldridge's assistant told me to come to the hospital. Dr. Aldridge was unable to take care of me because he had been called to operate on Queen Juliana of the Netherlands. On my way by taxi to Woman's Hospital, I dropped off a suitcase of clothing for Hans at his sister's. I had not the slightest pain from my contractions, but I was ordered bed rest in the hospital. In the evening, Hans paid me a short visit with Margrit. It was a brutally hot day. He perspired profusely and looked very stressed. There was not much to discuss, so I told him to go home and I would let him know when the baby came. I was so exhausted from the many weeks of vigil over Hans that as soon as he left I fell asleep. Nurses would come in and monitor the painless contractions, but I barely opened my eyes while they did their work.

At five in the morning, I was wheeled into the labor room. Four other women were in there at the same time. I was the only one who didn't moan and groan. Just before the baby's head showed, I had five severe contractions. Then suddenly two nurses laid their weight over my legs and prevented me from pushing anymore. When I asked why they are doing that to me, they told me the doctor was late and they couldn't let me deliver without his presence. When the contraction started again I screamed and cried from pain. I was given an injection and I fell asleep.

When I woke up I found myself lying in my own room, the

doctor standing over me and saying, "It's a girl, everything is all right." But it wasn't. They brought the baby in and her head did not have a normal shape. It was elongated like a small watermelon, from lying in the birth canal longer than it should have.

I cannot put into words how shocked I was when I saw my baby for the first time. What should have been the greatest moment of my life was reduced to utter pain and agony. I held her in my arms and kissed her while my tears washed her distorted head. I was terribly afraid she might have brain damage, and how Hans would react when he saw the baby's head. Now I had a new worry. I felt so alone. No one was there who could comfort me in my troubles. I was furious at the doctor and cried. Later, when he came into my room, I took my slipper and threw it at him, daring him to enter my room ever again. From then on a young intern visited me daily. He assured me that the baby would be okay, but I was not sure. The pediatrician confirmed, after having checked her neurological reflexes, that everything was fine, but I still didn't trust anyone.

Hans paid me a short visit during his lunch hour with Margrit, and brought me flowers he had bought from the corner street vendor. He said he was glad it was over and went with Margrit to see Hope through the window of the nursery. I was relieved that he didn't discover her peculiar head shape. I was not going to tell him, so as not to burden him with another worry.

In the afternoon, many beautiful flower arrangements arrived from friends and business associates, as well as from Aunt Gerda. There wasn't enough room for the many bouquets, and they had to be placed on the floor of my small hospital room. After Hans's visit I lay there all alone, surrounded by those gorgeous flower arrangements, and I broke down and sobbed, feeling sorry for my baby and me. The nurse brought in my baby. I couldn't breastfeed her because, after my many months of mental anguish, I had no milk. Crying, I held my child in my arms, hoping and praying her head would regain a normal shape and her brain would not be damaged. With all those beautiful flowers around me it looked to me as if they were meant for a funeral parlor rather than for a happy occasion. I felt utterly lonely and abandoned.

Every evening Hans and Margrit paid me a short visit; in all my eight days in the hospital Hans never came alone. When I was discharged, the nurse I had hired took us home. She took care of the baby for a whole month. Hans stayed with his sister for another week. He was too nervous to deal with the new routine. In a way, I was relieved that he was not there. I could relax and could bond with my beautiful baby, whose head had developed into a normal shape by now.

Somehow, I felt a peculiar distance between Hans and me. I had noticed when I returned from the hospital that he had put locks on all the cabinets where he kept his financial papers. When I asked him about it, he replied that he did not want any strangers snooping around. I had the feeling that Margrit had something to do with it, but I could not tell what it was until I later found out through our lawyer and friend, Stanley. While I was in the hospital Hans had signed over all his life insurances, some bankbooks and stocks to Margrit and Johnny. If anything had happened to Hans in those years, I would have had to contest his action in court. Only eleven years later, after a traumatic experience in a mental institution, which almost cost him his life, did he tell me what he had done, and finally, he changed everything back.

Not quite three weeks after the baby was born, Hans insisted that I go with him to the Ullmann Farm to take a week's vacation, while the nurse stayed home with the baby. Julian, his best friend, thought it might be good for both of us. I reluctantly agreed to go, although I would have rather stayed with little Hope. That vacation was the worst thing we could have done. It was a lonely place, with hardly any guests, and no entertainment. It gave Hans too much time to brood. We took walks for hours, during which he expressed his fears about the future, especially now that the baby was here. During that week

I tried to give Hans some hope and suggested that we could move to Vineland and start chicken farming like many of my relatives were doing. I could work in nursing, and Aunt Kate could take care of Hope. I was sure Aunt Gerda would give us a loan to buy a farm, just as she had done before when Hans needed help to buy into the business. That idea always helped to quiet him for a while.

Our doctor had hoped that Hans might overcome his anxieties once the baby was here, but he was wrong. On countless times Hans wanted me to explain to him why I wanted to have a baby. He told me again and again how stupid I was and how much more common sense his sister had. In his eyes she was a queen in comparison to me. Ultimately I lost all the respect and admiration I had for him, in spite of the fact that I realized he was ill. Sometimes I would weep and other times I would be numb and would treat him, as any nurse would have, by not reacting to his question, and insisting that he take his medication. Hans's doctor had warned him not to blame me or I might get post-partum depression, but he did not listen and, ultimately, I did. Except for my friend Emily and the nurse, nobody knew how much I had to endure. I could not let my parents know. They thought I was happily married.

When we came home from the Ullmann Farm, Hans went to the office again as usual. The nurse stayed only a few more days with us. Hans despised her because she tried to get him interested in his baby by placing little Hope in his arms. But he refused to take her, claiming he was afraid to hold her. The nurse interpreted that as a sign of jealousy. I was doubtful but one day I foolishly repeated to Hans what she had said. He became so incensed that he told her to leave immediately.

Our first night alone little Hope slept in our bedroom in a basket next to my bedside. Hans grew restless everytime Hope made a sucking noise or I got up to feed her. When she started to cry, he got up, paced the floor, smoking his cigarettes (his daily consumption was two packs a day), and announced that this couldn't go on. He needed his rest. He ordered me to have our beds moved into the living room first thing in the morning. The baby should sleep in our bedroom alone, which was at the end of the hall. Because of the street noise, one could not possibly hear the baby from so far away. His suggestion did not make sense and when I told him it wouldn't work, he became extremely upset. I made him sleep alone in our bedroom, and the baby and I spent the night in the living room. Before retiring he uttered in an emotional, quivering tone, "I wished the baby would have a better life. I love her but we can't keep her. We should find a better home." This was all I had to hear. I knew this was insane. I did not contradict him. But all night I tried to figure out a way to fix things.

Long before the baby was born, the doctor had suggested shock treatment. At one time, arrangements hade been made for Hans to be admitted to Doctor's Hospital, but Hans had backed out at the last minute. It was clear in my mind that our current situation was impossible and we could not continue so. Shock treatment seemed to be the only hope for Hans. I decided to call Dr Kallmann's office for an appointment first thing in the morning.

When Hans was ready to leave for the office in the morning, he came into the living room and again said, "*Nebbich* ("so sorry"), but we should find her a better home. Maybe Aunt Gerda will take her." Again, he wanted me to have our beds moved into the living room for the time being. For me this was out of the question to do.

As soon as he left I called my friend, Emily, and asked her to come immediately to help me get the baby out of the house. I had inquired at Woman's Hospital if they would take my baby while my husband was undergoing shock therapy. They gave me the name of a facility in East Orange, New Jersey, that took in infants.

The separation from my one-month-old baby was painful, but I had to be strong. With tears in my eyes I kissed her goodbye and Emily and little Hope drove off to East Orange. The baby was to stay there until Hans had recovered from his depression. I felt much more peaceful knowing that she was in safe hands.

I called Dr. Kallmann's office, but he was out of town. His associate advised me to bring Hans in for shock treatment the next day at noon, and I agreed. Hans was very disappointed when he came home not to find the beds in the living room as he had wanted me to do and asked me, "Where is the baby?" I told him what I had arranged, and he was very angry. How could I dare to make arrangements without his consent! But I told him in no uncertain terms that he either would undergo the treatments or I would leave him. He understood I really meant it. We hardly spoke that night. In the morning he called his office and said he would not be in.

Hans's Injury

It was August the twentieth, exactly one month after Hope's birth, when Hans and I walked to the doctor's office in scorching heat. I was dressed in a swirl (housedress) and Hans in short-sleeved shirt and Bermuda shorts. He repeatedly told me that he was doing this only for me. He felt he really didn't need to be treated, but for the sake of peace he would undergo this treatment. The doctor took Hans immediately and asked me to stay in the waiting room. I prayed that getting those treatments would help him, but my prayers were not heard. After a very short time the doctor appeared in the door and said, "Something happened to your husband. He fell off the table. I am waiting for the ambulance to take him to Park East Hospital nearby."

Oh my God! For a moment I blacked out. How was that possible? I burst into tears. When I regained my composure, I asked the doctor how that could have happened. He was in a great hurry to go back to attend to Hans. I told him, "But Hans is not going to Park East Hospital" I knew the hospital to be a second-rate institution. "I want Hans to be sent to the orthopedic division of Presbyterian Hospital." I had served on that ward years ago. Obviously, this doctor was embarrassed to have Hans admitted there, since he was associated with the psychiatric division of the Presbyterian Hospital. However, he had to conform to my wishes, and the ambulance drove to Presbyterian Hospital.

The doctor did not want me to see my husband after the accident, claiming he was under heavy sedation, nor did he allow me to accompany Hans in the ambulance. I took a taxi to the emergency room of Presbyterian Hospital, where I waited anxiously for a long time, in my housedress, not having had any food or drink since the night before. Finally, Hans was wheeled out of the emergency room on a stretcher, and I got a glimpse of him. I saw a pale face beaded with perspiration with eyes wide open staring at the ceiling, oblivious to what was going on. To me he looked as if he were in shock and dying. He was transferred to a ward and admitted, while I waited for the attending physician to tell me the diagnosis: Hans had suffered eight fractures in both hip sockets (accetabula), located in his pelvis, and was in shock.

I was allowed to stay at his bedside. For many hours I sat there looking at him, a continuous intravenous trickling into his arm, doubting he would stay alive. I blamed myself for causing this tragedy. Had I not been so forceful in demanding that he undergo shock treatment, he would not have sustained this injury. But, at the same time, I felt relieved that I had at least brought Hope to safety. It was early evening and getting dark when he first moved his head. He saw me and said angrily, "Take the baby and go to your parents. I never want to see you again."

This was like a dagger piercing my heart. He confirmed my belief that this accident was my fault. This was the end for both of us. I was sure he was going to die soon, and even thought it might be a blessing. I left his room and walked to the elevator in a daze. There, I met Dr. Hallock, chief of service, for whom I had worked years ago. He asked me what I was doing here. I told him what had happened and asked him to look after my husband.

Suddenly, I felt something warm and wet trickling down my bare legs. Dr. Hallock saw the pool of blood on the floor of the elevator. I was hemorrhaging. He called for a stretcher and I was rushed into the emergency room, where I was packed to stop the bleeding. I was given the choice either to stay in the hospital or call someone to take me home. My former head nurse from the Jewish hospital in Germany, Schwester Hedwig, came and took me to her place, which was a ground floor apartment with a small garden on the West Side. She cared for me for several days. Doctor Gabrilove visited me daily at Schwester Hedwidg's place and he also saw Hans at the hospital. After all that had happened to me, my mind had snapped. The doctor could not convince me that Hans had not died. They had to show me the daily obituaries in the *New York Times*, where I was sure I would find Hans's name. For hours I paced that garden and could not find any rest.

Our lawyer and good friend, Stanley Schindler, came and succeeded in assuring me that Hans was alive. However, I was plagued with guilt and blamed myself for what had happened. I had moments when I was seriously contemplating ending my life by jumping out of my twelfth-floor kitchen window.

Although I never confessed these plans to Dr. Gabrilove, he knew I was sick. When I left Schwester Hedwig to return to my apartment he felt it was not safe to leave me alone there. He ordered nurses around the clock for some time. They finally convinced me that it wasn't I who had caused the tragedy, and eventually I stopped blaming myself. One elderly night nurse, who exuded a lot of confidence, comforted me by repeatedly assuring me, "Do not ever worry what the future will bring. Always say to yourself, 'God put me here into this world and, therefore, He'd better take care of me.'" I subsequently made this my motto.

Later, when I didn't need her services any longer, I found that many of our whiskey and cognac bottles in our bar were almost empty, but I did not mind. This old nurse had helped me in many ways to overcome my guilt and despair.

After four weeks I was allowed to visit Hans in the hospital. He had asked to see me. Although I was apprehensive at first, I gathered enough courage to face him. There he was sitting in a wheelchair and, oh, how he had aged! His hair was now snow white. I embraced him, and he said everything would be all right. He asked for the baby, who was still in the nursery in New Jersey. I continued visiting him daily for a short while.

Little Hope was almost ten weeks old when Emily and I

brought her home. She was beautiful, with chubby red cheeks and dark brown eyes. It felt wonderful to have her back and to hold her in my arms.

During her absence I had exchanged the layette and baby carriage that I had originally ordered for a much smaller and less expensive one. Aunt Gerda had mailed me a baby carriage and pillow cover, which I exchanged for credit because I had one already and I did not need two. I realized we could not possibly continue to live the same expensive lifestyle as we used to, so I tried to economize wherever I could.

Aunt Gerda and her companion Mary were vacationing in Switzerland until early October. After Hans's injury I had not heard from her, and I found this strange. I suspected the senior partner in Stanley's law firm, Mr. Otterbourg, who was a friend of Aunt Gerda, had notified her about Hans's injury. Could it be that she had heard that Hans's depression necessitated shock treatments and she did not want to deal with anyone who had a mental illness? In the past she had had bad experiences. Her own husband, Uncle Herman, and several members of his family had committed suicide.

When she came home from Europe, she paid Hans a very short visit in the hospital. Then she called me, and I invited her to dinner. When I asked her what she would like to eat, she wanted boiled beef with horseradish sauce. I must have been still too nervous to prepare a meal. Instead, I served simple small steaks. Even that exhausted me. I was tired as we sat at the dinner table while baby Hope was sleeping in her crib in the bedroom while we ate.

Gerda wanted to know what happened. I was unsure what Hans had told her and was afraid to tell her that the injury happened during shock treatment. So I told her that Hans, after months of anxiety, suffered from chronic diarrhea, and more than once he had actually had embarrassing accidents. So Hans finally consulted a doctor but during examination he fell off the table onto a concrete floor and broke his pelvis. I should have told her the truth but I was afraid it might ruin Hans's reputation.

I told her how nervous Hans was and how he worried about the future. I was always able to calm him by suggesting to him if everything failed he could go into chicken farming like many of my relatives. Timidly I asked Aunt Gerda, "If it ever should come to that, you would help us financially, wouldn't you?" Sternly she replied, "Absolutely not, because Hans could never be a farmer. He is much too educated for that."

Shortly after we finished our meal she was ready to leave. She went to see Hope, who was lying in her crib, and when I asked her whether she was going to be the godmother as she had planned, she answered with a cold voice, "No." I did not dare ask her why. Now I was certain Mr. Otterbourg had told her what really had happened with Hans and me, and I was sorry I hadn't been more truthful. When she left she said, "You seem to have taken Hans's worries onto yourself. You need to rest, Frieda."

After that, we never heard from her, except at Christmas time, when she sent greetings and little presents for Hope. For Aunt Gerda's birthday we sent flowers every year, which she acknowledged with a cold thank-you note. She never invited us to her house again. She was a strange, most unpredictable person.

At the end of October, Hans came home from the hospital in a wheelchair. He was happy to be home. He was able to use crutches to go to the bathroom or sit at the dining table. Often he was in pain and I suffered with him, still feeling a great deal of guilt for having helped cause his injury. Nervous energy drove me to work hard. Slowly he gained his strength back and eventually learned to walk with a cane, but he walked with a limp for the rest of his life.

I had my hands full helping Hans with his bed bath, and shaving, while the baby fed herself with a propped-up bottle. After everybody was dressed and fed, I would wheel Hans to the street in front of our building where he could read his

newspaper in the morning sun. Then I would get my little Hope,
who was by now napping in her carriage. While I did the shopping,
they both enjoyed the warm November sun. In the afternoon I
tried to straighten out the cramped apartment and do the laundry,
including diapers, in my newly purchased washer and dryer, which
were a great help, but barely fit into our tiny kitchen. I even
washed and ironed Hans's white shirts and cleaned the place
without help. During that time we lived frugally. Hans had asked
me to economize and to not spend more than twenty-five dollars
a week for food and household expenses, which was difficult. I
learned to cook inexpensive food like beef goulash, chicken
gizzards, lung stew, and skirt steaks. I baked *challe* bread and cake—
enough for the week. I was often working late into the night,
because in the daytime I preferred to go with Hope to the
playground in Central Park, where I would have the chance to
talk to other mothers. We did not have many visitors, except
Margrit, Johnny, and Julian and his wife, Ilse, who came on
Saturdays or Sundays. In good weather, we would picnic on the
lawn in Central Park, and sometimes our friends would join us. I
was constantly busy in those days but I did not mind. There was
peace in our home at last. After all the turmoil in our marriage,
we were content with our simple life.

Unfortunately, since Hans's illness he had been on
antidepressants and as a result, was unable to be sexually active.
We consulted Dr. Gabrilove on that issue, but in those days
there was no treatment for male dysfunction. This condition
remained to the end of his life. Naturally, I missed the intimacy
in our relationship but I derived my greatest happiness from
seeing my Hope develop beautifully, and I enjoyed the restored
tranquility in our relationship. Hans remained my best friend
and companion till the end.

By late November, Hans was able to walk with a cane and
went by taxi to his office for a few hours daily. The negotiations
with McGregor dragged on for another two years, during which
time he received the same high salary, but we tried to
economize wherever possible.

One day when Hope was about two years old, I took her grocery shopping at the A & P store down the street. She had helped putting the items in the cart and I was standing at the checkout counter when I suddenly discovered my Hope was not with me. When I called out her name and she didn't respond I was terrified. The store manager and other people helped look for her all over. Afraid she might have slid on the conveyor belt into the basement, we even looked for her there, but we could not find her. I was desperate and ran out of the store and to my apartment house. I asked the doorman and the elevator man, "Have you seen my Hope?" No they hadn't. Oh, my God! By now I was in panic. I screamed, "Where is my child? Help me, God!" I stepped out of the elevator onto the twelfth floor, and found my little Hope sitting in front of my apartment, playing with a toy, unaware of the agony she had caused. What a relief when I saw her! Crying for joy, I hugged and kissed her. The next morning I wrote her a letter in the name of Santa with a colorful painting of him, which I have kept to this day. Santa warned her not to get out of mommy's sight ever again or he would take all her toys and dolls away forever. He reminded her to be a good little girl and make her parents happy. She was to promise not to run away ever again or she would be punished severely by Santa.

The panic I felt at that moment was indescribable, and every time I see on television the desperate faces of people who have lost their children, I can empathize with them by remembering the knot I felt when I had lost sight of my Hope.

A Major Problem

Although there was now peace in our home, there were other major problems to cope with that still caused Hans a great deal of mental anguish and despair. He was greatly upset that Aunt Gerda had lost interest in us. She was a very important person in his life, and for years she had maintained a caring relationship with us. The only way we could explain her attitude was that she did not wish to associate with people who were mentally unstable.

Another troubling problem arose when, in the summer of 1955, he received a ruling by a German court against his request for restitution.

Hans had instituted a lawsuit against the German government in 1952, for having refused to pay the pension and back pay he was entitled to as a federal judge, after having been forcefully put into retirement by the Nazi regime. After Hans had been forced to resign from the bench in 1933, he had found employment in a Jewish bank as an in-house council. The German government contended that Hans would not have returned to the position of a judge after the war because the bank position would have been more lucrative.

Dismayed at having lost his lawsuit against the German government, he immediately hired a prominent lawyer, Dr. Kempner, one of the prosecutors in the Nuremberg trials, who appealed the decision. Hans prepared his own brief for the appeal. He worked feverishly on it for days, and when it was finished, Hans consulted with Dr. Kempner, who approved the brief. Without the influence of this highly respected attorney, it was doubtful that he would have won his appeal, but in 1957 the lawsuit was settled favorably for Hans.

After that, life was much more pleasant. At last Hans received his monthly pension and back pay from Germany, which helped alleviate his constant worries about the future. Hans began to take interest in Hope, now three years old. He played with her and took her out for walks without me. We began to see our old friends again, and I could leave him babysitting as I went shopping or, occasionally, to the movies. I was amazed at seeing a large panoramic screen, which had come out some three years earlier, for the first time. We purchased our first black and white television and we bought room air conditioners. Sometimes Hans would even offer to push the baby carriage, into which Hope hardly fit any longer. She was a big child when she was three, and looked ridiculous in her carriage, but she would not let me get rid of it. One day, while she took her nap, I gave it to a junk dealer on Second Avenue, about four blocks away from where we lived. When it was gone, she carried on and insisted I should get another one. I bought her a stroller, which she refused to sit in and she would only push it. Several months passed without the old carriage. Then one day Hope and I walked by the junk store and she spotted her old carriage standing in front of the store amongst other furniture. She screamed and cried and wanted it back. I walked away from her, and when she saw me at the end of the block she finally gave in and came running.

Around that time the polio vaccine was invented and parents were advised to have their children vaccinated. I was scheduled to bring her to her pediatrician, Dr. Rogatz, for a polio shot. It was a cold day and Hope had on a heavy quilted, green warm-up suit, which she refused to take off. As soon as we were called in to receive the shot she ran out of the doctor's office onto Park Avenue and lay down on the pavement, screaming, kicking, and refusing to come back into the office. Dr. Rogatz came out to try to convince her to get the shot, but to no avail. I was embarrassed and angry with her. I pulled her by the hand and began the walk home. After a little while, we passed a man with crutches, and Hope wanted to know why this man had crutches. I told her he probably had polio. After hearing that, she insisted on going back to Dr. Rogatz, who was finally able to give her the shot without any objection and without one tear from her.

Hans wanted to go to Asbury Park for Decoration Day Weekend. Since it was too cumbersome to travel by train with luggage and a three-year-old, I suggested that he and Margrit should go without us. They went on Friday, but that evening he called me saying that he missed Hope, and would try to get accommodations for us. I felt happy that he had finally bonded with her, and the next morning Hope and I took the train to Asbury Park. Hans was waiting for us at the station. Unfortunately, he could not find any decent hotel room for us; the only room available was on the top floor in another small hotel. Margrit could not climb three flights of stairs, so I had no other choice but to take that hot room on the third floor. Climbing up with Hope was not easy. That night, the fire alarm went off. Hope would not wake up, so I threw my heavy child over my shoulder and descended the staircase, ever so cautiously, while people were pushing behind me in panic. As I reached the smoke-filled foyer, I collapsed from exhaustion. Smoke from an electrical fire had risen from the basement. It was a long time before it was extinguished and we could return to our rooms, but I was unable to fall asleep again.

When I told Hans the next morning what had happened, he felt sorry. He had meant well by asking us to join him. The rest of the weekend was pleasant, basking in the warm sun on the beach and wading with Hope in the ocean, which she saw that weekend for the first time.

In those days I was grateful that harmony was restored in our lives, and even from my parents I heard good news. My father had found a lot of work doing repairs for customers, and Gerhard had gone back to Germany to study landscaping at an agricultural school in Hanover, as part of German restitution. I was happy that my family did not need my support anymore, since I would not have been able to give it anyway.

The Years in Dover

But soon new problems arose. Rumors leaked out that McGregor would soon take over the business. Before the end of 1957, McGregor Company bought out Lissner Company, and Hans was offered a meager salary of seven thousand dollars a year as an assistant manager in the accounts receivable department in Dover, New Jersey. The other four vice-presidents of Lissner Company had found jobs elsewhere. But Hans was now fifty-one years old, and he felt he was too old to find other employment. I encouraged him to take the job in Dover, since it would be less taxing for him. Besides, it might be good for Hope to grow up in a small town. I looked forward to a new beginning. Hans, however, was apprehensive. He never liked any change and was fearful of the outcome. McGregor paid for the moving expenses, and in the spring of 1959 we moved to 49 North Sussex Street, Dover, New Jersey.

It was a culture shock for both of us. Because neither of us could drive a car we had to rent in the center of town. We found a two-bedroom apartment in a walk-up tenement building on one of the busiest thoroughfares. It was a convenient location, close to a shopping center and about a fifteen-minute walk to the factory, the McGregor workplace. The supermarket was right across the railroad tracks, which were in the back of our parking lot. We literally "lived behind the tracks." But despite the convenience, we soon found out that it had a lot of drawbacks. Two gas stations at both corners of the street sent fumes into our windows when the wind blew in the wrong direction. Next to us was a bar, which was open all hours of the night. Below us was a paint shop with highly flammable material. Luckily we had brought our room air conditioners from New York so we could sleep at night. Our landlord had recommended a reliable housekeeper, and I was fortunate to find a trustworthy woman who helped me unpack because I had suddenly developed severe back pain and could hardly walk straight. This woman, Helen Weisflog, was a godsend. She was a neat German woman, who lived with her husband in a small house near Hans's workplace. Not only was she very efficient, she was very likeable and readily available anytime I needed her. Oh, did I need her a lot in the years to come!

The first night in the new apartment I was awakened by a scratching noise coming from the kitchen. I got up to investigate and found mice. I screamed, and that was the end of my sleep for the night. I called the landlord first thing in the morning, and he sent an exterminator immediately.

Unfortunately it was too long a walk for Hans from the apartment to the factory. His arthritis had bothered him a lot since his injury, and walking for fifteen minutes twice daily was too hard for him. Helen offered to drive him to and from work until we bought a car. I had already taken a few driving lessons in New York, but we were not prepared to purchase a car until we were sure this new position would work out for Hans.

Hans and his boss became good friends in a very short time. Hans did not earn much money, but the job was not demanding either. This was great for him; he needed to be able to work without stress.

Everything was very convenient. Dover was only an hour's bus ride away from New York. The bus stop was just a few yards from our house, and the train station was not much further. We joined the local synagogue, which was also within walking distance. Soon we befriended other couples with children Hope's age. Up the hill on our street was a beautiful pond where Hope and I went to swim in good weather. But we still missed New York.

After a short time we purchased a car, a second-hand Buick Star Chief. I will never forget my first ride through the Lincoln

Tunnel to New York City, after just six weeks of driving. My heart was pounding. Only self-preservation instincts and prayer helped me get through the tunnel unharmed.

With our car, we were now able to visit Margrit every few weeks. I did not particularly enjoy driving, but it helped improve my relationship with Margrit, who appreciated our frequent visits to the city.

Soon another problem arose for Hans, concerning the impending negligence lawsuit against the doctor who had caused his injury during that one shock treatment in 1954. Our lawyer, Mr. Lipsig, a prominent negligence lawyer, informed us that he had received favorable depositions from the doctor's nurses, who stated that they were not present while the doctor gave the shock treatment. But he could not find a single psychiatrist anywhere who would be willing to testify against the doctor as to the correct procedure for shock therapy. Without the testimony of a qualified doctor, it would be difficult to win the lawsuit. I suggested, having had some experience in psychiatric nursing while in training at Bellevue Hospital, that I should try to find a job in a psychiatric hospital where shock treatments were given. Perhaps then I would be able to testify on Hans's behalf. Mr. Lipsig thought that was a good idea and encouraged me to do that.

Greystone Hospital, about twelve miles away from us in Greystone, New Jersey, was a state mental institution with five thousand five hundred inmates. It happened to have an opening for a part-time position as a nurse in the insulin shock treatment department, and I eagerly accepted it. Sixty shock treatments were administered in four hours daily. I learned the exact procedure that was necessary to secure safe treatments. It required six medical assistants to aid in the performance of each treatment. (In Hans's case the doctor apparently had performed the treatment alone.) While the job required extreme alertness and fast presence of mind, it often was scary to be locked into a ward with very dangerous patients. While I worked, Helen took care of our Hope for fourteen months, until the negligence trial in New York was scheduled in 1959.

On that day, Hans and I were walking up the steps of the courthouse when our lawyer approached us. He had already informed the lawyer for the opposition that I was ready to testify and immediately a settlement out of court was offered, to which Hans agreed. It was not nearly as much as he would have gotten had the case come to trial, but he was happy that at last the waiting was over. But soon after this problem was solved, we were confronted with a most unpleasant situation, which caused a rift between my parents and us.

Gerhard's Illness

Just as soon as our lives again became less stressful, my brother, Gerhard, caused us an incredible amount of anguish and worry. Gerhard had immigrated in Spring, 1959 to join his wife Judy and sons Uri and Danny, who had come here in 1957 under the sponsorship of Judy's brother Isy Kleiner. Judy settled here in Irvington, New Jersey, while Gerhard studied landscape architecture in Germany. After he had finished his course in Germany he asked me to send him an affidavit, so he could join his wife and children, to which I readily agreed.

I was sure Judy and Gerhard would be able to make a good living and I was looking forward to having my brother close by.

The day he arrived, Judy, her brother Isy, and I greeted him at the pier, but I noticed Gerhard was not very affectionate towards his wife. He did not embrace her as one would expect from a husband after a long separation, but I disregarded it, thinking perhaps he was tired from the trip.

I had prepared a special lunch for them at home, which they enjoyed: a homemade dish of chicken livers and pastrami on rye bread. Soon after lunch Judy and Isy had to go back to work. They planned to call for Gerhard after five o' clock to take him to their home in Irvington.

I was happy to have my brother to myself. After all, I had not seen him in twelve years, since my short visit to Palestine when I was a ship's nurse.

But being alone with my brother was very strange and disappointing. I had to drag answers out of him about my parents and what he had experienced in Germany. I asked whether he wanted to rest but he declined and just sat in the living room chair motionless and with a blank stare in his eyes. He seemed so strange that I felt uneasy being alone with him. I could hardly wait until Judy and Isy came to get him.

Gerhard had settled with his family in Irvington, New Jersey shortly before we had moved to Dover, New Jersey, which was only a short distance away. The move was a huge adjustment for us. We didn't have a car yet so we hadn't seen the family since Gerhard's arrival. Whenever I called to inquire how things were going, Judy always answered that they were fine. Isy had found Gerhard a job nearby working in a lighting fixture store, with a gardening job on weekends. I was happy that at last Gerhard and Judy were able to make a decent living.

They invited us to a lovely Bar Mitzvah party for Danny in August, 1959, and it seemed, that without my mother's constant interference, they were getting along well. It was nice to see the family united again.

But a few weeks after the Bar Mitzvah party, Gerhard called me. Apparently he had had a dispute with Isy and wanted some legal advice from Hans about taking Isy to court. I told him that Hans did not know anything about the laws here in America, and that Hans had enough troubles of his own. He'd better leave Hans out of it.

Shortly after, I received a phone call from Isy on a Sunday morning telling me that Gerhard was mentally disturbed. Gerhard was demanding money from Isy and other members of his family and had threatened to kill them. From all the excitement Isy was hospitalized with symptoms of a heart attack. Even Judy and the boys were afraid, and had to seek refuge in Judy's sister's apartment, in the same apartment complex in Irvington, New Jersey. The same morning that Isy called me the family had decided to have him committed to a mental institution.

On Judith's request a psychiatrist had arrived at Gerhard's apartment accompanied by an ambulance and the police, who waited in front of the building. While the doctor was preparing an injection for Gerhard, he climbed onto the fire escape and fled.

Isy urged me to notify the police if Gerhard should come to our house, which he presumed he would, and warned me he might be dangerous.

We were shocked and scared. I could not believe that my brother could do such a thing and that he was sick and dangerous. We had just gone through enough problems in our own lives. We certainly did not need any new ones. I felt embarrassed and angry that my family could not settle their own problems. But now, what were we going to do? My first inclination was to avoid any confrontation with Gerhard and to go to New York for the day. But on second thought, I decided to go to the Dover Police Station, which was located next door to us and inquire whether the Irvington police had notified them. While I was present, the Dover police called the Irvington police and they confirmed that Gerhard had eluded them. The officer in Dover urged me to notify the police as soon as my brother arrived. I told him we would rather not be involved in the situation and would like to leave Dover for the day. However he advised me to stay home, because Gerhard was ill and could be dangerous. He assured me the police would come as soon as we notified them of Gerhard's appearance.

Hans and I were so scared to be alone that we called in neighbors who stayed with us while waiting for Gerhard's arrival. Hope was staying in her room and playing with her toys quietly but I was sure she was aware what was going on.

At noon, the doorbell rang. It was Gerhard. I was shocked and afraid to open the door and called the police as I was told. At the sound of the doorbell little Hope ran to me screaming and did not stop until the police took Gerhard away. It took some time to calm her. The poor child was shivering with fear. For weeks she would not sleep alone and woke us up because of bad dreams.

Worried about what was going on with Gerhard at the police station, I brought him lunch, but the policeman did not give me permission to see him. He claimed Gerhard was very agitated because the police took away sharp scissors and gardening tools he had had in his possession.

A short time later, I heard the sirens of the Greystone ambulance arriving at the police station to take Gerhard to the same hospital where I had worked learning to assist in shock therapy. Curious people leaned on their window sills, watching as Gerhard was placed in the ambulance on a stretcher. I was very sad, but relieved that now Gerhard might get the right care.

Nobody was allowed to visit Gerhard for the first two weeks but I kept in touch with Judy, who was able to inquire daily about his condition. I felt sorry for her and visited her in Irvington. I was wondering what prompted his nervous breakdown and I mentioned Gerhard's strange behavior the first day he arrived here in America. Only then did Judy tell me Gerhard had been ill, suffering from periodic depressions, ever since he was wounded during the Israeli War of Independence in 1948. Gerhard had been on night patrol when a bullet grazed his temple. For many months he remained in shock, and he did not communicate or eat, and would just stare into space. My mother did not recognize the severity of his illness and she took it upon herself to care for him alone. She didn't allow Judy to call in a psychiatrist, who might have been able to help him in the beginning of his illness. He continued to suffer from anxiety for years and was often unable to work. My mother, who always had a strained relationship with Judy, eventually turned Gerhard against his wife. Judy was powerless and had suffered for years before her brother, Isy, was financially able to give her and her sons an affidavit to immigrate to America in 1957.

All those years my parents kept Gerhard's illness a secret from me. Maybe they were ashamed, just as I was to tell anyone about Hans's nervous breakdown.

After Judy had left for America my parents sent Gerhard to Germany in the hope his fear of war might subside when he left Israel. Judy thought that if he were safe in America, without the influence of my mother, Gerhard would be able to overcome his depression. Unfortunately his illness (manic-depressive) worsened.

A few weeks after his admission to Greystone Judy and I were allowed to visit him. We were encouraged by his progress. He seemed pleased to see us and the following week we even took little Hope along. He played with her and she was not afraid and even sat on Gerhard's lap.

But a few days later, his condition worsened again. Hans received an angry letter demanding money and threatening us by a drawing of a human head and an ax, showing us what would happen if the money were not received by a certain date. He also threatened to notify McGregor Company about what we had done to him and that he was going to sue us for libel. We repeatedly received these life-threatening letters, stating that he would deal with us as soon as he was released from the institution. Because Judy and her family, the Kleiners, were deathly afraid of Gerhard, they had, unbeknownst to us, convinced my brother that Hans and I were the ones that had committed him to Greystone. This was the reason his anger was directed primarily towards us, and not that much towards them.

After three months Gerhard was released from Greystone, but was forbidden from entering the city of Dover. We lived in constant fear.

One day he became so enraged, he threatened to come to Dover and kill us. Judy's relatives had a hard time talking him out of it, and finally persuaded him to go back to Israel and to tell my parents what a terrible thing we had done to him. The Kleiner family and their friends decided to whisk Gerhard out of the country as soon as possible. They pooled their money for a one way ticket to Israel and presented it to Gerhard.

As soon as Gerhard had left for the airport to return to Israel, Judy called me to let me know that we were safe now. All of us could breathe a sigh of relief. The next day I went with Judy to the U.S. immigration office in Newark, New Jersey, where she requested that he be blocked from ever reentering the United States. When my parents heard from Gerhard what I had supposedly done to him, they sent me a very angry letter, in which my mother accused me of having committed a sin against my own flesh and blood. She said she would never forgive me for that. This letter hurt me deeply, and made me feel immensely sad. Hans helped me write a letter responding to their accusations, explaining in detail what had really happened. We did not hear from them, not even a birthday card for me in March 1960. A half a year later, a formal greeting card came from them with the word Shalom ("Peace") for the High Holidays and about a year later, friends of my parents visited us. Hans and I explained to them the tragic events that had happened with Gerhard while he was here, so they could tell my parents in detail on their return to Israel.

They told us that soon after Gerhard's return to Israel my parents sent him again to Germany to work there. While in Germany, Gerhard made several attempts to obtain a visa to reenter the United States from Canada and Mexico. But his return to the United States was forever blocked upon Judy's request, and after staying a short time in Germany, Gerhard returned to Israel where he was placed in an institution not far from my parents' retirement home. He was allowed to do outdoor gardening there, and occasionally was permitted to visit my parents with supervision. They must have finally realized that Gerhard was ill.

The information relayed by this couple must have helped convince my parents of our innocence, because they resumed sending us friendly letters. Unfortunately, Gerhard's condition later deteriorated and he had to be placed in a higher security institution in Acre, where he remained until his death in 1980. He died of a heart attack at the age of sixty-seven.

Another Scare

While Gerhard was still here in America and causing us so much anxiety, I had discovered a small lump in my left breast. Needless to say, I was frightened and feared the worst. I did not tell Hans, since I did not want him to worry. The local doctor did an aspiration, but the lab lost the specimen. He suggested immediate surgery. Knowing I should first consult another doctor, I made an appointment with a doctor from Sloan Kettering in New York for the following day. Extremely worried, I took the early bus to the city, while I left Hope under Helen's care for the day. The doctor at Sloan Kettering also advised immediate surgery.

I was scared and couldn't decide. Uncertain about what I should do, I walked aimlessly along Park Avenue for many blocks. I stopped for a moment in front of a building with ground floor doctor offices, and spotted Dr Aidair's shingle. I remembered him from Sloan Kettering. He was at that time a great authority on breast cancer. I was desperate and walked in without an appointment. I told the receptionist that I knew Dr. Adair and she let me wait. In the meantime I let Helen, the housekeeper, know that I was delayed and would not be home for dinner. The waiting room was full of women, all sitting in silence. I looked at their faces and wondered whether they also were packed with fear as I was. I waited in suspense for nearly two hours, pleading with God that He should spare me from that dreadful disease.

Finally I was called into the treatment room. Doctor Aidair recognized me and greeted me with a friendly smile. I told him that I had consulted two other doctors, who advised immediate surgery. Carefully he examined the lump and said,

"The tumor is movable. The verdict is not guilty. I don't see any immediate need for surgery. Go home. I want to see you in three months again. If it is not gone by then, we will excise the tumor, but I don't think this is a malignancy."

I jumped from the table happily and gave him a big hug. It was dark when I got home, relieved but very tired from the harrowing experience of the day.

After three months the tumor had disappeared just as Dr. Aidair had predicted, and I was grateful to him for having advised against an unnecessary operation.

From 1960 on we enjoyed a tranquil time. Hans was content in his job, although it was a drastic change for him. We lived frugally. I kept busy sewing dresses, draperies, and slipcovers for the apartment. Our Hope was always dressed in the prettiest dresses, and we often wore similar outfits. On Sunday mornings Hans usually brought her to Hebrew school at the Temple. It gave him a chance to befriend other fathers or chat with the rabbi while waiting to bring the little ones home again. Hope also attended glee club once a week. During the holiday season they sang Christmas songs. I always enjoyed watching the kids singing to their hearts' content. Some of her friends had Christmas trees in their homes and she wanted one too. I told her I couldn't put a tree in our living room because it might offend some of our Jewish friends. However, I allowed her to have a small tree, which she could decorate and keep in her room. She was very happy with that tree, until one day Hope and I met the rabbi at a store and he asked whether he could pay Hans a visit in a little while. I assured him Hans would be pleased. But as soon as we parted, Hope was anxious to get home. She immediately went into in her room and stayed there until the rabbi's visit ended. Then she grabbed me by my hand and pulled me into her room. Right away I noticed the tree was missing and I asked, "What happened, where is your tree?" Smiling, she opened her closet door and showed me where she had hid the tree from the rabbi. The pretty little tree lay there squished into the narrow closet, devoid of many of the ornaments; many needles had fallen off onto the carpeted closet. She never asked for another Christmas tree again.

Quite often Margrit and Johnny used to visit us in Dover and spent the weekends with us. Both were very fond of our Hope.

Johnny was thirty-six years old and had established a practice as an optometrist in Portchester, New York. He wanted to get married and had met a lovely young girl, a teacher, named Marilyn. They came to Dover to meet us. She was vivacious, a pretty redhead, smart, with a great sense of humor. Hans and I liked her, but Margrit didn't approve because she came from a poor family and was American, not from the old country. Margrit became distraught over this impending marriage and began to show signs of dementia. She accused the painters of stealing her valuables. The doctor hospitalized her immediately and she received a series of five shock treatments. Luckily she snapped out of it just in time for the wedding.

I sewed all our dresses for the happy occasion. I wore a beige satin cocktail dress with matching hat. For Margrit, who was hard to fit because of her scoliosis, I made an exquisite imported beige lace dress. Even she was pleased. From then on I became her seamstress. Hope looked adorable as a flower girl in her white organza dress. Hans looked very distinguished in his white tuxedo. The wedding took place in New York on the Fourth of July, in 1960, on a hot summer day. It was a lovely celebration and we all had a good time.

A New Opportunity

As time went by, we got used to our lifestyle in Dover. We grew accustomed to Hans's modest income of seven thousand five hundred dollars a year, which was not easy, compared to the high salary Hans had earned as treasurer of Lissner Company. I wished I could have improved our situation by earning some money, but nursing did not pay enough for us to be able to afford a babysitter, and the hours were not flexible. Just then the most unexpected thing happened to me.

One morning I read an advertisement for electrolysis treatment in our local newspaper. Some time before I had sprouted a few ugly hairs on my chin, but there was no electrologist to be found in Dover. I had had this hair problem after childbirth, but a physician had removed it with just a few treatments. Now, after six years, new hairs had shown up. Unfortunately, I could not go to the city, and besides, I could not afford the doctor's fee. So when I saw the electrolysis ad I was eager to get rid of my embarrassing hairs. The small ad in the newspaper seemed odd; it did not give the name of the practitioner, nor did it give the address, just the phone number. Assuming it was a doctor, I called immediately for an appointment and I was glad the person could fit me in during her lunch hour on that same day.

In the blazing sun, I walked up a steep hill to the address she had given. It was a modest little house, apparently in a non-professional area. There was no shingle indicating the name or profession. I wondered whether I had reached the correct address.

A young woman in her thirties, dressed in a lab coat, opened the door and introduced herself as Mrs. Moorhead. She took me up one flight to her neat-looking office and after asking me a few pertinent questions, worked on me for fifteen minutes. When the treatment was over I asked whether she was a doctor. She told me it was not required to be one. I asked her how long she had to study to be qualified, and she said it took two years to learn. The fee for the fifteen minute treatment was five dollars. While she went out of the room to get change, I spotted her diploma hanging from the wall. It was issued by Dr. Baer's Institute of Electrolysis, Newark, New Jersey. I thought I would be interested in learning electrolysis too. Perhaps I could take evening courses? I wouldn't mind if it took two years. It would be something I could do at home. The more I thought about it, the more I liked the idea. In the evening I discussed it with Hans. He told me to look into it. The next morning I called the Electrolysis Institute in Newark and was told to come in that afternoon.

The school in Newark looked shabby. It did not make a good impression on me. Dr. Baer interviewed me and told me the training would only take two weeks, not two years. I didn't need a license to become an electrologist and I could buy the necessary equipment from him at a cost of two thousand dollars. After passing a test I would get a diploma from him. He also told me the going rate was five dollars for fifteen minutes and fifteen dollars for an hour-long treatment. Some professionals in the field earned more than a medical doctor. I told him I had to talk it over with my husband and left.

I could not believe that only two weeks of training was sufficient to do the invasive procedures this work required, and that I would not need a license to practice. Even a manicurist, like Judy, my sister-in-law, needed a license.

Dr. Baer's Institute was not far from the office of the Board of Nursing in Newark, so I walked over and asked them whether they could give me any information about learning electrolysis. They informed me that one does not need any formal training. All I had to do was buy the equipment from the manufacturer who would give instructions on how to use it, and I could open the office anytime thereafter. I was very excited, and I could not wait to tell Hans what I found out. He encouraged me to look into it further.

I found another school in New York—the Kree Institute— that looked much more professional and offered similar training and equipment. The president of the company encouraged me, saying that that I would have a greater chance of succeeding than most, since I was already an RN. That made sense to me, because people would have more confidence in a professional nurse. After all that I had seen and heard, I was determined to become an electrologist.

Excited about our new project, Hans and I made plans about how and where we could open an office in our small apartment. The only possible place was the seven-by-ten-foot dinette. For privacy, it had to be closed off from the rest of the rooms by accordion doors. Hans enjoyed planning my new activity tremendously, especially since it involved organization, advertising, and management, in which he excelled.

The next Monday I signed up for the course and started my training. I commuted daily by bus. While I was in the two-week training program, Helen took care of Hope, staying with her until Hans came home from work.

The people who were treated at the school did not have to pay for treatments because the students learned while practicing on them, under the supervision of a teacher.

Although I had given many injections while working in nursing, on my first day of practical training at the electrolysis school my hands were shaking with the first insertions. My patient asked me how long I had been a student. I told her that I had just started this morning, and that she was "my first victim." She did not ask anything more and I wondered if I had scared her. Evidently I had not, because the following Monday she appeared in school, starting as a student too. She greeted me with a smile, and told me I had given her the inspiration.

The theoretical part was easy for me because of my medical

background, but the practical side was not so simple. It required enormous dexterity and hand-eye coordination for exact insertion into the hair follicles. Most importantly, it required precision needles, which were not available in the school, as I later found out.

At school I met two fellow students, Lucille and Joe, from Connecticut, which was one of the few States in the United States that required licensing. Lucille was a bookkeeper and Joe was an engineer for the Beckon and Dickinson Needle Company. He was already very experienced in electrolysis, having treated his wife for a severe hair growth. He was taking this course so that he would be able to open an office in Connecticut, for which he needed a license. Little did I know then how much Joe had helped me in becoming successful as an electrologist. After the ten days training period I bought the equipment, which we were told was the best in the world, and I received my diploma. I proudly hung it, framed, in my converted dinette, which would now be my professional office. I was ready and eager to perform my newly acquired skill.

The first ad in the local paper appeared on a Monday morning in March 1961. It read: "Frieda Lefeber, RN Nurse Electrologist—Unwanted Hair Removal—Graduate of the famous Kree Institute—Member of the American Electrolysis Association—For Appointment, please call—." The first inquiry came around noontime. The lady made an appointment for the next day. Oh, was I excited! Hans called a few minutes later. I told him that I had just received my first call, and made him get off the line because I did not want to miss any calls. Well, no one else called for the rest of the day.

The next day, Mrs. Ackerman arrived for consultation. She was a matronly, heavy-set woman with hair growth like a man's beard on her round, double-chinned face. She had to shave at least once a day. This had bothered her all her life. She recently had become a widow. Her husband had left her a nice pension to live on and she decided to use some of it to take care of her problem. She came faithfully for a one-hour treatment every week. Soon, some of my Temple friends came too, and many others came as a result of ads in various newspapers and telephone books. Within a short time I was making as much money in a ten-hour work week as RNs made in forty hours.

Most of my patients came in the evening after work, and the living room became a waiting room. So Hans and Hope had to stay quietly in their bedrooms. We could not cook our meals in our kitchen because of cooking odors. I made an agreement with the butcher across the street to cook either pot roast, meatloaf, or chicken for us and then have it delivered. The owner of a luncheonette next to the butcher made us homemade soups and cooked other tasty meals and salads.

Everything was very well-organized. Every Wednesday and Saturday afternoons and all day Sundays I took time off and went swimming with Hope and Hans or we went to New York to see Margrit and friends. I enjoyed being my own boss in my new profession, and tried to be exact and conscientious in my work. But after a few months I noticed that the hair on my patients returned on the same spot where I had taken it out. What was wrong here? The teachers had told us that initially, a small percentage of hairs would return, but that these treatments were eventually permanent. This was utterly disappointing and embarrassing, especially since some of my patients were our friends. I was at a loss to explain to them why this happened, and many of my patients stopped coming.

Hans told me I should close my office as soon as I recovered the expenses for the equipment. I should write it up as another aborted career just like my massage, my modeling, and my draping and designing career. I thought he was right. After all, I did not want to ruin my reputation.

I was very discouraged about my failure. However, just then the most unforeseen thing happened, which changed my life forever.

I received a letter from Lucille, with a fine needle taped on the sheet. (I still have her letter.) She explained how easily the insertions were made with this "probe" as it was called in the profession. Joe had invented it. He had successfully used it on his wife and now was offering it to six hundred electrologists across the country for trial. The cost of each probe was twenty-five dollars. Lucille was going to be the distributor. She herself had used it on some of her patients with unusual success. I was intrigued by this offer but somewhat skeptical because of my disappointment with the Kree Institute's promises of success. I asked to meet with Joe, so he could give me specific instruction on how to make the insertion into the skin with this uniquely constructed probe.

Lucille invited Joe and me to her home in Connecticut. I also learned why it was so much more expensive than the Kree probe, which cost only five dollars a dozen and broke easily. Joe's probe was made of platinum and was extremely pliable and break-resistant. He had bought the metal before the U.S. government stockpiled it for military use, making it unavailable for trade on the open market. I told Joe that I would try out the probe I had received from Lucille. If it proved to be successful, I would order more.

This visit turned out to be extremely important for me in developing the proper technique. Joe encouraged me to call him with any questions I might have in electrolysis. I really appreciated that suggestion and made use of it in the years to come.

I tried Joe's probe on just one person, my first patient (Mrs. Ackerman, the lady with the full beard), and in three month's time she was permanently free of unsightly hair. What an unexpected success! Hans and I were newly encouraged in continuing our business venture.

Unfortunately, soon after my meeting with Joe and Lucille, she lost her husband quite suddenly. She had to go back to her bookkeeping job to support her three children. She did electrolysis for extra income only in the evenings, and had decided not to use Joe's needle, since she simply could not afford to finish with her patients so fast, and then have to wait for new ones to come.

I figured that if my patients were satisfied, the word would spread fast. I wouldn't mind even if I had to wait for new clients, but I was right not to worry. Soon, after my success with Mrs. Ackerman, I called Joe to place an order for more needles. He was very discouraged that so far no one else had reordered his needles, so I told him that I would buy his entire stock of platinum needles if he could quote me a reasonable price.

I bought his entire platinum needle stock for several thousand dollars. I still have the letter he wrote in which he stated that I was the sole owner of this probe. Hans, my manager, sent a copy of his letter with my resume to every dermatologist, endocrinologist, and gynecologist in the surrounding area.

Our ads in the various newspapers and telephone books now read: Frieda Lefeber RN Clinical Electrologist— Outstanding results in Permanent Hair Removal in a fraction of the usual time. In a very short time I became so busy that we decided to open a more spacious office in nearby Morristown. I would maintain the Dover office for late afternoon and evening appointments.

Now that I was successful, I became a slave to my work. There was no stopping me. Patients came from everywhere: the West Coast, as well as other countries like England, France, Italy, Greece, and even the Middle East—Jordan and Kuwait. Some flew directly into Morristown airport in their private planes. One patient's husband was a high-ranking officer in the Pentagon; she arrived in a military plane. Even Mrs. Jacqueline Kennedy asked for my services. But she requested that I should treat her in her home, which I couldn't do because I could not transport my equipment to her home

Now that our finances had considerably improved, I would have loved to buy a house in a good neighborhood, rather than remain living in a busy, commercial area. But I could not get Hans to move out of the apartment. He had never learned to drive and felt comfortable living in the center of town. I worked hard in those days, often until nine o'clock. Hans and Hope had to stay in their rooms during that time. I wished I could have devoted more time to them and I always felt guilty. However, it was difficult for me to refuse patients who needed my service, and I worked because I knew how much it meant to Hans to be financially secure again. He was very proud of my success. Although my earnings were much higher than his were, he didn't show any signs of jealousy. Without Hans's fine managerial skill and his complete control of our finances, at which I was totally inept, I doubt I would have done as well.

Besides being a good manager, he was a great companion to our Hope and a most loving father. Hans spent all his free time with her. After school they played games like chess or Monopoly, or they went for long walks with our dachshund Schatzi, which she had gotten for her eighth birthday. She was the cutest little animal and Hope adored her. We took Schatzi along on vacation whenever we went—to the shore or the Pocono Mountains. She lived with us for seventeen years. At bedtime Hans and I tucked our Hope, our *motek* ("sweetness"), into bed with Schatzi, who slept with her.

Hope was growing up to be our pride and joy. She was a pretty girl with dark brown eyes, curly brown hair, and a rosy complexion. She had nice friends, none of whom lived nearby. Often Hope's friends invited her to their house after school, but none of the girls could visit us because I was working. On weekends we spent time together as a family. We had joined a swim club at nearby Lake Hopatcong. Hope could swim and play there with her friends, while Hans loved to play cards, and I was just happy to relax in the fresh air. Often Margrit came to Dover. Now, that I brought in so much money, I was, in her eyes, the most wonderful sister-in-law.

During the winter, we drove to New York on Sundays. Hope could skate at Rockefeller Plaza, and then we would meet old friends and Margrit for dinner, usually at the Tavern-on-the-Green.

For the first time in my life, I experienced a tremendous satisfaction in what I was able to do. I had restored the stability to our lives that had been missing for so many years. I felt extremely fortunate to have found a profession I was suited for. It gave me a sense of accomplishment to be able to help my patients, who were inflicted with excessive hair growth. Over my nearly thirty years in practice I received many letters from grateful patients, who wrote that I had changed their lives forever.

However, after few years of harmony and health, new clouds appeared on the horizon.

The Day
of My Father's Death

It was still dark outside on the morning of the day of Succoth (the Jewish harvest holiday) in October 1965. When we awoke we were surprised to find that every single light in our apartment—even our closet lights and table lamps—were lit. Who could have turned them on? Hans and I certainly hadn't done it, neither could have Hope, who never left her room during the night. We were puzzled and to this day I have not found an explanation for this mysterious occurrence.

Late in the afternoon on that day, I received a telegram from Israel with the sad news of my father's sudden death. He had died of a heart attack approximately around the time we woke up in Dover and found all the lights turned on. My father was a pious and very religious Jew. Could those lights have had anything to do with his passing?

I always had great love for him, and now that he was gone I was truly sorry not to have made it possible to visit him. I had last seen my parents nineteen years before for just one day, when my ship was anchored in Haifa in 1946. I regretted not having gone to their eightieth birthday celebration in 1964, just one year before. But I was too afraid of Gerhard, who at the time lived in an institution near my parents. He might have been permitted to attend the celebration. Now it was too late. I was deeply shaken and overcome by guilt and sorrow.

But those lights in my apartment on the day of my father's

death, could this have been a supernatural phenomenon?
Every year since then, when I light a *Jahrzeit* candle (memorial
candle) for my father on the Eve of Succoth, I wonder about
it.

Hans's Illness Returns

It was just a few days before Hans's 60th birthday on January 6, 1966, when I noticed him lying on his bed listlessly staring. He did not want to eat dinner with Hope and me. When I asked him what was wrong, he answered, "Nothing. I don't want to talk about it." I was hoping it was not another depression, and suggested he should see Dr. Gabrilove.

A few weeks before, I had made plans to spend the weekend of Hans' sixtieth birthday in New York at the Greystone Hotel, and had ordered tickets for the opera, *Carmen*, at the Met for all of us and Margrit. I also had made dinner reservations at Hans's favorite restaurant, La Poulardier. We were looking forward to that special day.

It turned out to be a very sad celebration. Hans could not sit still in his seat in the opera. Finally, he left the compartment and walked restlessly in the foyer until the performance was finished. At the restaurant he hardly ate anything. He looked sad and apologized for having spoiled the celebration we had arranged for him. Even Hope was unable to cheer him up, and he would not tell us what was bothering him. I was glad when Margrit convinced him to stay with her and consult with Dr. Gabrilove on Monday, while Hope and I returned to Dover.

Doctor Grabrilove advised Hans to seek help for his depression at the well-known private Psychiatric Institute of Living in Hartford, Connecticut, to which Hans readily agreed. I was relieved that he was willing to go, hoping that he might find relief from this state of anxiety. He stayed there for ten days while they made all kinds of tests and prescribed medication. But apparently, he did not feel better, and he signed himself out. Greatly disappointed, I called for him and took him home. In those days, insurance did not pay for mental illness. The medical expenses amounted to eighteen hundred and fifty dollars, which was a great amount of money at the time.

Once home, his condition got worse. The medication Chlorpromazine, which our local doctor, Dr. Porfido, had prescribed for his anxiety, was useless, and when a complete blood count was taken the doctor found that he had now developed diabetes. Our doctor sent him to Memorial Hospital in Morristown, which had just opened a new psychiatric facility. There he received a number of newly approved gas-shock treatments, which were much milder than the electro-shock therapy. No visitors were allowed during that time, and after a three-week stay in the hospital at an enormous cost, he was released, but again without any improvement in his condition.

In my despair I called on Dr. Felger, head of insulin electro-shock therapy at Greystone State Hospital, where I had worked in 1959 to assist in Hans's negligence suit against the doctor who had let Hans fall off the table. Dr. Felger never made house calls, but he made an exception with Hans. He came twice a week. Hans liked and respected him, and I felt greatly relieved.

By the summer of 1966, his depression had not improved. He looked very haggard and was unable to concentrate at work. He feared he would lose his meager job at McGregor, although he knew it would not affect us financially. Dr. Felger felt his visits were fruitless and suggested that Hans sign himself into another private mental institution at Fair Oaks in Summit, New Jersey, where the minimum stay was again three weeks. No visitors were allowed for the first ten days. Little did I know how helpful that would be for me.

After dropping Hans off at Fair Oaks, I felt very ill. I had a high fever, chills, and pain in every joint. Helen, who came in the afternoon, rushed me to her doctor, who diagnosed me with the flu and pneumonia. He wanted to admit me to the hospital, but I insisted on staying home, so Hope would not be frightened by having both parents hospitalized. Helen took her to and from school and cared for her while I slept for most of the first few days. Eventually, I began to feel a little better but was still very weak.

It was now the beginning of fall. The nights were cool, and I preferred to sleep and rest by open windows, rather than hear the constant humming of the air conditioner. But the street noise and the music from the bar next door made it impossible to sleep. A woman who lived above my apartment suffered from cancer and also seemed to be unable to sleep. No sooner had I fallen asleep than her walking on the squeaking wooden floor awakened me. Also, the wind brought in fumes from the two gas stations on the near-by corner. And every now and then a long freight train would pass behind our house. So, I was forced to use my air conditioner all night and day.

While I was convalescing, I took a good account of my life. There I was making a lot of money, but living like a pauper. I decided that this had to change. I deserved a better home than we lived in now.

Move to Morristown

For years I had tried to convince Hans that we should move out of our dismal neighborhood. I called Dr. Felger and told him about my intention to move. He was of the opinion that if I didn't do it now, while Hans was still at Fair Oaks, I would never have another chance to get him out of Dover. He assured me Hans would get over it, once he was confronted with the reality.

I was determined to make the move. I called the owner of a newly built luxury apartment building in Morristown, New Jersey, where I had seen one apartment some time before. I asked him if I would be able to sign a lease if I could give him satisfactory financial references. He agreed and sent a messenger to me with the lease. Within days the movers came, and with Helen and her daughter's help, Hope and I moved into Apt. 5E on 2 Hamilton Road in Morristown. The apartment was beautiful and spacious; it had a huge living room and dining area, two bedrooms and baths, a kitchen and a large terrace overlooking a magnificent garden full of flowers and fruit trees.

I was still too weak to do anything, but I could rest on the terrace in the sunshine, and that felt good. I was proud of myself for having had the courage to make this drastic change alone, although I was uncertain how Hans would react to the move. Frankly I was afraid to tell him and procrastinated to the very last moment.

All the while I told Hans that I was still not well enough to visit him, because I was recuperating from the flu. He seemed very concerned and warned me not to start working too soon. I promised and called him every day.

Helen was in charge of unpacking the many boxes, and

every day she drove Hope to and from school in Dover, because I wanted Hope to finish the school year there. After two weeks I felt strong enough to go back to my office, which now was within walking distance of our home.

A week later Hans was released from Fair Oaks, again without marked improvement. The attending psychiatrist told me that Hans should remain under the care of a psychiatrist. I still had not told him that I had moved out of Dover and had given up my office there. As I drove him home, I became increasingly afraid to tell him. I knew he would be upset. Finally, we arrived in Morristown. As I drove the car into our parking lot, he questioned me, "What are you doing here? Why are you stopping here, Frieda?" I looked him straight in the eye and said, "This is your new home, Hans. I couldn't stand it in Dover any longer." He was fuming with anger; his lips quivered. "How dare you do that without my knowledge? Have you gone mad? How will I be able to go back to work, have you ever thought of that?" When he reached the apartment he started pacing the floor of the apartment and then slammed the door to the bedroom, cursing and rumbling in there. He was so upset that I had to call Dr. Felger, who came immediately and sedated him. Again the doctor started to pay house calls.

Hans had suffered a setback and was unable to go back to work. He was angry with me, wouldn't talk to me, and didn't even get dressed or shave for days. In nice weather he would lie on the beautiful terrace in a very sullen mood, staring into the air. When I asked him what he was thinking, he didn't even answer. Sometimes, our neighbor would bring her old parrot in his cage out to her terrace before she went to work. The parrot would start talking, "Hello—Hello." There would be a long pause, then, "You idiot." And then the bird would burst out into hilarious, loud laughter for a while. It was so infectious that even Hans had to chuckle.

Hans had lost interest in Hope as a result of his depression. She knew he was ill, and I tried to keep her out of the house as much as possible. Her friends used to invite her to their homes after school, or Helen would pick her up from school, because I was busy working. On my days off I spent time with her, bringing her to ice-skating, swimming, or visiting friends. After dinner she usually played with Schatzi until it was time to sleep, and I then tucked her into bed. I am sure Hope was affected by Hans's illness. One day, I was called to the principal of the Dover Elementary School. Her teacher complained about Hope's disruptive behavior in the classroom, and that she was the instigator of a lot of unruly doings by her classmates.

I explained to the principal that we had problems and I attributed her behavior to the tense atmosphere at home. She must have been trying to find an outlet by encouraging other students to misbehave and do silly things just to have some fun in her life.

I felt uneasy leaving Hans alone in the new apartment while I went to work. Helen was there daily for several hours, cooking and cleaning. Perhaps, my absence from home contributed a lot to Hans's loneliness, but I had to work in order to pay for his hospital expenses, his medication, and Dr Felger's visits. Nothing was covered by insurance, and the new rent was high, and I also had to buy a new car.

One morning, the newspapers reported that the police had raided the very building we had lived in, on 49 North Sussex Street, in Dover. They had arrested several men who lived on the third floor for possession of drugs. Now Hans changed his opinion about my decision to move to Morristown. He realized it was the right move. Slowly, he got used to living in our new and comfortable quarters, and his condition improved so that after five weeks of absence he was able to work again. But he still resented having to drive to work in heavy traffic. I drove both Hope and Hans to Dover at seven thirty in the morning, then I went to work, returning to pick them up again at five. After dinner, which Helen had prepared for us, I went back to work until late in the evening.

After a few months of two weekly doctor visits, Hans felt that he didn't need Dr. Felger anymore and he discharged him. Eventually, Hans could even do without his medication and stopped taking it. Soon I noticed a decline in his health, but he refused to seek further medical help. Hans claimed the commute was too strenuous and he quit his job. I was at a loss as to what to do for him. He talked to Margrit daily on the phone.

In June Hope finished her school year in Dover and I enrolled her in the Morristown Middle School for fall. I was glad Hope spent the summer months at day camp. She had gone to that camp since age six and she loved it there. The owner, Sam Hollander, had a good relationship with Hans. He too suffered from depression at times and Hans often confided in him.

One morning, after a sleepless night, Hans expressed the wish to see his old doctor in New York. We went to see him, and later we visited Margrit. Hans seemed to be especially nervous that day. On the way home he did not want the radio on and seemed nervous. Suddenly he became very fidgety, and I asked, "What's the matter, Hans?" I saw him grab the door handle, mumbling, "Enough, I can't stand it any more. I have to get out." I was driving on the highway at fifty miles an hour. Scared, I screamed, "Don't do it, please!" and quickly brought the car to a halt on the shoulder of the highway.

Shaking from fear, I said, "Hans, if you were the driver of this car and someone next to you told you he wanted to jump out of the car, wouldn't you realize that person is very sick and needs help?" He nodded his head. "Then let's drive to Greystone Hospital before you cause any harm to both of us, and let's ask Dr. Felger for some medication." He agreed and we drove off. I was fearful he might change his mind and do something drastic, and was relieved when we arrived and saw the doctor.

The doctor persuaded him to stay in the hospital for a few days. Hans was able to get a room next to the nurses' station, rather than in a ward with all the other male patients. I was glad that he consented to stay.

Dr. Felger called the next day and advised me not to visit Hans because he was angry with me, and felt that I had tricked him into staying at Greystone.

I was glad that I did not have to go see him. I was worn out and badly needed a rest from him. My friend Emily came to stay with me for the week Hans was hospitalized, and when she visited him at the end of the week, she couldn't believe her eyes. There was a miraculous transformation in Hans. He greeted her smilingly with open arms and was in the best of spirits. He was his old self again, as if he never had been sick. He was happy and he had just heard from the doctor that he could be discharged.

When Emily told me the news I could hardly believe it and called the attending doctor. He told me what had caused this sudden change in Hans. A few nights earlier another inmate had attacked Hans and nearly choked him to death. But, because his room was so near the nurse's station, they could hear peculiar sounds coming from Hans's room. They rushed in and were able to rescue him. This shock, the doctor explained, was worth more than a hundred electro-shock treatments. He had instantly snapped out of his depression and became his normal self, and he could be discharged and return home.

I was surprised, but doubtful that this would be permanent. Because of the constant stress of his illness, I had developed a bleeding colitis. I had lost a lot of weight in a very short time and was too exhausted to take him back so soon.

I called Margrit and asked her to care for him for a month while I got treated for my colitis. She agreed. He came home for a day in very good spirits, packed some clothes and went to New York to stay with his sister. He called me daily and told me Margrit was teaching him to cook, so he would be able to cook for us when he came home.

While Hans was staying with Margrit and my colitis was slowly improving, I thought I would take a vacation. With my doctor's permission, I decided to take Hope to visit my mother in Israel.

It was one year after my father's death. I felt I should pay her a visit and it would be good for Hope to meet her only grandmother. My mother was eighty-two years old, and was not in good health. I was still afraid that my brother might learn that I was visiting her, and, although he was in an institution, he might be able to escape and do us harm. From time to time, since his return to Israel, we had received incoherent but threatening letters. So I did not make the journey to Israel with enthusiasm, but more or less I felt it was my duty to visit my mother.

We greeted my mother with a bouquet of long-stemmed red roses, but I was shocked at how she had aged. It was sad to see her so pale and lifeless. She smiled when she saw us, but I could not detect any great joy. She lived in the infirmary of a retirement home in Haifa and rarely went out of her room. She sat by an open window all day and did not participate in activities that were offered there. She told me she had lost all desire to live, especially because of my brother, who was still in a mental facility. She could not understand why he couldn't be released. However, when she told us that he sometimes sneaked out to visit her and always behaved normally, I immediately felt very uneasy. Hope tried to be very loving to her grandmother, despite the language barrier; I always had to do the translation. I carried most of the conversation. My mother was not very talkative and usually after an hour's visit she fell asleep. We visited her early in the morning and early evening. During the day we went on sightseeing tours of that beautiful country.

One evening however, after leaving my mother, I saw a figure in the dark, running right past us and disappearing in the woods. For a moment I was scared but brushed it off. Could it possibly have been Gerhard? But my fear of him made me decide to change our itinerary. Years later when Gerhard's son, Dan, visited his father in the asylum, Gerhard confirmed that he had seen us that evening.

We said goodbye to my mother. I felt good having seen

her. I promised her that if all was well, all three of us would visit her in two years, and we did. She gave me two silver Sabbath candles, which she had received from her parents as a wedding gift in 1912, and other silver religious articles (a Menorah and a Havdolah box) and small jewelry. The candles are lit in our house every Friday night to this day.

We stayed in Israel another week and traveled to Jerusalem and Tel Aviv, and then took a most spectacular guided bus ride through the desert on a narrow road to Elath, the most southern part of the Negev, where we stayed in the newly built Queen of Sheba Hotel. On our way back to the States, we stopped in Paris for three days at the Grand Hotel, on the Rue de Rivoli. I had to be very careful of what I ate. Perhaps from the excitement of traveling, my colitis had gotten worse. I could hardly leave the hotel. I lived on croissants and tea, and even that didn't agree with me. The Rue de Rivoli had lots of souvenir shops and I sent Hope to buy presents while I was resting in the hotel. I would have liked to show her more of the beautiful city, but I was not able to. I was glad when we reached home.

Hans was anxious to come home from his stay with Margrit. His health was completely restored. Finally, we were a family again. Hans did the shopping and the cooking. He walked Hope to school and brought her home. They played chess and Monopoly again. He walked our little dachshund, who was his constant companion. Across the street was a brokerage firm where he watched the tickertape daily and occasionally played the stock market.

I worked in my office for at least ten hours a day. I would come home for dinner and then go back downtown to my office. In 1967 race riots broke out. Morristown had a large black population. My office was in the center of town, at 8 de Heart Street, and I didn't dare to go to work.

Luckily, there was an office apartment available on the ground floor where we lived. I cut a deal with the landlord, and within days, I had the whole new office redecorated, my equipment moved in, and the necessary security arranged. Hans sent out hundreds of letters on new stationary to doctors and patients, notifying them of the change of address. All newspaper ads, telephone books, answering service, etc., had to be changed, but it was worth it.

Now I was busier than ever. I wanted to train another nurse to help me, but Hans was against it. He feared she might ruin my reputation.

Everyday Hans brought a beautiful lunch tray to my office. Some women in the elevator would tease him about spoiling me like that. He would reply, "She deserves it."

We had joined a local synagogue, where Hope went to Hebrew school. One week when we arrived for Friday night services, something strange happened. We saw our rabbi putting his suitcase into the trunk of a car belonging to our doctor's wife. Rumor had it that she was having an affair with the rabbi, and now we had witnessed it firsthand. Hans did not condone such behavior. He called the rabbi a hypocrite and we withdrew from the Temple.

We joined another synagogue, B'nai Jeshurun in Short Hills, New Jersey. The cantor, Norman Summers, had a magnificent voice, so we looked forward to hearing him every Friday evening, and enjoyed meeting friends for Oneg Shabbat, which was always celebrated with coffee and delicious cake.

Twice a year, we went on vacation, traveling to California, Europe, and visiting my mother in Israel in 1968 and 1971. Winters, we went to the Dorado Beach Hotel in Puerto Rico and played tennis or we traveled to other Caribbean islands on cruises, or went to Bermuda. We never went away without our Hope. Hans didn't worry about money any more. It was truly a miracle how he had recovered from his illness and had regained his sense of humor. He told me, after experiencing near death at Greystone, he decided he'd better not worry anymore because he didn't want to end up in an asylum again.

When I asked him what had brought on the last depression he confessed. He had lost forty thousand dollars of our money in the stock market and had blamed himself for it. How sad! The damage he had inflicted on himself and the enormous medical bills far outweighed the financial stock losses.

After he felt well again, he changed his life insurances and bankbooks back to me, which had been in Margrit's possession ever since his depression in 1954. The next eight years we spent together in harmony. Again he became my closest and most trusted friend. Our Hope brought us much joy. She always had excellent marks in school and had many friends. I wished I could have devoted more time to her, but I knew she received quality time and love from Hans. She spent summers in tennis camps before joining us in our travels. When she was in eleventh grade, we went to visit colleges and traveled to Harvard, Brown, Yale, and Cornell. Her SATs were high enough to consider these fine schools. In the end she chose the University of Pennsylvania, mainly because she didn't want to be far away from home.

In the fall of 1972, Hope entered college. We were proud of her achievements, but it was lonesome without our Hope, and every two or three weeks we visited her. Hans especially missed his *motek* ("sweet child").

We had joined a tennis club, where I would play while Hans played cards. Often he watched me playing tennis and was proud when I won a game. It was a beautiful country club with lovely condos. Silently I thought, if ever anything happened to Hans, I would love to live there. I was grateful for the good life we were having since Hans's remarkable recovery.

My Mother's Death

After we visited my mother in the summer of 1971, we received only one short note on the High Holidays. It was written by an attendant who let us know that she was too weak to write herself and she was sending us greetings. I became concerned when I did not get a card from her on my birthday. Soon after Passover holidays, Isy Kleiner, with whom I had not been in touch for years, mailed me a black-edged envelope, which always indicates a condolence note. My first thought was that it might have been Gerhard who possibly had died. But when I read the formal condolence note I was shocked to find that it was my mother who had died.

I couldn't understand why the nursing home in Israel did not notify me of her death. How did she die and when? I called the administrator, Hannah Weiss, whom I had met during our last visit eight months before. Hanna told me that she had not seen my mother since then and explained to me the reason why.

When we visited Israel in 1971, Hans, Hope, and I spent our final weekend in Jerusalem. During our absence, my mother called in her attorney and insisted on having her will changed. My father had left his money, about twenty-eight thousand dollars, to my mother. My mother told the lawyer that since I was financially secure, she wished to leave her estate to Gerhard. The lawyer tried to convince her not to do that because there was no hope that Gerhard would ever be released from the asylum. Instead, he advised her to leave her estate to the three grandchildren. She refused and insisted on having her will changed, and that only two thousand dollars should be paid to me in recognition of the help I had given my parents when they were in need. Hannah Weiss, who, with the lawyer, was witness to the changing of the will, also tried to convince her that what she intended to do was wrong. They again suggested that she leave the money to her grandchildren, but she was adamant and became angry with both of them. All Hannah knew about her death was that while an attendant accompanied her on the way to the bathroom, she had collapsed and died instantly. Hannah was of the opinion that the attorney who was the executor should have notified me of her death, which occurred on March 7, 1972.

My first reaction was anger. It was not about the money, but it confirmed the lack of love my mother had showed me all her life. If she had left me a note, explaining her way of thinking and nevertheless expressing her love for me, I would have understood. Although she did me wrong, I light a Jahrzeit candle every March 7, in memory of her, and I hope she rests in peace.

Sadly, immediately after my mother's death, the Israeli government confiscated Gerhard's inheritance because he had become a ward of the State, and my father's hard-earned money disappeared.

Hans's Final Year

During the Thanksgiving holidays in 1974, we enjoyed five lovely restful days at the Dorado Beach Hotel in San Juan, playing tennis with Hope and basking in the sun at the beach. We then spent Christmas vacation in Acapulco, Mexico, at the Princess Hotel. It was brutally hot in Mexico, the beaches were polluted with horse manure, and we could only find relief from the heat by swimming in the overcrowded pool. Hans preferred to eat his meals at the buffet, which were served outdoors. He loved that he could choose whatever pleased his voracious appetite. But one day he came down with "Montezuma's Revenge," which manifested itself in high fever, chills, and bloody diarrhea. He was very ill and needed medical care. We decided to cut our vacation short and return home directly.

Six weeks later, his rectal bleeding still persisted, and he consulted Dr. Ben Asher, who had his office on the same floor as I had mine. Hans had to undergo a Barium enema, but the test results were not good. The doctor had found a polyp in Hans's lower intestine, and advised us to consult with a surgeon. We were worried. How could it be that Hans could possibly have a malignancy? He looked so healthy and always had a hearty appetite. Being a pessimist as he was, he was sure he had cancer. I tried to tell him not to come to any conclusions until we saw a surgeon, although I was afraid Hans might be right. We went to see Dr. Kree, a surgeon from Mount Sinai Hospital in New York, who told us that a malignancy might be involved and urged Hans to undergo the operation. After getting a second opinion he was admitted to the hospital and was operated on at eight o'clock in the morning of March 17, 1975.

On the day before the operation, Hope came from

Philadelphia to Morristown, and together we drove to New York very early the next morning to be by his bedside before the operation. A blizzard made driving conditions almost impossible, and the drive took several hours. Unfortunately, we were unable to see him before he was wheeled into the operating room.

Waiting seemed like eternity. I said my silent prayers over and over. Finally, Dr. Kree came and told us the crushingly sad news. It was a cancerous tumor, and a rather old-growth one. He was not able to remove it entirely and had found liver involvement. Hans would need chemotherapy. Upon hearing this, Hope and I cried and held onto each other for support.

Hours later, Hans came down from the recovery room. He was groggy and had tubes connected everywhere. We held his hands and wiped the beady perspiration from his forehead, while his private nurses took care of his medical needs. We stayed with him until all visitors had to leave. Exhausted from the horrendous day, we tried to find rest at the Gotham Hotel, where we stayed for a few nights. Although Hans was very brave and endured the discomfort after the operation remarkably well, it was pitiful to see him suffer. I was glad that the doctor had not told him that the cancer had spread to his liver.

Hans was hospitalized for two weeks. During that time I found in an article in the *National Inquirer* that a doctor in Japan was treating cancer patients with a new drug and achieving amazing results. I called the doctor in Tokyo, but he advised me not to bring Hans to him because he had no cure for liver cancer. I was constantly on the lookout for alternative treatment for this dreadful disease. I had heard about a natural supplement called "Laitril," which was derived from the seeds of apricot pits. It contained some small amount of cyanide, which is an antioxidant, and was supposed to reduce cancerous tumors. It was illegal in this country, but available in Mexico and Europe. I went to a health food store nearby and read in a health newsletter an ad, which read: Are you suffering from cancer? Call #538—. I recognized the Morristown area code number and called the number immediately. A woman answered, and said she might be of help, and would like to see me. A short while later, June, a tall, friendly, young woman in jeans arrived in her jeep. She told me that her mother had been treated with radiation for a metastasized, inoperable throat cancer at Sloan Kettering without improvement. As a last resort, she took her mother to Dr. Hans Nieper, a renowned cancer specialist from Hanover, Germany. He had treated her mother in his clinic with Laitril and other cancer-inhibiting drugs, and, after a few months, she was declared cancer-free. She was so impressed with Dr. Nieper's unconventional approach to the cancer treatment that she decided to try to persuade other patients inflicted with this disease to seek the same treatment.

After all the discouraging news about Hans's illness, I now had some hope. June came like a godsend. I clung to everything that might save him. June offered to visit Hans, and the next day drove her jeep to Mount Sinai Hospital and spoke with him. She visited him several times while he was there. When he was released from the hospital, June stopped by daily to see him at home. She even brought her mother to us to show him how well she was doing. Hans became very fond of June. She was a great support to all of us. She knew where we could obtain Laitril, which was illegal in this country.

After Hans felt strong enough and Hope had finished her semester in May 1975, we all went to see Dr. Nieper in Hanover, Germany. Hans underwent all sorts of treatments in his clinic, but Dr. Nieper told Hope that there was nothing he could do since there was liver involvement. Still, we did not give up hope. Hans had a special rapport with Dr. Nieper, who made our two-week stay rather pleasant. On the doctor's 46th birthday he invited us to an elaborate party at his country home.

After the treatments ended, we took Hans for a restful vacation in Baden-Baden, a beautiful resort in the Black Forest, and he felt strong again when we returned home.

In August, his health deteriorated rapidly. He realized that his end was near, and instructed Hope fully about our financial affairs, putting everything down in writing. I admired how brave he was. Once more Hope and I made a desperate attempt to save him. By ambulance, we went to New York to a clinic where electro-magnetic therapy was performed to shrink the tumor, but he was too weak to endure the treatments. We had to transport him to Morristown Hospital where he spent the last four weeks of his life with nurses around the clock.

He called upon the rabbis and his beloved Cantor Summers to give him spiritual comfort. He admitted to me that he was not always as good a husband as he should have been, but he wanted to let me know he had always been faithful and loved me deeply. I knew that, but upon hearing it, I could not hold back my tears. For the last days of his life, Hope came home from college to be at his bedside, but he was in a coma at times.

December 9, 1975 was a cold, snowy day. Hope had decided to return to college. Early in the morning, before leaving, she dropped in to see her father and then called me to come immediately, because the end was very near. I rushed to his bedside. His breathing was labored and intermittent. The moment I touched his hands, he drew his last deep breath and he was gone.

Hans had made all the arrangements with the rabbis for his funeral himself. His coffin was placed on the bema ("the altar") of our temple and Cantor Summers gave the eulogy and sang *Kadish* ("the prayer for the dead").

In the temple I was choked up with grief but couldn't shed a tear. I felt drained and numb and thought it was a blessing that Hans was relieved of his suffering, but later that night, alone in my bedroom, I was overcome with sadness and it was a relief when I was finally able to cry.

We sat shiva for a week, as is customary in our religion. Hope's friends from Penn attended the funeral and comforted her. I felt badly for Hope. She was only twenty-one, too young to lose her beloved father.

I was alone now and had to learn to manage my business without Hans. It took many hours to write out checks, to pay bills, and totaling daily receipts and entering them into logs, but I learned. I went to bed very tired every night. Being constantly busy helped me in getting over the grieving period.

After Hans's Death

Hope took her father's death courageously. After the funeral she intended to stay with me for a while, but I convinced her that I was strong enough to carry on alone. She had applied to four law schools, Penn, Columbia, NYU, and Rutgers, but her applications had been submitted rather late. She graduated in May of 1976 from Penn magna cum laude. I attended the ceremony in Philadelphia, beaming with pride as she graduated. I wished Hans could have witnessed this proud moment. After graduation, Hope and I spent a few restful days in Saint Thomas.

The University of Penn rejected her because all openings had already been filled. She was deferred from Columbia and waitlisted at NYU. So she went to Rutger's Law School in Camden, which was just outside of Philadelphia. I was glad that she had chosen that school and could live in a secure apartment in Philadelphia. We found a lovely studio at the Dorchester on Rittenhouse Square. I had it furnished by a New York decorator in modern decor and with fine Kerman rugs. Hope loved living there. I loved to spoil her by buying her beautiful clothes and providing her with luxuries. She spent one semester in Oxford, England and when I visited her in the summer I bought her a five-piece set of the finest Wedgewood china for twelve, which she uses for special occasions to this day. I always remembered how difficult life was for me when I was her age, and I wanted my child to have better memories than I had. It gave me much pleasure to give her the things I never had; in fact, it was the only pleasure I had.

After Hans died my life changed in many ways. I kept myself

busy from early morning until late at night. The hours were long, but I wanted it that way. I enjoyed going to temple every Friday night. When listening to Cantor Summers' beautiful voice I found solace and peace, but it felt strange sitting with couples we used to be friendly with on Oneg Shabbat ("the get-together") after Shabbat services. Eventually, I befriended a few single, widowed women. The couples at the tennis club rarely invited me to join them for dinner. Without Hans watching me, I lost interest in playing tennis.

Even Schatzi, our dog, behaved strangely. She obviously missed Hans. She always used to sit next to him in a comfortable chair in the living room, but now Schatzi sat there alone. Whenever I sat in that chair, she would jump off growling. Some weeks after Hans died she suffered a stroke. While she was ill, I kept her in my bed. If she became restless I would carry her down in the elevator in the middle of the night so she could eliminate outside. Miraculously, she recovered from her stroke after one week. After that her behavior changed, and she became my constant companion. I even took her downstairs to my office while I was at work. She greeted every patient by waggling her tail. When she died in 1977, I had her cremated, and her remains are still kept in an urn in my cabinet.

Two years after Hans's death, Schatzi died at the age of seventeen; I was unable to work for days. I felt lonesome in that big apartment. I thought it would be good for me, now that I was single, to move to New York, where I would be able to enjoy the cultural aspects of the city on weekends. My accountant advised me to buy an apartment as an investment. I soon found a suitable place on the Upper East Side. I gave up the large apartment in Morristown and moved some of my furniture into my office apartment downstairs; it was large enough to hold a few cabinets and a sofa bed, allowing me to sleep there during the week.

In June 1978, I moved into a lovely apartment on the twenty-second floor at 118 East 60th Street, with a view of the Manhattan skyline and the George Washington Bridge in the distance. From the kitchen window one could see the 59th Street Bridge. The view was magical at night. I could see Bloomingdale's display windows on the street below. My large terrace overlooked Central Park. As I moved in, I said to myself, *These are the fruits of my labor!* I decorated the place with fine wallpaper and mirrors, and bought a new bedroom set. This was my Shangri-La, and I loved it! I soon befriended a few interesting women who lived in my building. I joined a swim club where I could also dine and entertain. On Friday nights, after services at my temple in New Jersey, I would drive to the city and stay there until early Monday morning. It felt as if I had a vacation every weekend.

Hope loved coming on weekends. She clerked with a federal judge in Philadelphia in her last year of law school, and graduated in 1979. I was very proud of her and gave her a party at the club, inviting all her friends and some of our relatives. She found a job with the Security and Exchange Commission, where she worked for two years.

Saturday evenings I usually went to the opera or to Carnegie Hall. I looked forward to spending weekends in New York. Still, I often felt lonely. I would have liked to meet a decent man, just for companionship. I had joined Temple Emanuel and had gone to their singles' functions, but never met anybody there. I found singles' socials awkward and stopped going to them. Perhaps, it was my fault. I was shy and not aggressive. I rather would have liked to be introduced to someone, but I didn't know the right people.

In October 1980, I thought I ought to seek out a *shadchen* ("a Jewish matchmaker"), one who could introduce me to someone. I could learn that person's background and interests and see a photo before I agreed to meet him. "Helena" ran such an agency from a swanky office on 400 Madison Avenue. One day, I mustered enough courage to consult with her. She told me that she usually didn't take women over fifty but since I didn't look my age (I was sixty-five), she would make an exception. She just happened to have the perfect man to introduce me to. She showed me his picture and told me about his interests and education. It all sounded great. If I agreed to meet him, the fee would be two hundred fifty dollars. I thought I would give it a try.

Hank was retired, living in Philadelphia, and was a graduate of Penn with a degree in law and accounting. He was sixty-eight years old. In the photo he looked very distinguished, tall and slender, with a white beard. Everything seemed right and I agreed to meet him. A day later he called me from Philadelphia and sounded charming. With a deep, warm voice he said, "Please make a reservation in a nice restaurant for lunch on Saturday. I will be in New York and am looking forward to meeting you." I had not had a date with a man since my first date with Hans in 1934, and now it was 1980. I felt all excited like a young girl, and could hardly wait until Saturday.

On Saturday, at noon, the doorbell rang and when I opened the door I saw a very tall—6-foot-3—handsome, well-dressed gentleman with a big white beard, a smiling face, and deep-set eyes. He looked very distinguished. I was pleasantly surprised and wondered why this man would have needed a dating service to find a suitable partner. I offered him a drink and we sat for a while and talked. He told me that he was a patron of the arts, and supported other charitable causes. He had worked for the I.R.S. in art appraisal and was especially interested in modern art and music. When it was time for lunch we went to Reginette, a cozy restaurant on Park Avenue and 59th street where we both ordered hamburgers at $7.50 a piece; he complained about the food, although it was prepared to perfection. I could not understand why he didn't like it. When I asked him what was wrong, he said, "It should be twice as big for the price they charge." I didn't agree, and thought his complaint was not justified.

I found it strange that he didn't want to stay after we had eaten. We took a long walk in Central Park, and when we returned to my apartment for a cup of coffee he criticized the decor in my apartment. He said bluntly, "What a gaudy place you have! But I am impressed with the view." I thought it was totally inappropriate for him to say that to me. I felt he had no manners and was upset. I said to him, "You have quite a nerve to tell me that. But since you are so blunt let me ask you why did you engage Helena's services and pay her two hundred fifty dollars? I would think a man like you shouldn't have any trouble finding someone on your own." He promptly denied paying her a fee, saying he knew her socially. He apologized for having insulted me but he did not like the oriental pictures that decorated my wall. We spent a few interesting hours getting acquainted. He told me about himself. He was a native Philadelphian from a poor family. A widower, he had lost his wife fifteen years ago. They had no children. From May to October he resided in Philadelphia and spent winters in Florida, where he lived with his sister.

He wanted to know about my daughter. Hope, at the time, was working for the Security and Exchange Commission. When he said goodbye, he took both of my hands and kissed me and said, "Let this be the beginning of a beautiful friendship." He asked for my daughter's phone number because he wanted to tell her what a lovely mother she had. He was a charmer.

After he left I felt as if I were on cloud nine. He was a little awkward, but I really liked him. I could not wait to call Hope. She immediately began to investigate among people she knew who were art collectors, from whom she received favorable information about him.

When Hank did not call me for ten days, I became disappointed. He finally called, and wanted to see me again; he came the following Saturday. This time he did not want to go to a restaurant. He said he was a good cook. We should buy the food and he would prepare a gourmet meal.

In the supermarket I found out what a cheapskate he was: he made me pay for the groceries! Now, I understood why he did not like the hamburger at Reginette on our first date. The $7.50 for lunch was too much. In the evening he prepared an excellent meal. I enjoyed his company and he was very helpful in cleaning up after dinner. I thought, *This guy is well trained.* We became a little cozier. After dinner we went to Carnegie Hall to a concert, for which he paid.

The following week I visited Hope in Philadelphia. He invited us to his spacious apartment, which was sparsely furnished, with lots of modern, abstract art on the cold white walls. It looked like a gallery. No wonder he did not like my cozy apartment. We talked for a while and then Hope left for a dinner date. He was very charming and amorous. Later he took me to a very nice restaurant. There he kissed me in public. I felt embarrassed but liked it. Hans would never have done that. I hadn't felt like that in many years, and I did not even want to resist him. We spent an unforgettable evening together.

Hank visited me one more time the following weekend before leaving for Florida. We enjoyed each other's company very much and I was happy to have found a lovely companion, even though he was reluctant on spending any money on me. I wondered if I had fallen in love or if it was just a momentary infatuation. In any case I was happy and was physically attracted to him. We were both sad when we kissed each other goodbye.

Every night he called from Florida and told me he missed me. He had told his family about me, but when I asked him whether I should visit him in Florida, he inexplicably did not want me to come. He surprised me on Valentine's Day by coming directly from Florida to New York. He brought me a small replica of a modern steel sculpture featuring the letters L-O-V-E. We spent a lovely time together. Again he was very romantic and I loved it. The following day he had to go to Philadelphia to see his mother-in-law and to take care of some business, and after staying there for several days, he came back to New York to visit some galleries. He had made an appointment to see some paintings for his clients.

It was a bitter-cold day when he called me to accompany him. I was elegantly dressed in my mink coat, but he wore an old frayed fur-lined cloth coat with torn pockets and sleeves and an old Russian fur hat. I told him that I was embarrassed to

walk with him, but he persuaded me to come with him to view
the paintings. At the galleries, the owners, who all seemed to
know him, greeted him with great respect. As we left he told
me how unimportant it is what you wear. He said, "People will
always respect you for what you know, and not what clothes
you wear."

It was time for lunch. We were walking on Lexington
Avenue, and he spotted a Fish and Chips restaurant. That's
where he was going to take me and I refused to have lunch
there. "I am not going to eat in that fast food place," I told
him. "But they have the best fish chowder, Frieda." "You can
eat there, H. I will eat something later at home." We sat on a
narrow bench at Fish and Chips and he consumed his soup in
a plastic bowl with a plastic spoon. I tried it, and found it flat
and watery. What nerve he had to take me to a place like that!
I felt insulted and angry about this eccentric behavior, but I
just kept quiet.

After that we walked to Bloomingdale's, where he tried
several fur coats and fur-lined coats, some of which looked
good on him. But he did not decide on any of them and we
left. I had a slight suspicion that he expected me to buy him a
coat.

At home I ate my lunch and did not offer him anything.
He tried to make up but I told him that I wasn't going to tolerate
the way he treated me. It was insulting and he better shape
up. He apologized and even shed a few tears when he was
telling me that he was a child of the Depression. He couldn't
help being so stingy, even with himself. I should forgive him,
he was trying to change, he kissed me and I gave in.

That evening he took me to a charming restaurant. I rarely
drink wine but that night I drank just one glass and became
quite tipsy. While going down a steep staircase in that
restaurant, I tripped and twisted my ankle. Luckily he grabbed
me in time or I would have fallen down all the way. I was in
considerable discomfort that night and nursed the leg with
ice compresses.

The next morning I was still miserable. It did not make sense for him to just sit around and see me suffer, so I told him to go back to Philadelphia. He did and I drove back to Morristown in pain to get some medical attention. My doctor in Morristown took an X-ray. I was lucky; it was not a fracture.

Hank returned to Florida the next day. He called often, but he did not come back to see me until his birthday on June 18. I had looked forward to that day, and had made lunch reservation at Le Cirque, a fashionable restaurant on the East Side. He arrived on that very hot day with two big cartons, not a suitcase, in which he had carefully packed several jackets, pants, underwear, and toiletries. I could not believe it when I saw it. How odd! He told me he had theater tickets for the evening performance of *The Fifth of July*, which was playing downtown on 45th street. *That was nice*, I thought.

The food at Le Cirque was excellent. I treated him to lunch (the bill was eighty-nine dollars with wine for the two of us), and he thanked me. When we left, he asked me what I would give him for his birthday. I thought he was just teasing. Was the lunch at Le Cirque not enough? What chutzpah! He wanted me to drive him to Simms, a men's clothing store, which was located across the George Washington Bridge. When we got to the tollbooth, he took my wallet out of my handbag, took out a dollar and handed me the money to pay. I thought, *How cheap can you get!*

At Simms, he tried on ever so many sports jackets. All looked good on him, but he could not decide on any. We were just about to leave, when he spotted a black trench raincoat on a mannequin. It was a Bill Blass designer coat. He tried it on and asked me how he looked in it. Jokingly, I said, "You look like a gangster." He wanted that coat. But then he told me, "I don't have enough cash with me. Can you pay for it?" I wrote out a check, and as he carried the coat out of the store he said, "This ought to be my birthday present." I answered, "You've got to be kidding." At home he made no attempt to pay me back, and later I forgot to remind him of it.

When it was time to go to the theater, he warned me he wasn't going to take a cab. We would have to go by subway, which would get us there much faster. In the 1980s, a lot of crimes happened in the subways. I had not used the subway in thirty years and was reluctant to give in to his wish. I purposely wore no jewelry and took no handbag. I was dressed casually with a light white cotton blouse and a print skirt. It was still oppressively hot. Luckily the subway was full of passengers, so I was not afraid anymore and in just three stops we arrived at our destination.

The theater was old, and had no elevator, and we climbed up the staircase to the very top, to the very last seats. The air-conditioning, if there was any, did not reach that high. It was stifling hot. I fanned myself constantly with the playbill. The people on the stage looked miniscule. When it was over, I could not wait to get out of there. It was eleven thirty in the evening. I begged him to please call a cab. He refused, took me by the hand and literally dragged me down the subway staircase. I called him a jerk and cursed him and told him I had enough of him. The subway tunnel on 42nd Street was filled with homeless people and all kinds of shady characters. He did not know his way and couldn't find the right track. I was petrified.

When we finally found our way through that labyrinth, we had to wait on the deserted platform until the Lexington Avenue train arrived. We sat opposite a big fat man, dressed only in an undershirt. He held a large wooden hammer in his hand, but he looked benevolent. I thought this man was prepared for any eventuality. I was fuming and angry as hell. When we reached home, I told Hank to pack his clothes and leave. He pleaded with me to let him stay until morning because there were no more trains leaving for Philadelphia that night. I allowed him to spend the night on the sofa in the living room. I could not sleep all night, as a result of all that aggravation. What a loser he was! Early the next morning he knocked at my door to say goodbye but I didn't open the door to my bedroom and he left with his two cardboard boxes and the raincoat.

I never expected to hear from him again, but he called to apologize. I told him that I had no desire to continue the relationship. I could never live on his level, and he should just forget about me. He told me he couldn't forget me and would call me from time to time. I was still angry and hung up.

Needless to say, it took me a while to get over this affair. I tried to forget about Hank by working hard in my office. Deep in my heart I knew I had made the right decision, and I had the feeling that this man was out to exploit well-to-do women, and that was why he had contacted Helena. When he went with me to look for a fur-lined coat at Bloomingdale's or for jackets at Simms he must have expected me to pay for it. He actually tricked me into paying for the trench coat. He has not yet paid me back. After this experience I never dated another man. It was not worth the heartache.

The Years 1980=2002

Even after I broke up with Hank in June 1981, he continued to call me periodically. But I had no intention of renewing our relationship. I knew he was a womanizer or perhaps even a gigolo. I told him what I thought of him, and of course, he denied it.

I put all my energy into my work, and contemplated opening another office. I would have to look for an assistant first, and had planned to take in my good friend and colleague from nursing school, Ilse Beck. She would have been best suited for this type of work. Unfortunately, her son suddenly developed a long-term illness, and I could no longer count on her. It was difficult to find the right person. I finally asked two patients, Joan and Pat, to join me. They had received their practical training by doing insertions on my niece, who had excessive hair growth over her entire body, due to a metabolic disease. After months of training, Joan and Pat had acquired enough skill, and I sent them to an electrolysis school for two weeks in order to get a diploma. But Pat demanded a higher percentage than I was willing give her, so I let her go. She opened an office twenty miles away, as was permitted under the contract I had had with her.

But, without my needle, she was unsuccessful and was forced to close her office in a short time. Years later, she came back to me as a patient, and told me how much I regretted having left me.

The other girl, Joan, stayed with me. She had a winning personality and patients liked her. I was happy to have trained her, and had full confidence in her. She eased my workload schedule considerably. Now I was able to take time off from work without worrying.

Berlin Revisited

Because Joan was very capable, I was able to accept an unexpected invitation from the mayor of the city of Berlin to honor and to welcome two hundred eighty former citizens. It included airfare, hotel accommodation for eight days, and fifty dollars daily allowance.

First, I was hesitant to accept the invitation. I hadn't forgotten the last time when we had visited Berlin, in 1968, and I had had an awful nightmare the first night at Hotel Kempinski. I dreamt that Nazis were goose-stepping in our courtyard in Kuestrin, followed by many rats. Some of them were already breaking into our house and were approaching my bedroom. I woke up screaming. It took a while until I came to my senses and realized it was only a dream, and I was trembling with fear. Hans and Hope had tried to quiet me. We had left Berlin the next morning and spent the rest of our vacation in Rome, Italy.

But this time the temptation to see Berlin was too great, and in May of 1982 I went. It turned out to be a most memorable experience.

When we arrived in Berlin, I was assigned to stay at the Hotel Excelsior. It was the very place at which Hans and I had met almost a half a century before. What a coincidence! As I looked out the window of my room, I saw the dance floor where we had met and danced for the first time, in May 1934. Forty-eight years had passed, but I remembered the time as if it was yesterday.

The welcome address by the mayor, followed by a banquet at the Reichstag, was most impressive. The following day we were given a tour of the western part of the city, parts of which were still in ruins. The Berlin Wall, built by the Soviet Union during the 1960s, divided East and West Berlin. We were not permitted to enter East Berlin, the Russian zone.

The houses on Kurfurstendam, the most elegant street in West Berlin, still showed signs of the devastation from the war. I tried to find the house on Geisbergstrasse 41 where Hans and his sister had lived, but it was not there anymore. It must have been destroyed. A new house stood in its place. It felt strange not to be able to find familiar places.

A boat ride took us to the notorious Ploetzensee prison. Many righteous Germans and prominent political prisoners were tortured and assassinated there during the Hitler regime. The guide told us, in chilling details, of the brutalities that took place there. The images of what I saw there haunted me long after the visit to that prison.

One day, I visited the Jewish hospital of Berlin where I had trained. Miraculously, it had survived the ravages of war unscathed, but was now in dire need of repair. It brought back many memories. I sat for a long time on a bench on the lovely grounds of the hospital compound and reminisced. It had operated during the war years under most difficult conditions, with a small staff of Jewish doctors and nurses. In the final years of the war, the buildings that housed the laboratory and the morgue had been designated by the Nazis as a gathering station for deportation of Jews. From there, they were loaded onto trucks and then transported by freight trains to Auschwitz or other concentration camps. As I stood in front of the door to the morgue, where I had sneaked out on Kristallnacht, I shuddered, thinking how many weeping souls had passed through here.

The people in charge of our stay, who accompanied us everywhere, were all young Germans. They expressed their regrets that we had been driven out of Germany. One could sense their feeling of guilt and shame. Visiting Berlin was a bittersweet experience, but in a way, a healing process. I was glad I had the courage to have revisited my former city.

My New York Office

When I returned from Germany, Hank called me again, still trying to convince me that I had a totally wrong impression of him. I still had feelings for him, but my common sense told me I should not rekindle that flame. I would be better off to put my energy into my work.

Now that I was living in New York and had a trustworthy assistant, I decided to open an office in the city. I found a suitable place on 133 East 73rd street, where professionals could rent medically equipped office space on an hourly basis for twenty-five dollars per hour. The switchboard secretaries made all the appointments. Three hundred doctors, dentists, and other health-related professionals participated. The set-up involved very little financial risk. I sent out letters to doctors in New York to announce the opening of my office and about my unique service, and also received a number of referrals from dermatologists, endocrinologists, and gynecologists in the building. It was a good start.

One of the participating doctors was the psychologist Dr. Ruth Westheimer, who at that time also rented space there. Since she was a "Landsman," we occasionally spoke in the lounge. One day she suddenly became well known because of a Channel Six television interview at that medical facility, the only one of its kind in New York. This happened when the television crew arrived at the building on the morning following a blizzard. Because of the storm, everybody in the building, except for except Dr. Ruth, had cancelled their appointments for the day. She and one switchboard operator were the only persons there when the crew from Channel Six arrived. Dr. Ruth agreed to be interviewed. She was charming, witty and, in her squeaky voice, very outspoken about sex, which in those days, was not discussed as explicitly as it is today. When I turned on the six o'clock evening news, I saw her and was amused and admired her free spirit. She became a radio personality instantaneously, and was soon well known in her profession.

My practice in New York grew steadily. Soon it was more advantageous for me to rent office space, rather than continue to pay by the hour. I found a suitable place on 14 East 60th Street, which I shared with a Chinese acupuncturist three days a week. Many doctors had their offices in that building. It was very convenient, just minutes away from where I lived. While I worked three days a week in New York, Joan managed my Morristown office.

My Visit to Israel and Egypt

Around Christmas 1982, I took a trip to Egypt and Israel, organized by the Council of Jewish Women for Jewish singles over forty. But there was no chance for me to meet someone. The few men on the tour, most of them in their sixties or seventies, were looking for forty-year-old women. Nevertheless, I enjoyed the trip very much. It was a year after Israel had made peace with Egypt. I found this ancient country extremely fascinating, with its many treasures. The people who had been hostile to Jews for years were now extremely friendly. Our Egyptian tour guide showed us the treasures of King Tut at the museum in Cairo, and went with us to his tomb with its well-preserved paintings deep inside. I sat on a camel in front of the pyramids, but was afraid to ride it. I should have known better than to attempt to do this, because I always was afraid to ride our horses at home. It stemmed from an incident my brother had with a Shetland pony that my father had just bought for us. Enthusiastically, Gerhard climbed on the pony without a saddle, but the animal forcefully threw him off, and my poor brother landed in the deep manure. While helplessly screaming for help, I had watched him sink, when finally the workers in our stables rescued him. From that moment I never rode another horse again.

Later I went into the pyramid, but before long I developed a tremendous headache and had to leave. The ride on the Nile and the majestic sculptures in the Valley of the Kings left a lasting impression on me. We were saddened when we visited the only Jewish synagogue in Cairo and an ancient cemetery, both of which were in terribly poor condition.

Israel had changed since I had last been there in 1971. It

had been built up quite a bit. We toured its many historic sites and enjoyed its magnificent landscapes. I always loved to return to Israel, but knew that I could never live there, because of the constant unrest. One day I visited my parents' graves in Haifa and Gerhard's grave in Chedera. He had died in 1980 in the asylum in Acre. What a tragic life he had led!

It was Christmas Eve and we wanted to take in the festivity in Bethlehem, surrounding the Church of the Nativity, but were greatly disappointed. Manger Square was filled with a huge crowd of people. Beggars and little children were constantly asking for money and merchants were offering their goods by yelling out loud in Arabic. There was too much commotion, and we soon returned to the hotel and watched the church ceremony, which was televised all over the world. The day before our departure, we were caught in an ice storm while walking on the Via de la Rosa in the old city of Jerusalem. It was treacherous walking on the slippery cobblestones. It hadn't snowed in Israel for many years. The very next morning we boarded the bus and drove on the icy road to the airport.

When I came home from my trip, Hope had some news for me. She had quit her job in a private law practice because her boss wouldn't give her a big enough increase in salary. In the two weeks that I was away she had already opened her own office. I was stunned and only hoped it would work out. In the beginning, she earned money by writing briefs for other lawyers. Of course, I had to supplement her income at first, but soon she was able to make a good living, and I was proud of her.

Last Rendezvous

Unexpectedly, Hank surfaced again. I had not heard from him for a year. He phoned from Florida and told me he was interested in getting an apartment in New York, and if I could send him the real estate section of the *New York Times.* I teased him and asked him, "What's gotten into you, are you becoming a spendthrift?" He told me he was a changed man and was spending his money. A few weeks later he called from New York and said that he had rented an apartment with a friend in Greenwich Village and would like to see me for dinner at a restaurant of my choice. I was curious and thought, *Why not?* Perhaps, he had changed as he said. We met at Vivaldi's on 58th Street and 2nd Avenue, a lovely Italian restaurant. We had not seen each other in almost two years. As always he was charming and pleasant to be with. He was surprised and couldn't understand why I had opened an office in New York; it surely was not for the money. He wanted to know whether I had met someone. I told him, "No Hank, after you I gave up on men. My main interest in life is Hope, who, by the way, is visiting me this weekend."

He obviously was disappointed. I didn't invite him to the apartment after dinner, but I told him to come for tea and see Hope the next day, which he did. She didn't care for him at all anymore, knowing that he had taken advantage of me. Her conversation was short with him and when she wanted to drive back to Philadelphia before it got dark, I accompanied her to her newly purchased car, which was parked on Park Avenue. Hank didn't make any attempt to come with us. When Hope kissed me goodbye she warned me, "Don't get involved with that creep again. I have an uneasy feeling about him." When I came back, Hank told me he had to leave soon because he had to go home to his friend for dinner. In a way I was glad. He had not told me whom he had rented the apartment with, and I was under the impression it was a gentleman friend. But when he said she had invited him for dinner I questioned him, "You haven't told me—who is that friend you are living with?" First he seemed hesitant. He was obviously annoyed that I had asked and said, "Listen, just because I live in New York, I want you to know I am not going to account for everything I am going to do here, and don't expect me to be around you all the time."

Secretive, as he always was, I was sure it must be someone he didn't want me to know about. I told him, "You know by now I have no intention of renewing our relationship. I don't expect anything of you. We will just remain casual friends. So, if you want to tell me who she is you are going to have dinner with, it's okay. I don't really care." Finally he came out with it. It was his former girlfriend, an art professor from Yale. She was twenty years younger than him. When we first met he had told me about their relationship. She was now married and lived with her husband in an apartment in New York in the village. While her husband was away on business she had invited him to spend some time with her.

Apparently that gigolo had the habit of keeping in touch with all his former lovers, including me. I had judged him right all along. He wanted to embrace and kiss me, but I felt nothing but disgust for him and told him, "It is over," and he left. That was the last time I saw him, although he still called every now and then.

At Dr. Reder's

After a nasty cold, I suffered from bursitis in my right shoulder, which caused me great discomfort while working. On recommendation of a patient I went to see Dr. Reder, whose office was just a few blocks from me, on 62nd and Park Avenue. He was known to perform "miracles." He had treated my patient, and her pain disappeared with just a few treatments. When I arrived at his office I was told Medicare did not cover his treatments, and I had to pay twenty-five dollars in advance. Every seat was taken, and some of the patients were even sitting on the floor of the large waiting room, which was decorated with antique furniture, precious paintings, and fine porcelain urns. I was ushered into the treatment room. It had three dental chairs, two of which were occupied by gentlemen. I sat in the middle one. Metal rods stuck out of their nostrils. Soon they started a conversation with me and even introduced themselves. I felt awkward sitting there with them.

The man on my left was the famous composer, Julie Stein. He was in his sixties. He was pale faced and sitting crouched over in his chair. He looked like death takes a holiday, and told me he had been coming to the doctor daily for thirteen years. He praised the doctor and said that without him he would not be able to walk or work. Why so long, I wondered? I was told one needs only a few treatments. The other gentleman, a bank president, was less talkative.

Soon, the doctor, a little man in his eighties with thick eyeglasses, appeared. First he took care of the two gentlemen by removing their rods from their noses and asking them to come back in the afternoon. Then, without washing his hands he came to me, and asked, "Where is your pain?" I cautiously raised my right arm until it hurt. Not saying a word, he then went to an old-fashioned sterilizer and retrieved two metal rods from the boiling water. He twirled cotton around them and dipped them into a small brown bottle. Then he inserted those swabs into each nostril, the same way the other patients had had them. "Go into the waiting room until you are called," he told me. After twenty minutes, I was sitting in the same chair again and Dr. Reder removed the swabs. He ordered me to raise my arm as high as possible. To my surprise I was able to raise it without the slightest pain. "How does it feel?" he asked with a smile. "It's a miracle," I exclaimed. Overjoyed, I jumped up from my chair, grabbed the little doctor's face, and kissed him on both cheeks twice. Right away, I was embarrassed about my uncontrolled behavior.

He asked me to come twice a day for a week. But I couldn't do that. I had to return to Morristown by Monday at noon. So he agreed to see me that same afternoon, and again on Sunday and Monday morning. I thought perhaps I could insert the cotton swabs at home if my dentist would give me this numbing agent.

When I left his office I walked on clouds. I cannot describe the euphoria I now was in. It was a different feeling than from drinking alcohol. I pranced along Park Avenue without a care in the world, and oh, so happy! I had the feeling everybody noticed my happiness. I liked when people turned around, and never felt so exhilarated in my life. After walking in my high-heeled shoes for a long time in this state of delirium, I went home and slumped into bed.

By the time I returned to Dr. Reder's office in the afternoon, I was my own self again. Apparently, the tincture had lost its effect and the pain started to return, though not as severe as before. With the second treatment I did not experience such sublime happiness. The next day, on Sunday, while sitting in Dr. Reder's waiting room with my rods in my nostrils, I met Jack Nicholson, who had come from California, to be treated by this famous doctor. He had just gone through a divorce and was very talkative about it. Everyone was sociable.

An elderly gentleman told me all about himself. His son was running on the Democratic ticket for the vice presidency, but lost. Then he was sobbing because he had lost his wife recently and could not get over her loss.

A woman whose husband was the owner of the Twenty-One Club chatted with me. Her name was also Frieda. She had her little dachshund with her, whom I happily patted. Before she left, she asked me to meet her for lunch at her club, but I couldn't accept the invitation.

On Monday morning before leaving for Morristown I innocently asked the doctor to sell me a bottle of his tincture because, as a nurse, I was familiar with inserting swabs. That way, I could continue doing this at home during the week, and I would come back on Friday. He looked at me, frowning, and abruptly said, "No, I can't give it to you." I wondered why, but didn't ask any further. I thought, *Oh well, my dentist probably has the same tincture. I am sure he will let me have it.*

When I returned to Morristown I called my dentist and asked him to give me a vial of Xylocaine (the numbing agent dentist's use). He just said, "Frieda, I have bad vibes," and he refused. Then I called a former patient who was a pharmacist and told her my experience. She answered, "You are naive, Frieda, you had sniffed cocaine." Of course, she didn't give me the tincture. I had to endure the discomfort of bursitis pain until it naturally subsided on its own.

A year later, on May 14, 1984, the *New York Magazine* wrote an article about Dr. Reder with the headline: "Dr. Reder meets cocaine on Park Avenue." (I still have the article.) It said that he was legally permitted to dispense cocaine but only in his office. For me it was a drug whose efficacy lasted but a few hours and then wore off; but it was an experience.

Hope Finds Her Soulmate

Hope often visited me in New York on weekends. She was almost twenty-eight. I had the feeling she was lonely and was looking for a meaningful relationship. Whenever she came, I tried to make her stay very pleasant, taking her to nice places to eat and buying her clothes.

Sometime in spring 1983, a young man, Howard, called her for a blind date. A mutual friend had given him Hope's phone number. They talked for hours on the phone and when he asked her where he could pick her up for a date, they discovered they both lived at the same place, "The Dorchester." They met and soon fell in love. Hope and some of her friends shared a summerhouse on the beach in Ventnor, New Jersey, and now her new boyfriend, Howard, joined the group. The weekend before the Fourth of July, Hope invited me to come to the shore and meet Howard. I arrived by bus from New York, and he and Hope met me at the station. Howard, a handsome, dark-haired young man with a warm bright smile, made a good impression on me. He had impeccable manners, and he opened the door to the car for me as we drove off to have lunch. All afternoon we spent a relaxing time at the beach. Howard had a winning personality and persuaded me to stay overnight. The next morning, all three of us relaxed and enjoyed the beautiful sunshine at the beach.

In the early afternoon, Hope expected a client, so she had to leave us for a while. Howard and I decided to go for a walk along the beach, and he told me about his family and his plans for the future. I was surprised when he suddenly asked whether he measured up to my expectations. Hope had not yet confided in me whether Howard would be her choice to marry, so I told him that he was a very nice young man and that I was glad he and Hope were sharing a beautiful friendship.

I had a good feeling about their relationship. He was intelligent, soon to finish his chief residency in radiology at Penn, and from a good Jewish family. I knew he would be right for Hope. When I spoke with Hope on the phone the next day, I told her that I would approve of Howard very much.

The next week was the Fourth of July weekend. It was a hot summer day. I had no plans but to relax by the pool at the club and watch the fireworks from the roof terrace later that evening. Shortly before noon, Hope called, "Mom, what are you doing today?" My first thought was, she couldn't possibly ask me to come out to see her? I told her that I just intended to take it easy. Then there was a pause : "Mom, Howard and I want to come and see you. We have something good to tell you." I knew right away the reason for their coming to New York.

Oh, was I thrilled! After she hung up I did not know what to do first. I was too excited to prepare a meal for them, so I made reservations at a steak house, the Coach House on 61st and Madison Avenue. Then I phoned a friend who was in the jewelry business and asked her to bring over a cultured pearl necklace, the finest quality she had, to give Hope as an engagement present. A few hours later the happy couple arrived with a big bouquet of flowers and announced their engagement. With tears of joy we kissed and embraced each other. Both called Howard's parents in Cleveland to tell them the good news. We spent some happy hours at the restaurant and then the young couple returned to Philadelphia. I was very happy and grateful that my Hope had found such a lovely young man to share her life with.

A few weeks later, Howard's parents came to Philadelphia to meet us. Wedding plans were made and the date was set for February 4, 1984. The wedding was going to be in Philadelphia at the newly built Four Seasons Hotel, with the religious ceremony at Temple Rodeph Shalom. Hope made all the arrangements herself.

Thanksgiving Day weekend, Howard's parents invited us to come to Cleveland and meet all of their relatives. It was an exciting time.

But nothing in life goes smoothly. There is always something that mars a happy occasion. I had trouble in my office with Joan. She had been with me for two years and had earned a good salary in the first year, and in the second year, her income rose to thirty-two thousand dollars, which was excellent for someone without a professional degree. She always seemed to be appreciative and satisfied. I had full confidence in her and treated her like my own daughter. But, on her vacation in August, she had met a young man, and after that I noticed a change in her. She seemed to be disinterested in working, showed up late for her appointments, and looked generally unhappy. I could not quite figure out what was bothering her. But, I wanted her to attend Hope's wedding and so, I gave her a beautiful black evening gown from Hope and custom jewelry to wear with it.

I noticed that since August my business had dropped, but I attributed it to the bad economy. I thought, now that she did not make as much money, perhaps she might be dissatisfied.

Two weeks before Hope's wedding, Bob, my accountant, discovered that there was an enormous decline in income. He thought something was very strange. He urged me to let Joan go immediately. But I was too attached and I could not do it myself. Bob and Howard volunteered to do it. They drove from Philadelphia early the following Monday morning and fired her on the spot. I was not present when it happened, but they told me it went well. They just told her that her services were no longer required. She did not ask any questions. Apparently she knew why. Of course, she did not attend the wedding.

The wedding was a beautiful celebration. Hope looked exquisite in her pinkish-white wedding gown and Howard was handsome in his tuxedo, but he looked so pale during the religious services, I was worried about him. As I watched with happiness and pride, the rabbi bestowed God's blessings on the couple in a solemn ceremony, while Cantor Summers from the Short Hills Synagogue sang. (He had come especially to chant at the ceremony.) I wished Hans could have been present. After services all guests were transported by trolley to the Four Seasons Hotel. The grand ballroom was beautifully decorated with flowers. Everybody had a great time dancing to a great orchestra until late in the night. The couple left on their honeymoon to the Islands, and all out-of-town guests were invited for brunch the next day.

When the party was over and I drove back to New York I was caught in a terrible ice and snowstorm on the Turnpike. After many hours of hazardous driving I finally arrived home, exhausted but happy to have given Hope and Howard a celebration that they will always remember with joy.

Soon after the wedding, Hank called me again. I had not heard from him for some time. I told him that Hope had married and he wanted to know why he had not been invited. He had "chutzpah." I told him that I had no reason to include him in our circle of friends. That ended the conversation.

After Joan had left, I worked hard in both offices and decided to ease my burden by hiring a secretary. She took care of appointments and bookkeeping. But in October 1985, my hectic schedule came to an end. My office building in New York had undergone major renovations. My rent was raised three times the amount I used to pay per year, making it unprofitable for me to continue to work there. In a way, I was glad the problem of juggling my time between two places had resolved itself. It was time to take life easier. I knew Hope was well taken care of and happy, which gave me great peace of mind.

Howard had finished his residency at Penn and had been invited by his professor to come to Sweden for four months fellowship at his hospital. It was an offer he couldn't refuse. Hope could not go with him. The thought of separation loomed heavily over the young couple.

I wanted them to enjoy the month before his departure in

July and so I rented a beach house for them in Brigantine. They invited their friends for weekends. The traffic made it difficult for me to drive to the shore, but I didn't want to miss seeing the happy couple, and we always had a great time together.

After the first month of separation, Hope and Howard met for one week in Paris, and again the next month they spent a week together in Italy. Each time parting was painful for them. Therefore, they decided not see each other again until his fellowship ended in October. Then he surprised us by coming home in September for an interview for a position as a radiologist at Jeanes and Fox Case Cancer Hospital in Philadelphia. It was around the time of the High Holidays, and we were very happy to have him home.

Howard had to decide within the few days he was here whether to accept the position. He was tempted to take the offer, but was faced with an ethical dilemma. While he was still chief resident at the University of Pennsylvania Medical School he had promised the medical board that he would accept a teaching position at their school after the fellowship in Sweden. He felt it would be unethical to back out of that commitment now and take this very promising position at Jeanes. With a lot of persuasion, we convinced him to accept this new offer, which was financially more advantageous than the professorship at Penn. The new position started in October, immediately after his return from Sweden. It was a good decision.

About two months after Howard's return, at Christmas time, the young couple visited me. While Hope and I were out shopping, Hank had called to wish me a happy New Year. Howard answered the phone. He knew what kind of a jerk Hank was and he told him not to call me again. Howard must have been very effective because I have never heard from him again. Years later, Hank told a mutual friend that the biggest mistake he made in his life was not having married me. Frankly, I never had any intentions of marrying. I would have been content just to find a meaningful relationship.

March 1985 brought my seventieth birthday. I had never had a major celebration on any of my birthdays. Hans had never given me presents until Hope was older and insisted that he bring me flowers. It wasn't important to me, anyway, and most of the time I was working. I remember my 60th in 1975. I was sitting at Hans's s bedside after his colon cancer operation at Mount Sinai Hospital. Now, I was going to be seventy and I awaited my birthday with some degree of trepidation.

My birthday fell on a Saturday, and Hope and Howard came from Philadelphia to spend the weekend with me, and take me out to dinner at the Essex House on Central Park South. We were all dressed in our finery, and when we arrived at the restaurant the maitre d' took us all the way to the end of the large dining room and then opened a door to a dark room. Suddenly, as we entered, all the lights went on. Surprise! Balloons decorated the entire room. Relatives and friends were singing "Happy Birthday," and I was shocked. It was a lovely party. I appreciated how thoughtful my children were to give me my first big birthday celebration.

Becoming a Grandmother

There was another surprise a few months later. I went to Philadelphia to celebrate Mother's Day with them. They gave me a beautiful album with photos of my 70th birthday. Just as I was admiring my present, Hope announced, "Mom, we have a better present yet. You are going to be a grandmother."

I was thrilled and embraced both my children. How wonderful to hear such good news! Of course, every mother is concerned when the daughter is expecting, and I was no exception. But I had good reason to worry. When I was pregnant with Hope, I had been given an injection, called Des (a drug to avoid a miscarriage), which was later withdrawn from the market because of severe side effects in the offspring. The one dose had left only slight changes in Hope's uterine lining but I was concerned that it could affect Hope's pregnancy.

On Saturday, January 4, 1986, little Rachel was born, a beautiful, healthy baby. It was an exciting day! I had just come home from Temple Emanuel when Hope called, "Mom, you are a grandmother now. We have a beautiful baby girl." I let out a scream of joy and told her I would leave New York instantly to come and see the baby. On the Turnpike, I told the collector, "I have just become a grandma. I am so excited I can't find my ticket, sir," and he let me go through.

The ride to Philadelphia seamed to take forever. It was beautiful to see my happy and grateful children with little Rachel, a sight I will never forget. As I held that precious baby in my arms I thanked God for the gift that He had given us.

Shortly before Rachel was born, Howard and Hope had moved into a two-bedroom condo in the suburbs. When Hope came home with the baby, she had a nurse helping out for several weeks. I came almost every week after the nurse left. I loved to bathe and feed Rachel. I began thinking of moving to Philadelphia, but did not quite know how I could work it out.

The condo they had bought was not ideal for raising a child. It was situated on the main thoroughfare at Montgomery Avenue and Cheswold Lane in Haverford. It didn't even have enough space for a sleep-in nanny, who had to sleep on a cot in the baby's room.

One evening, about three months after Rachel was born, Hope phoned me. "Mom, we found our dream house, but we need your help. We talked to our accountant and he agreed we should buy the house. Could you give us a bridge loan, until we sell the condo?" How could I refuse? I saw the house the next weekend. It was still under construction, so I could not see much, but as long as they liked it, it was all right with me.

A few months later they moved into their dream house. It was a spacious place situated on beautiful wooded grounds in a good residential area. Little by little they furnished some of the rooms. But Rachel's room was complete and tastefully done. It was a joy to see my little Rachel develop so beautifully. I couldn't wait to come out on weekends to see her. I spent less and less time in my apartment in New York.

Rachel was about five months old when one Monday morning, before leaving for Morristown, I wanted to kiss little Rachel goodbye. Unfortunately, I slipped on the steps leading into the sunken living room where she was lying in her playpen, and I hurt my back. For a moment I blacked out. At first the pain was tolerable. I didn't know what possessed me but I got into my car and drove off to keep my appointments in Morristown. By the time I reached my office I was most uncomfortable and was unable to work. My secretary took me to the hospital to see an orthopedist. The doctor found a fracture in the hip socket. He told me that there was nothing he could do but give me painkillers. It had to heal by itself. I was allowed to walk if I could stand the pain, but it was impossible for me to work. After few days, I told my children what had happened and Howard came immediately, and drove me back to Philadelphia. There I spent most of the time lying on the couch watching my adorable grandbaby in her playpen and crawling on the floor.

Unfortunately, my recuperation took longer than was anticipated. The pain did not diminish. Finally I consulted a doctor at the University of Pennsylvania who found the fracture was not in the hip socket but in the fifth thoracic vertebra. It was too late to do anything now. It had to heal by itself.

While spending a month with my family and enjoying that little baby, I asked myself, *How could I possibly continue living in New York without her?* I came to the conclusion I should give up my apartment in New York and move to Philadelphia. I talked it over with Hope and Howard and they thought it was a great idea. I wanted to live near my children but was not well enough to look for a suitable place yet. I called a real estate company and my New York apartment was sold within a week. I didn't even have to be present for the sale. Hope arranged for the moving people to put my furniture into storage in Philadelphia. When I was well enough to look for an apartment, I found one at the Green Hill Apartments on City Line, fifteen minutes away from my family. It was a beautiful, spacious two-bedroom place with a terrace overlooking the well-kept grounds of the apartment complex. It had all the comfort of luxury living, including an indoor and outdoor swimming pool, tennis courts, and a garage. I was happy to have made the move.

Soon I resumed my work in Morristown, and came on weekends to my new, beautiful place. I loved spending time with little Rachel. It didn't take long to befriend some single women where I lived. Although I never regretted the move, I missed New York, and even now I go back periodically to see the latest shows.

In 1988, little Dana arrived. Hope had to have bed rest for

ten or twelve weeks during her pregnancy, but everything went well and everyone was happy with the new arrival. She was a cute, healthy baby and reminded me a lot of Hope. I enjoyed bathing my little grandchildren on weekends, and tried to be helpful whenever I could. The long weekly commute to my Morristown office was very tedious. On one of my trips, I must have been very tired. For a second I had closed my eyes and suddenly found myself veering to the right side, heading into a ditch. Luckily, I was driving in the slow lane or I could have caused a serious accident. I immediately decided to hire a driver, which made life much easier for me. He is still driving my family whenever needed, which is quite often.

Retirement

Not to long thereafter I consulted a dermatologist, Dr. Herald Farber, for some minor skin problem. He had just opened a spacious office on 140 Montgomery Avenue, in Bala Cynwyd. After going to him for treatments a few times, I noticed that some of his rooms were unoccupied. I thought this would be an ideal place to do electrolysis and I asked him if he would sublet one of his rooms, and he agreed. Now I was excited about this new business venture.

I had, unfortunately, missed the deadline for advertisement in the telephone book. I also had strong competition here on Main Line in Lucy Peters. She placed huge, alluring ads in major magazines and newspapers. So the beginning was slow. I was hoping to close my Morristown office eventually. It was getting to be too much to hold two offices. Just then, a totally unexpected opportunity developed.

On a routine visit to my dentist in Morristown, his technician came in and introduced himself as the husband of a former patient, whom I had treated some twenty years ago. I remembered her. Dorothy was a young registered nurse about to get married, with severe facial hair growth, which I had successfully treated. When I asked how she was doing, her husband told me that they had four children and that Dorothy had given up nursing. She was now working in real estate. I suggested that perhaps she could find someone who would want to buy my practice in Morristown. I would be willing to train the person, and Dorothy could make a commission.

The very next morning Dorothy called me and said, "You are not going to sell your office to anyone but me." I was amazed at how resolute she was. I told her to come and we would talk.

She was an attractive young woman in her early forties with a pleasing personality, and, after testing her for good hand-eye coordination, I thought she would be perfect to take over my business. She was very eager to learn and applied herself remarkably well. The lawyers for both parties had worked out an agreement whereby she would pay me over a period of five years.

In January 1990, she took over my practice, using my special needles, and even retained the name Frieda Lefeber in all telephone advertisements and on the shingle at her office door. I felt my patients were in good hands with her. She still is very appreciative and visits me once a year. It had changed her life completely. She was able to send her four children through college without any help from her husband, whom she divorced shortly after she took over my practice. She told me she blesses the day she met me.

Now I was semi-retired and just worked in my Main Line office three days a week. But in 1991, Dr. Farber took in an assistant and needed my room. He only could let me have the room for one day, which was not enough. I was disappointed and after three and half years I closed the office. I simply no longer had the energy to start all over again, to look for another place. It would involve too much work. I felt that at the age of seventy-six I was entitled to retire.

Learning To Paint

At first it felt strange to be without work. My life was no longer regimented by constant appointments. Now I could sleep late in the morning, which I liked. But I soon realized that lazing around all day without any purpose was not satisfying. Almost all my adult life I had worked, and tried to accomplish something, and now I didn't know what to do with myself. I never liked to watch soap operas or television for any length of time. Card games, like bridge, were impossible for me to learn because I could never concentrate long enough on the game. Reading was hard for me because I have some eye muscle weakness. I was searching for something that might interest me, but couldn't find the right thing.

One day my friend, June, who had taught art at one time, visited me. She saw a small painting hanging on the wall in my living room that I had done when Hope was six years old, while she was sitting on a sofa in our living room. I had purchased a trial set of oil paints and a small canvas and finished the painting in one day. But my hands got so messy that I couldn't get rid of the dirt under my fingernails. Since I couldn't possibly treat patients with those fingernails I gave up my first and only attempt in dabbling in art, and threw out the paint set and brushes. I kept the picture, and placed it in a cheap, narrow metal frame. June was admiring it and thought it was charming. She advised me to take lessons from a teacher, Zelda, who taught art classes at the Green Hill Apartments on Thursdays.

I went to Zelda's art class the following week. She had set up a still life of a fruit bowl, flowers, and a wine jug on the windowsill, and she asked me to do a quick sketch of it. When I was finished with the drawing, she told me I had talent. I was not sure whether she meant it or whether she just wanted another student in her class. However, the following week, I showed up for class with the oil paints, brushes, and canvas she had asked me to buy. It was quite expensive and I hoped it would not be a waste.

I was eager to paint the still life, and Zelda helped me a lot. It took many lessons before it was finally finished, and I was proud of my accomplishment. Hope was amazed at what I had accomplished. She showed it with pride to all her neighbors and friends. I am sure the picture wouldn't have turned out as well without Zelda's help. I looked forward to my weekly lesson and was fascinated and eager to learn. In time I was accepted as a student in art appreciation at the Barnes Museum, where I had the great opportunity to view the magnificent paintings of the masters firsthand. The classes were held once a week for three hours and the course lasted two years. I never missed a class.

At one time I set up my own still life in Zelda's art class. I bought fresh vegetables: romaine lettuce, red and green peppers, carrots, scallions, a lemon, and a cucumber, and I placed them on a large pewter platter, which was resting on an embroidered tablecloth. Every week I had to replenish the vegetables for the art class at a cost of six dollars, because they had wilted or shriveled. It took me eight weeks to complete this still life. I received high praise from everyone. Although the painting was expensive, I was pleased that everyone liked it. It was placed in a prominent spot in our den.

Soon, I realized that painting only once a week did not satisfy me. I was happy that I had found an interest in art and wanted to learn more. I heard that Rosemont College was offering painting and drawing classes twice a week. Senior citizens only had to pay fifty dollars per semester, so I signed up. Pat Nugent, the head of the department, gave me encouragement and I learned a lot. I turned out many paintings, and every one was hung in fine, decorative frames in Hope's house. I never got tired of painting and was looking for further instruction.

Eventually, I enrolled in continuing education classes at the Pennsylvania Academy of the Fine Arts. The hours were evenings twice a week from five to nine-thirty. Oliver Grimley was my first drawing teacher there and Pat Traub my first figure painting instructor. I was a real novice in figure painting. I had never drawn or painted a nude figure and did not even know how to begin, but slowly I learned. I wondered what those teachers thought I was doing there with so little experience.

In the summer of 1992, The Pennsylvania Academy of the Fine Arts offered students a one-month course in Florence, Italy, at the Sacci International Art School. Our life-drawing teacher, Toni Visco, taught eight students from the academy.

We roomed on the fourth floor of an old fourteenth century house. It was very primitive, but we didn't care. Sometimes we cooked our own meals, and often we ate out with Toni, who was our constant companion. He showed us the treasures of that magnificent city. Although the teachers from Sacci were not wonderful, I enjoyed being able to paint all day. It was a great experience and we had much fun.

Later that summer I accepted an invitation from my former roommate, Edith. We had been student nurses in Berlin. She now lived in Laguna Beach, California. I had not seen her since the early years in New York, when we roomed together at 100th Street and Broadway, but we had kept in touch. She was always a character, a free spirit that had a very active sex life before her marriage. At one time she lived with a young German refugee doctor, a gynecologist who had fallen madly in love with her. His office and living quarters were on the ground floor of an apartment building on the upper West Side of Manhattan. After a short courtship the young couple had decided, on the spur of the moment, to get married, and they asked me to be their witness at city hall. The ceremony was brief, and after quick lunch in a cafeteria, we parted.

A few days later, Edith appeared at our landlady Mrs. Lange's, with all her belongings, very distraught and red-eyed.

At first she did not want to talk about what happened, but after much prodding she told us.

On the night of the wedding, the groom had an emergency call from Mount Sinai Hospital. One of his patients had gone into labor, and he had to leave his bride. After hours of waiting, Edith called in the elevator man and celebrated her marriage with a bottle of champagne. When the groom returned to his home he found the bride in bed with the elevator man. That was the end of their marriage.

A few years later, Edith married another doctor, formerly from the Jewish hospital of Berlin. When war broke out in 1941, her husband joined the U.S. Army as a captain. They were stationed in New Mexico and lived there after the war.

I had not heard from her in those years. When she surfaced again in New York, she was a widow. Her husband, Gerhard, had died of a heart attack at a very young age, but had left her a sizable life insurance policy and pension. She grieved over him, but not for long.

Next, she married an Italian man who was the retired chauffeur of a reputed New York mafia figure. They were only married a short time when he died. Now she mourned two men. She went back to private duty nursing at Mount Sinai and lived in an integrated neighborhood on West 96th Street. One night, she was attacked in her hallway. That's when she decided to move to Laguna Beach, California.

The visit with Edith was a total disaster. Edith was a different person now from when I had known her. How she had changed! She was a nut case. Not only did she arrive at the airport late, telling me she couldn't find the entrance, but after she picked me up, she couldn't find her way home. It took her an hour instead of the fifteen minutes it should have taken to get from the airport to my motel. As soon as we arrived, she asked me to change into my bathing suit to go swimming with her. Because she had to pick me up at the airport, she had missed her swim session. She had a daily routine of a one-hour walk, one-hour aerobic exercise, one-hour stretch exercise, and one-hour swimming. It was a compulsive behavior.

After swimming, she served dinner, a fatty lamb stew, which I did not like and ate only a small portion. She was insulted and asked, "Why, you had told me that you weren't a fussy eater and would eat anything that is put in front of you!" I had to explain that I could not digest fatty food and I wasn't hungry.

She tried to impress me by telling me what a remarkable and charitable person she is. She was donating the monthly checks that she received from the German restitution office to children's organizations. She also was a member of an organization for planet and wildlife preservation and was on the board of directors of many Jewish welfare organizations. When I told her she probably was the Jewish "Mother Teresa" she smiled. She said she was a concerned citizen and was constantly writing to senators and presidents trying to improve conditions. She belonged to the Democratic Party and found President Regan stupid. When I told her I belonged to the Republican Party, she was outraged. It made no sense to argue with her. I soon changed the conversation topic and we reminisced about our life as student nurses in Berlin and the early years in New York.

It was late in the evening and I was tired. The motel was only a five-minute ride away, but she said it would be easier for her if I lived in her house. That way, she would not have to take me back every night. Although I would rather have stayed in the motel, I agreed to move in with her the next day. That was a major mistake. She repeatedly let me know how much effort and planning she had put into showing me a good time. She had made out the menu of what to serve for the next few days. But, when she saw that I did not like her lamb stew, it upset her greatly. Fortunately, I convinced her that it would be better if we ate our meals on the road when she wanted me to see the surrounding, so we could order what each one desired. She went along with that.

But she insisted that I had to conform to her regimented daily exercises and swimming. I could not believe when she asked me to take my daily shower at the swimming pool because she had not turned on her hot water in years, in order to conserve energy and help the environment. While I was on the West Coast I had intended to visit my cousin Joachim and his wife, Enci in San Diego for a day or two. When I told her my intention she was upset. I should have told her that before she had made so many plans. Actually she had not made any plan other than her daily routine of exercises, which exhausted me and was not my idea of a vacation. She constantly criticized me. I finally could not take it any more, and after three days I left.

I went back to the motel and called my relatives in San Diego. They told me to come and I stayed with them a few days and recuperated from Edith. I had a lovely time in San Diego after those stressful days with her. I never heard from her again.

Israel Revisited

Later in 1992, I had an opportunity to join a group of representatives of the Jewish federation for a one-week mission to Israel. I had not been there since the late seventies, and was amazed at how it had grown. To visit that historical land always evokes sentimental feelings in me, both because it is where my family found refuge from oppression and where they had labored for many years to make the country what it is today, and because of the significance of its history in regard to the identity of my people.

As representatives of the Jewish federation, an organization that contributes financially to Israel, we were welcomed and escorted by the Israeli government. They proudly showed us their country and explained their valiant history. As I had done on previous visits to Jerusalem, I visited the memorial (Yad Vashem) for the six million Jews who perished in the Holocaust. It always moves me and fills me with deep sadness.

While in Jerusalem, I visited my cousin Hertha's son, Jehuda Oppenheim, and his family. His parents had died in Australia. Jehuda practiced psychiatry at Hadassah Hospital in Jerusalem. He lived in the part of the city where only orthodox Jews live. I intended to call on him on a Saturday, but he did not permit me to come, because he did not want me to travel on Shabbat. I had to choose another day to visit him for lunch. His pretty wife wore a *scheitel* ("a hairpiece"), which is a sign of orthodoxy. I was sad to learn about the fate of his grandparents (my Uncle Adolf, Aunt Bertha, and their son Herman, formerly from Kuestrin). All three perished in Auschwitz.

The visit to Israel was most informative. It was amazing to see the determination and enthusiasm that the people showed.

They can indeed be proud of their achievements in the fields of medical science, computer science, and engineering. It is too bad that the constant unrest in Israel has prevented me from even considering living in that beautiful country.

The following year, in June, my friend Pearl, a fine watercolorist, and I, joined a group of artists who painted for four weeks in Monet's garden in Giverny, France. We were permitted to paint in it from five to eight in the evenings and all day Monday. It was the first time that I painted without the supervision of a teacher. We had a most delightful time, enjoying painting outdoors all day and attending parties at night. Monet's stepdaughter once occupied the house we lived in, just a short walk away from Monet's garden.

Sometimes, we would take a train ride to Paris, which was less than an hour away. One day, coming home from Paris, I was shocked when I discovered that my wallet had been stolen. It was just three days before we were to go home to the United States. It must have happened while I was making a phone call in a pub near the train station in Vernon. I was desperate. I reported it to the police in Giverny, who thought I might have just lost it in the pub or in the train station. The policeman offered to drive me back to the pub to ask the proprietor to look for it. Some of my friends came along to search. Was I happy when Pearl found the wallet in a trashcan! Only my money (about two hundred dollars) was missing. All my credit cards and credentials were untouched. Very happy and greatly relieved, I invited everyone in our group, including the nice policeman, for lunch the next day.

After a month of rest at home, I took a two-week workshop in portrait painting with Frank Covino, in Pueblo, Colorado. I learned a lot from him and decided to follow him to Meeker, Colorado, the very northern part of the state, for another workshop. The camaraderie among the students was great. I painted portraits of Rachel and Dana from photographs, which showed a good resemblance to the children. After the course in Meeker I rented a car and drove, in a torrential rainstorm, from the northernmost part of Colorado to surprise my family in Snow Mass, where they were vacationing. When it got dark I discovered that the high beams didn't work, which made driving extremely hazardous. Totally exhausted, I was lucky to find the last hotel room available in a Snow Mass motel. After few hours of sound sleep I surprised my family. They immediately came over to my motel for a hearty breakfast. Proudly, I presented them with the portraits, which they all loved. They hang in a prominent place in our family room. Unfortunately, I was unable to tolerate the high elevation at Snow Mass. My pulse became irregular and I had to return to Philadelphia after three days.

I don't know what it was that made me always eager to learn more about art. I had a tremendous drive to acquire more knowledge and skill in painting. Often, I lost track of time and painted into the early morning hours and every so often I forgot to eat a meal. I was happy that I had found a hobby that brought meaning and interest into my life. In October, I took two more workshops with Frank, one in Seattle, Washington, and the other in San Diego, California. Since then, I have painted a number of group portraits for my family and friends.

I always enjoyed my learning vacations, and in June 1994, I signed up for a four-week painting workshop at Lake Como in Northern Italy, one of the most beautiful parts of the world that I have ever seen. The teacher, Diana Willis, taught me a different technique. It always amazes me how much there is to learn in art. It seems endless.

On weekends, when we had no classes, my classmates and I took excursions to Lake Lugano, Lake Maggiore, and St. Moritz, Switzerland. I enjoyed that workshop and in 1998 and 2002 I joined again Diana's workshops in Italy.

Hope was always worried about me driving to evening classes because they were in an unsafe neighborhood. I had already taken two years of lessons at the academy when I decided to enroll in the day program for the fall semester in 1994. I was happy to be accepted into their four-year certificate program at the age of seventy-nine.

The following four years at the academy were some of the happiest in my life. They gave me a real sense of accomplishment and a feeling of self-esteem, and invoked in me a freedom that I had never experienced before. I met some wonderful people who had the same desire as I had: to express themselves through art.

Aunt Gerda's Inheritance

In late 1994, Aunt Gerda died at the age of 101, leaving behind twenty-six million dollars. Most of the money was bequeathed to the city of New York, but her lawyer informed me that she left me fifty thousand dollars. I must say I was surprised! Why me? I felt she should have left it to Hope, her grandniece, or better yet, made her executor of her estate. But she didn't, and I felt I shouldn't benefit from that inheritance alone. I decided that I would use the money to celebrate my 80th birthday and invite my family on a trip to Paris.

In May of 1995, all five of us flew to Paris in business class, and spent almost half of Aunt Gerda's inheritance in one week. We enjoyed a memorable eight days vacation in luxury at the Ritz Hotel, visiting museums, enjoying French cuisine, and visiting Monet's Giverny. The children were impressed and loved Paris. It was money well spent. I planned to use the rest of the money for my 85th birthday.

After the family left Paris, I joined a group of fourteen students from the academy in Aix en Province, in the south of France. Doug Martinson was our teacher. We stayed in an old, dilapidated castle in Saint Remy, but the food was excellent. Every day we drove in a van to the sites near Mont St. Victoire, where Paul Cezanne used to paint, or to Arles where Van Gogh had been hospitalized and painted magnificent pictures.

One beautiful morning, while sitting on the terrace of the castle eating breakfast, a young couple sitting at the next table engaged in an argument in German. I turned around and jokingly said in German, "Don't say anything bad about me, because I can understand every word you are saying." They were startled and amused, and we began to converse. They told me they were on their honeymoon. Their wedding had been the night before and they had driven by car all night from Pyrmont, in northern Germany. That's why they were cranky. Both spoke English very well. Christiane was educated in England and Andreas had studied farming in South Africa for several years. He had taken over his parents' property in northern Germany, where he was going to farm and live with his bride. They were a handsome, young couple. Our group invited them to join us after dinner for drinks, and we talked and laughed long into the night.

After two weeks, the rest of the group returned to Philadelphia while I took a painting course at the famous Ecole des Beaux-Arts in Paris. I stayed at a small hotel, the Brighton, at 218 Rue de Rivoli, in an attic room with a small balcony overlooking the Tuilleries, and the D'Orsey Museum. It was just a short walk to the Louvre, where I had dinner every night in the basement restaurants.

I felt like a young student, and walked every morning over the Pont de Noeuf Bridge to school. We painted nude male and female models sitting side by side in lounge chairs on the lawn in the beautiful garden, while students not belonging to our class walked by and looked on.

The young couple, Christiane and Andreas, who had become my friends, surprised me with a visit in Paris and took me to a beautiful dinner party in Versailles. The host of that party was Andreas' school friend. When we arrived at his house I discovered that the man had a Pennsylvania license plate on his Mercedes. He explained to me that he had just recently moved from Philadelphia, where he had worked for a chemical company, and that his children were still attending college there. What a small world! I kept in touch with Andreas and Christiane after they left, and promised them I would visit them the following year.

My Move *to* Flat Rock Road

While attending the academy, I usually spent all of my time outside of class with my family, helping Hope prepare dinner or attending to the children's needs, and returning home to my apartment late to sleep. I had hardly made use of the lovely place at Green Hill in all those years.

So it was no wonder when Howard and Hope asked me whether I would like to give up my apartment and live with them. I was delighted. They engaged an architect and enlarged the house to 8,000-square-feet with enough room for me to have privacy. (They built for me a spacious living room, a bedroom and bath, and a beautiful studio with ski lights.) The renovation took four months, and in January 1996, I moved into my new quarters.

Life with my family has been a very happy and rewarding one. Most of the time we get along fine. Howard is especially kind to me. I receive a lot of love from all of them. It is a joy to see the girls grow. I am never lonely having them around me. I am included in all their parties, even my children's friends invite me to their festivities. I try to be helpful whenever I can, by going food shopping, sometimes carpooling the children, or taking them to doctor's appointments, because Hope is busy with her legal work.

I have always liked tradition and on Friday nights I would prepare a festive table with a fine tablecloth, flowers, my parents' silver candles, and wine. I always baked the challah ("braided bread"). After the children recited the *broches* ("blessings"), Shabbat dinner would be served. It was always a festive time and the family enjoyed my cooking. Now these lovely Friday dinners take place occasionally because the girls have dates to go out with their friends.

The years at the academy went by fast. In my third year, I was given my own studio at the Academy. I had to learn to work on my own, without a teacher's constant supervision. At first I was lost, but after a short while I felt comfortable painting independently.

The following summer, I visited Andreas and Christiana in Boerry, Germany for a few days. The young couple was very hospitable. I loved their beautiful and massive nineteenth-century red stone house with its bright, red-tiled roof. The huge, cobble-stoned courtyard was surrounded by storage structures built in the same style as the main building. They showed me the picturesque, sprawling countryside, which inspired me to paint.

From there I went by train to Berlin to join an Elderhostel group which was studying the post-war development of Germany. We stayed at a comfortable hotel in Berlin near the Kurfurstendam. It was amazing to see how much the city had been restored. It was quite safe to use the subway, so I visited the Jewish hospital again after nearly twenty years.

With the help of private donations, the city of Berlin had been able to restore and enlarge the hospital. The hospital grounds were well maintained, but the beautiful ivy, which used to cover all the buildings, was gone. The facade looked cold without it.

Sitting on a park bench on the landscaped grounds, I reminisced. Where had the years gone? It seemed like just yesterday that I had lived here.

Our old nurse's residence was now a center for drug addicts. I met with the current director of nursing, a male nurse. He showed me the new school of nursing, which was in another part of the hospital complex. He told me that students of all faiths were now accepted. They did not wear the uniforms and caps we used to have; they just had white lab coats and no caps. On the walls of the nurses' residence hung familiar photos of us, taken when we were students. Only a few of those nurses in the photos who had worked there during the war years, under most difficult circumstances, survived. It made me wonder whether I would have been strong enough to endure the hardships, if I had not made it out of Germany in time.

After my visit to the hospital, I went to see the famous Great Synagogue in the Oranianburger Strasse. It had been bombed during the war and was in the process of being restored, but the part of the annex where my Great Uncle Lembke and his wife had lived remained untouched. He was the chief cantor in that synagogue. I looked up to the windows of their apartment and wondered how and when they died.

In May, it was still cold and windy in Berlin and I got a nasty cold, but it did not stop me from eating the delicious white asparagus, which was in season. I visited the national museum and the famous Egyptian Pergamon Museum. In the evening, we went to see the opera, *Die Fledermaus.*

One Friday night, I was invited to the home of the charge d'affaire of the American Embassy, Joel Cohen. His wife, Carol, is the daughter of a friend of mine in New York. She invited me for Shabbat dinner in their home in the suburbs of Berlin, where I met the ambassador from Israel and an elderly lady from Russia who told us how she survived the Holocaust hiding on a farm with her infant daughter in Russia. It is incredible what human suffering can go through.

Another day, I took a train ride to Frankfurt on the Oder, where I had gone to school. It was a long walk from the train station to the school. Some of the streets I recognized, but many parts of the city had been rebuilt and I had to ask for directions to the school. The impressive, red stone building is a landmark now. It was built around the turn of the century. The principal took me through the old familiar halls and introduced me to some of the students who happened to pass by.

From there, I continued the train ride to Kuestrin, which now belongs to Poland. It was a dreary day. The train station looked dirty and was in dire need of renovation. Three taxis were standing on the street, but nobody spoke English or German, so I decided to walk. I recognized the old post office, but all the other houses along the road were post-war structures. They looked like shabbily built bungalows. When I came to the plaza where we used to live, the old white brick hotel was now gray and dirty looking. Across from there I recognized the two chestnut trees that stood in front of our balcony. They were in bloom now, and had survived the devastation of the war, but our house was gone. I was very disappointed, and felt as if I had been robbed. I had hoped to walk into my parents' former home, perhaps be able to talk to the present owner, and possibly see the old furniture my parents used to own.

I turned away, walked into the dreary hotel restaurant and ordered coffee, but it was too bitter to drink. I just sat there by a window and stared at the beautiful, white cone-shaped blossoms of the majestic chestnut trees that once stood in front of the house we lived in. I was sad and close to tears. It started to rain and I rushed back to the train station, hoping to return someday and find at least something familiar in my hometown.

When I came back from Europe, fall classes began. I was busy preparing for the third year student exhibition, which was going to be my first art showing, in May 1997. I worked hard for it. We had to learn to make our own frames. Each student was given a spacious wall in the beautiful museum of the academy to hang the paintings.

The opening night of the exhibition was an exciting event. Buyers came from around the tri-state area. My family and many of our friends came to the show. Six of my paintings were sold. In a way I was glad that people liked my paintings, but at the same time I was sad to part with them. After the opening, Howard and Hope invited our friends to a dinner party at the Napoleon Restaurant, whose owner had purchased two large paintings from me.

In July I met Christiane in Ascona, Switzerland, during the American Jazz Festival. We toured all over Switzerland, Lake Lugano, and Lake Maggiore, and Northern Italy, Lake Como. We stayed in small hotels. I liked especially Orta, a charming, old Italian village. There was a beautiful view of the lake from our terrace at the hotel, and I painted for hours to my heart's content.

When the fall semester began, I began working on paintings for the student exhibition in my fourth and final year. In sculpture class I had overworked my left thumb, and I tried to ignore the pain until it hurt too much. When I finally consulted a hand surgeon, I needed a painful ligament replacement. I was handicapped for six weeks, with a cast on my hand and lower arm. But, in spite of the cast, I managed to produce nineteen paintings for the show. It was a smashing success. I received the Arco Chemical Purchase Award, and, in another exhibition at Yellow Springs, which is connected with the academy, I received the Mable Woodrow Wilson Award. Out of nineteen paintings I exhibited, fourteen were sold, enough to pay my tuition for the entire semester.

Graduation
from the Academy

I remember the day of my graduation ceremony, when I was called to the podium to receive my diploma. The principal announced to the audience, "And now the 'youngest' of our students to graduate from here, Frieda Lefeber. Please come to the podium." The audience applauded and my fellow students stamped with their feet, while my grandchildren screamed with pride, "That's my grandma!" and everybody laughed. At eighty-three, I was the oldest student ever to graduate from the academy.

Those four years spent at the art school were well worth the hardships. It wasn't easy to drive in heavy traffic to and from school, but the teachers were very supportive, and I learned a lot and loved every minute of it. My art freed me from shy and insecure feelings. The years at art school helped me to achieve a sense of myself as an individual. I learned to express myself through my paintings, and I gained confidence and self-esteem. It changed my life and made me feel fulfilled.

Even after my graduation in May 1998, I was still not content and knew there was room for improvement. I intended to take postgraduate courses in the fall.

I painted again with Diana Willis at Lake Como, Italy in August, and then flew to Andreas's 40th birthday celebration in Berry, Germany where I presented him with his portrait, which he loved. It was a festive party, which took place in a tent out on the beautiful lawn. All their family members and many friends attended.

The following day Christiane and I drove back to Kuestrin (a three-hour ride). I was hoping to find at least some familiar sights in that town. Perhaps my father's garden? We drove all over the town but couldn't even find the big church, a beautiful Gothic structure. All of the houses we saw were built after the total destruction of the town, and the new streets were named in Polish. There was nothing recognizable anymore. The only things that had survived the devastation were those two chestnut trees, the rundown hotel, and the fortress in the old city, which dated from the time of Fredrick the Great's father, around the seventeenth century. (This was the spooky fortress, surrounded by a moat, with a bridge leading into a cave, where we used to burn candles and communicate with spirits using an ouija board.) It was incredible how the landscape had completely changed in just half a century.

The trip to Kuestrin was futile. I was disappointed and depressed. As a last attempt to find any trace of my former school-friends, we stopped at the town of Kuestrin-Kietz, which was still German territory, hoping to find the citizens' registration office, which might be able to locate some of my former classmates (if they were still alive). But the office was closed that day. We had spent many hours traveling and had accomplished nothing. I was tired, hungry, and very sad.

On our way home we spotted an inn, Under der Linde, an old, white-stucco house with geraniums in flower boxes on the windowsills, with tables and chairs for guests to sit outdoors. Written on a blackboard was the menu of the day, *Matjes* Herring with home-fried potatoes, or *pfifferlinge* with fried potatoes. That was just what I felt like having. I ordered a portion of the *Matjes* Herring and consumed it with great delight. But I could not resist the temptation to eat a portion of *pfifferlinge* too. Both foods are not available in America. Herring, an import from Holland, only tastes good when it is fresh. The *pfifferlinge* are mushrooms, which do not grow here in America. They also have to be picked fresh and prepared the same day. After consuming those delicacies, I felt better.

When we arrived in Berlin, Christiane's former boyfriend, Wolfgang, invited us to stay for three days at the Radisson Hotel where he was the manager. The accommodations were luxurious. He took us to a restaurant for dinner, and, afterwards, we went to the newly rebuilt Adlon Hotel for drinks. We had a great time. It was amazing how Berlin had again become the lively metropolis that it had been before the war.

Although I had experienced much sadness while I lived in Germany under the Hitler regime, my return to that country, especially to Berlin, always brings back memories of the good years I experienced there.

Who knows what would have happened if Hitler had never ruled? Before his rise to power, life in Germany was pleasant. The majority of its citizens were benevolent towards Jews. When I first came to America, I was amazed to hear that quotas existed for Jews who wished to enter certain schools or colleges. In old-time Germany, there were no golf or tennis clubs or hotels that excluded Jews. Germans mingled socially with Jews at all levels. But under Hitler's dictatorship, the German people were afraid. They had to stay silent while injustice and cruelty was done to Jews, or they and their entire family paid severe consequences. If the Nazis found out that a person helped Jews or harbored political fugitives, he was tortured. I don't know whether I would have had the courage to put myself in such danger for other people. I have given the matter a lot of thought, and I feel one should not condemn everyone. Christiane and Andreas' families remind me of the decent German people I used to know.

When I came back from Europe, it took me a while to decide what art classes I should attend. I heard that Osvaldo Romberg, an excellent art teacher at the academy, gave classes in his own studio two days a week and I applied there. He was very selective about who he took in. I don't know why he allowed me to participate, but in any case, I was flattered. To this day, I enjoy his classes immensely and I learn a lot. My drawing skills have greatly improved since then. I intend to stay with him as long as I am able to, in spite of the commute to Center City, which is difficult especially during the rush hour.

Rachel's Bat Mitzvah

In May 1999, we celebrated our Rachel's Bar Mitzvah at Temple Rodeph Shalom. She looked beautiful in her navy blue silk suit standing on the Bema with great poise. She recited the Torah portion and led the *Havdalah* service (the evening prayer at the end of Shabbat). We were all very proud of her. Many of our relatives and friends were invited to a beautiful celebration at the Four Seasons that evening. It took Hope months of planning and preparation for this event. The ballroom was decorated with magnificent flowers. Everyone was dressed in their finery. Rachel wore a lovely light blue gown fitted at the waist and decorated with beads and pearls. Hope had an elegant, deep red taffeta gown; Dana looked lovely in a long navy blue dress, and I was dressed in heavy gray-sequined satin.

Everybody danced to an excellent band and enjoyed delicious food. The following day, Hope and Howard invited out-of-town guests and friends to our house for brunch. It was a celebration that Rachel and all of us will remember always.

That summer I traveled to the magnificent Canadian Rockies, and after that, I embarked on a cruise to Alaska with the Holland-America Line. I saw breathtaking scenery. Later on I went to New York City for two weeks to take painting classes at the Art Student League. I did not care for the courses, but I enjoyed staying with my longtime friend Ilse, who lives on West End Avenue. We reminisced about our youth in Berlin and our lives as student nurses.

When I came home from my travels, Christiane called me. She had left Andreas and had asked for a divorce. I was sorry to hear that the marriage had ended because I felt close to both of them. When I talked to Andreas he was heartbroken. A few months later he visited us in Philadelphia, but was still very depressed.

My 85th Birthday

New Year's Eve 2000 was uneventful, although everybody was announcing this to be an important event because it was the start of a new millennium. I stayed home with my grandchildren and watched television until after midnight. I never liked to go out and celebrate New Year's Eve.

That year I traveled a lot. The first trip came at the end of March, after a quiet celebration of my eighty-fifth birthday. I took my family to Italy and Israel, using the money that was left over from Aunt Gerda's inheritance. We went on Al Italia business class. But, we were unable to continue after our stopover in Milan because of a pilots' strike. It was impossible to get hotel accommodations in the city of Milan because of the strike. With great difficulty, American Express got us into the Villa D'Este at Lake Como, two hours away from Milan. The accommodations were luxurious. It turned out to be a pleasant interlude. I was happy to show my family this beautiful part of the world where I had often painted. The weather was perfect, and we enjoyed an all-day water taxi ride on the beautiful lake, and stopping in charming villages along the way. After three days we were able to continue our journey to Israel.

We stayed in Jerusalem at the Hilton Hotel and hired a guide who drove us in her small van all over the country showing us major historical and biblical sites. We went into ancient caves, the holy shrines of all denominations, and Masada, the ancient fortress. The guide was well informed about the political situation. The tour was most interesting and educational for all of us. Howard and the grandchildren, who had never seen Israel before, were impressed and loved Israel.

After we returned, I again went on a painting expedition for three weeks with Marjorie Portnow at her studio in upstate New York. She is a great teacher and a good friend. We enjoyed painting "en plain air" every day for six hours. I turned out eight landscape paintings.

A few weeks later I traveled to England, and saw the charming Cotswold's, Cornwall and London. There I took in three shows, *Ma Ma Mia*, *The Graduate* and *Virginia Woolf.* Then I joined a group on a scholar's tour to Holland and Belgium to visit the museums of the old masters. After four weeks of traveling with one Pullman-sized suitcase, I was anxious to return home. Hope and the family were still in Colorado when I arrived, and I enjoyed the solitude at home until Labor Day.

In mid-September classes started with Osvaldo, and I finished my second year with him. We were now eleven students, all trying to improve our skills. There is much to learn in art, it seems never-ending, often frustrating and discouraging, but also very fulfilling.

Dana's Bat Mitzvah

The year 2001 did not start well. Rachel, my dear grandchild, suffered from an eating disorder—anorexia. Her weight had come down to such an alarming level that she had to be hospitalized. We all were worried about her serious illness and it caused great strain on all of us. I lost any desire to paint, but continued to attend Osvaldo's figure drawing classes, to in order get out of the gloomy atmosphere that prevailed at home. For many months I was unable to produce a single painting at home.

Since painting was impossible for me, I concentrated on writing my autobiography. I bought a computer to facilitate this time-consuming task. Two years earlier I had started taking classes at Main Line Night School with Vivian Grey and Virginia Newlin in autobiographical writing, and had written a few chapters in longhand. Virginia's criticism and that of my classmates helped me in improving my writing skills.

Rachel was still very sick and hospitalized at Renfro, a facility for women with eating disorders. But Dana's Bar Mitzvah was scheduled to take place on May 5, 2001. Hope was busy making preparations for it, so that Dana's celebration would measure up to Rachel's two years ago. New clothes were bought for everyone. A lot of details had to be worked out. The preparations for the event helped us to concentrate on something other than Rachel's illness. Rachel was released from the hospital for the event.

On her Bar Mitzvah day Dana recited her Torah portion and led the congregation in prayer with much poise and beauty. We were all proud of her. She looked lovely at the party at the Four Seasons, wearing a rose-colored evening gown. The orchestra was great and even I danced a lot. It was good to forget for a few hours the worries we had with Rachel, who looked pale, emaciated, and sad in her white gown. The following morning, out-of-town guests and friends joined us for brunch at home.

Soon after the celebration, Christiane visited me for a two-week vacation. I was determined to give her a good time. Knowing how tense the mood was in our house, I tried to stay away from home as much as possible and showed her the city of Philadelphia. We visited the Barnes Museum, the Philadelphia Museum of Art, the Academy of Fine Art, and other historic sites. She met my friends and colleagues who invited us for lovely luncheons. I even arranged a date for her with a nice young man, Michael. He showed her a very good time and brought her to visit the Amish country, Chesapeake Bay, and his country farm. Then I went with her to Washington for four days to show her our capitol. We stayed at the Harrington Hotel. My nephew Dan and his wife took us to a nice restaurant, and Howard's brother and his lady friend invited us to a French bistro and drove us around to see Washington by night with its illumination of impressive government buildings. On a rainy day we spent several hours at the National Museum. A friend drove us to George Washington's estate in Mount Vernon. Christiane was impressed with Washington, but she really fell in love with New York. She even wished she could have stayed and found work there for a year or so.

After four days in the Big Apple, we came home. Hope and Howard gave her a farewell dinner at the Prime Rib restaurant, which Christiane enjoyed. She had not eaten any beef for some time because of the outbreak of the mad cow disease in Europe. I was happy to have given her a good time because she always treated me so well on my visits to Europe.

A few weeks after she left I went abroad on a month's vacation. I stayed in the beautiful old city of Prague for four days and went to museums and attended concerts every night.

From there I took a relaxing six-day cruise on the river Elbe. The ship stopped in Dresden, which is known for its beautiful baroque architecture. The city had been heavily bombarded during the war and was now fully restored. We stopped at many other picturesque cities. The tour ended in Berlin. I stayed at the Hamburg Hotel, which was in a very nice section of city. It rained every day, but that did not stop me from visiting the Jewish hospital, which was a half-hour subway ride away. I walked around the familiar grounds and then went into the completely remodeled hospital. A doctor and a head nurse gave me a tour. Many new buildings had been added and equipped with the latest medical equipment. I walked in the familiar long halls of the old pavilion. It felt like homecoming; coming back to the place where I had labored for four years and received an education that had served me well.

After leaving the hospital I went to the Kate Kollwitz Museum. She was a famous sculptress and a world-renowned artist. Hitler boycotted her because she ignored Hitler's rules to shun Jews. When the famous German impressionist, Max Lieberman, died, she dared to attend his funeral. As a consequence all her paintings and sculptures were withdrawn from every gallery and museum in Germany and burnt, by order of the ministry of culture. Heartbroken, she lived in obscurity and deprivation until she died.

The next day, Andreas picked me up in Berlin, and we drove to his home in Boerry. He had taken time off from his farm work, especially to entertain me. All his friends in that little hamlet had heard I was visiting, and every day they brought fruits freshly picked from their gardens. One friend, the wife of the only doctor in the village, had baked a cheesecake topped with delicious fruit. Andreas gave a barbeque party and invited his friends. I was amazed how well he had adjusted to living a bachelor's life. I met his parents and sister, who invited us to a dinner party in their seventeenth-century house. The food was delicious and elegantly served on old Meissen dishes. I enjoyed my stay with Andreas. The next day he drove me to a spa in the resort town of Pyrmont, where I stayed for eight days.

It was not what I had expected of a spa. The room was comfortable but the place had the atmosphere of a sanatorium. Many very ill patients were there to recuperate and I had the feeling I was the only healthy person. Christiane's father had recommended this place. I was too tired to move to a hotel. Included in the spa were daily massages. The masseur was terribly rough. I had to tell him to be gentler, but unfortunately I had told him too late. The next day I had black and blue marks on my arms and legs. From then on I allowed him to massage only my back and do reflexology on my feet.

Christiane's father, Franz, lived in the same resort. He went all-out to make my stay enjoyable. Everyday he drove me to lovely outdoor cafes in picturesque, old fourteenth-century villages and castles. I always ordered either *pfifferlinge* or *Matjes* Herring. Because of the mad cow disease, I did not dare to eat beef or pork in Europe. I did not mind having the same food every day, but everybody else ate meat without being afraid.

After my eight days in Pyrmont, Christiane called for me and drove me to Hamburg, where I spent the next three days at the five-star Hotel Elysee. There I had the best massage I ever received. In the evening, I met for dinner all of Christiane's friends, at an outdoor Italian restaurant. We had a great time. The next day Christiane showed me the city, and in the evening we went to an open-air theater by the river Elbe. The following day my twenty-six day journey ended. It was great. If God will grant me the strength, I hope to be able to see even more of this wonderful world and meet interesting people along the way.

After spending seven weeks at Renfro, our Rachel was released, but was still very frail and under constant medical care. She was our greatest worry. She had missed classes because of her illness, but with special tutoring during the summer months she was able to graduate from tenth grade. She was not happy at Baldwin, a private school for girls, although she was an A student. It was too intense, so we enrolled her in a public school. It was a good move; school was much less demanding and in no time her health improved. Within half a year she started to eat like a normal person and now she has returned to her normal weight. We are all grateful and relieved. She is very interested in helping others who are suffering from that disease, and gives lectures in schools and synagogues and on public television, disclosing freely her inner struggle during that time. During the summer of 2002 she interned with a professor at Penn, who is a renowned authority on eating disorders. We are very proud of her.

9/11/2001

It was early September 2001 when classes began with Osvaldo. Like everyone else, I have a personal recollection of the moment we heard of the bombing of the World Trade Center disaster on 9/11. As usual, I was at Osvaldo's drawing class at eight thirty that Tuesday morning. The model was posing, the students were standing at their easels, and Osvaldo was making the rounds. The ringing of the telephone interrupted the silence that always prevailed in the studio. Osvaldo answered his cell phone and spoke in Hebrew in a very excited voice. Then he hung up and yelled in his broken English, "They are terrorists, these dammed Arabs, quick turn on television, they bombed, listen to—" as he mumbled and hastily plugged in a small black and white television. It was his daughter who had just called from Israel telling him he should turn on the television immediately. She had just heard that a plane had flown into the Word Trade Center. Now with the television on we saw with horror the burning of the first building and a short while later the second plane crashed into the other. Stunned, we watched in silence at the devastation while Osvaldo was cursing the terrorists. He knew who did it; having lived in Israel, he automatically accused the fanatic Muslims.

I could not imagine how a human being could possibly inflict such pain on others. I was petrified watching those desperate victims jumping out of windows. The fear of what else might yet happen made us decide to get home as soon as possible to be with our loved ones. We all stayed glued to the television at home until late into the night. The horror gripped us all and made us feel sick, utterly helpless and afraid. Our lives had changed, and there was sadness and deep pain in all of us. When will brutality, hate, and destruction ever end?

Christiane and Andreas called from Germany to let me know their concern and prayers were with us. In sad times like this, I appreciated their caring.

Of course, my grandchildren were also very frightened. The children were dismissed from school and all of us remained glued to the television all day. The uncertainty of the future scared us terribly.

In time of crisis people turn to religion, and so did I. One day, after visiting my podiatrist, I saw an awning across the street that had the inscription: KABBALAH. Vaguely remembering that it had to do with the Bible and Jewish mysticism, I went to inquire. It sounded fascinating and I signed up for ten lectures for beginners and enjoyed the teachings of kabbalah. It basically tells you how to conduct your life peacefully, receiving light and energy from the Creator. It is amazing how many prominent people like Newton, Plato, Einstein and many more, have found strength from studying kabbalah. A book, called the *Zokor*—written by a kabbalah scholar more than two thousand years ago—interprets the beginning of the universe in the way scientists now believe it started. It is a fascinating study, although, I am not sure I understand the concept of reincarnation or the superstition about angels and the devil. I have real doubts about that. But it is amazing what seemingly modern discoveries were already hypothesized so many years ago, and the guidelines the kabbalah offers to achieve inner peace are profound. I even signed up for Hebrew lessons, because there is great meaning in the Hebrew letters.

Later, my enthusiasm for studying for kabbalah diminished when I realized that the center expected me to pray for hours and to show my support by eating expensive luncheons and dinners on Shabbat with the congregation. Constantly new lectures were offered, which were expensive. I was expected to buy the Zokar at a cost of five hundred dollars, which I did. But when I was asked to contribute the same amount again so that the center could spread the study of the Zokar to non-Jewish corporations, I became suspicious about the integrity of the center and so, I stopped going.

A course in "Dynamics of Major World Religions" was offered at Rosemont College in January 2002, and I signed up for it instead of continuing the kabbalah study. I also enrolled for classes in Pilates exercises twice a week, to improve my posture. Soon I'll be off to Europe, painting in Bologgio, Italy with Diana again and then I'll be going to a spa in Switzerland to get pampered. For fall, I already have signed up classes in writing, painting, drawing, and Bible interpretation.

Life has been very rewarding and I am grateful to have been able to participate in activities that interest me. I derive much of my strength from the love I receive from my family and friends.

Epilogue

Sophocles wrote: "One must wait until the evening to see how splendid the day has been."

I am content with what I have accomplished in my long journey through life, but I will never stop searching for new things to learn and will look to tomorrow with confidence and joy.

In my life story I have spoken openly about myself, revealing my innermost thoughts. As I relived my life by writing about my past, it helped me to cleanse my mind, heal old wounds, and understand and forgive myself and those who hurt me.

Although I experienced great sadness, hardships, and disappointments, I always tried never to despair but to face my challenges with faith in God, courage, and determination. It made me stronger and perhaps wiser.

I am grateful to have always enjoyed good health by having been blessed with good genes, and by trying to maintain a healthy lifestyle through daily exercise and yoga practice.

The sources of my greatest joy and pride have been you, my family: Hope, Howard, Rachel, and Dana. God bless you!

With great love, your *Naggie.*

Grandpa Louis at 80 years old

Mother, 20 years old

Gerhard and I, 1919.

Mother, 1920.

My parents with us at the beach, 1921.

With Grandpa, 1922.

Mother and I, 1923.

Mother and I, 1926.

In school uniform, 1928.

In our garden, 1929.

My best friend Dorothea, Gerhard and I

My parents with Gerhard shortly before he fled

Hans, 28 years old, when I met him in 1934.

Myself, 19 years old.

Student nurse.

Student nurses with Professor Rosenstein

Dorothea gave me that picture before my first trip
to America in 1937 inscribed to my very dear friend Frieda.

My first picture in America, 1939.

My first job at Knickerbocker Hospital, 1939.

Off duty on board the SS Carp, 1946

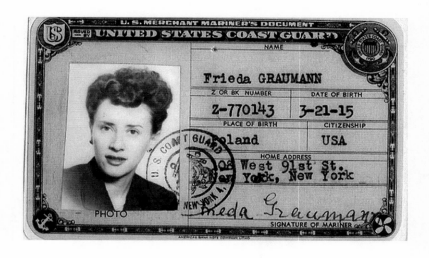

My coast guard ID

Off duty in Egypt aboard SS Carp with new acquired fez.

Just married. Nov. 24, 1948

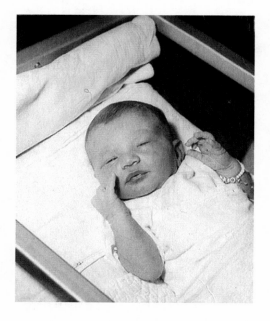

Hope born 7/20/54 in Hospital nursery.

Hope, 8 months old.

Hans and Hope

Hope's first school day.

At the beach, 1961.

Myself and Hope, 1961.

My parents 80th birthday, 1964.

Hope, mother, and I on our visit to Israel in 1966.

Visit with mother, 1971.

Hans in Spain, 1972

After cancer operation at Dr. Nieper's
in Hanover, Germany in May 1975.

A few months before Hans died in Dec. 1975.

Hope's graduation at the University of Pennsylvania, 1976

Aunt Kate's 96th birthday in 1979.

'Bittersweet' Return To Germany

By SHIRLEY LAZARUS
Staff Writer

Staff Photo by JOHN BELL

Frieda Lefeber of Morristown fled Berlin after 'Kristall Nacht,' but was invited back recently for a tour of her homeland — at the West German government's expense.

BACK IN BERLIN. More than 40 years after fleeing Berlin, Frieda Lefeber, (far right) sits with others at a luncheon hosted in the Reichstag in honor of the 260 Jews who were week-long guests of the Germans. "Looking out the windows from this big hall," she explains, "is all barricaded East Germany."

'Bittersweet' week as guest of Berlin

Although she had "cold feet about it to the last minute," Frieda Lefeber of Morristown did accept an invitation from the West German government to be, along with approximately 260 others, its guest for a week in Berlin early last month. She was assigned, she told The Jewish News upon her return, to the very hotel at which she had first met the man whom she was to marry, after both had had harrowing experiences but had managed to escape the Holocaust.

The week of touring and planned events — a "bittersweet experience" — was part of a project the West German Senate has sponsored for several years now. Nearly 12,000 Jewish people have taken these expense-paid trips, a fact which Mrs. Lefeber believes, "helps the Germans alleviate their guilt."

Yet, she added, she also felt the sincerity of the Germans she met, particularly those under the age of 40, who were making this effort to reach out to Jews, partly as a way of under-mining neo-Nazism. "The seemed deeply moved by our coming," she said.

She was studying nursing in Berlin in the late '30s. Hans Lefeber was a judge in Berlin. Fleeing alone, she came to the U.S. in 1939 with a work affidavit as a children's maid. The job fell through, but she managed to get a position as a private nurse.

He fled to Sweden in 1940, later they met in New York City, where they were married. Lefeber, who first worked as a shipping clerk but studied accounting and became a business executive, and died five years ago.

FRIEDA LEFEBER

By SHERRY KIRSCHENBAUM
Jewish News Staff

Nov. 9, 1938 — Kristallnacht, the "Night of the Broken Glass."

Jews of Berlin huddled in their homes and the back rooms of their shops as members of the Nazi Party smashed the windows of every Jewish store and then looted their contents. Every synagogue and Jewish institution burned. Stray Jews pulled off the street and out of their homes were herded towards trucks which carried them to concentration camps.

For Frieda Lefeber, a nurse at the Jewish Hospital in Berlin, it was a night of terror. She and the other Jewish nurses stayed inside the hospital for safety.

"I lived in the nurse's quarters of the hospital," recalled Mrs. Lefeber. "They were going to burn the hospital on Kristallnacht, but they made a mistake and burned down the Catholic hospital next door."

Mrs. Lefeber, now a resident of Morristown and a member of Congregation B'nai Jeshurun of Short Hills, returned to the site of that horror-filled night in late April as a guest of the city government of West Berlin.

The 12-year-old, good-will program sponsored by the Berlin Government has already brought 12,000 former Berliners back to their native city on a one-week, all-expense paid trip.

"It is a way for West Germany to alleviate its guilt," said Mrs. Lefeber.

"Their guilt never quite leaves them, but this helps to lessen it. They want those who had been persecuted to have fonder memories," she continued.

The government only invites former residents of Berlin who are over 65 years of age. Mrs. Lefeber's home town was actually 1½ hours outside of the city, but her late husband, Hans, was a native of Berlin and the initial invitation was addressed to him.

Mrs. Lefeber contacted the Berlin Government in 1981 to inform officials that her husband had died, at which time the invitation was offered to her. "Cold feet" caused her to decline, but when the invitation was reissued in 1982, she decided it was time to confront her fears and see Berlin once again.

Bittersweet return to Germany.

Hope & Howard engaged, July 1983.

The Wedding, Feb. 4, 1984.

My family.

My associate Dorothy Moreno
at my Electrolysis office
in Morristown.

Evening classes at the Academy, 1992.

Art instructions at Rosemont College, 1992.

3rd year newspaper clippings.

Photo for Main Line Life — PETE BANNAN

Frieda Lefeber, of Penn Valley, 83, will graduate from the Pennsylvania Academy of Fine Arts, where she has been a student since 1994. On April 21, one of her paintings will be auctioned at the patron party for the May 16 gala to benefit the Rock School of Ballet.

YOUNG AT ART

FREDA LEFEBER *AGE 84*

Freda Lefeber

4th year student exhibition & newspaper clippings

Still life.

Early paintings 92'-98'

Dana, 3 years old, 1991

Self portrait, 1992

Self portrait in Italy

Rachel

Dana, 5 years old.

Rachel, 7 years old

My grandchildren and I in Israel, 1995.

Arco Chemical Purchase Award, 1998

In Bellogio, Italy, 2000

Italian market, 2000

Photo with teacher

En plein air painting.